EAST ASIAN TRANSFORMATION

From the re-emergence of Japan as an industrial power in the 1950s through to the rise of China as a potential economic and political behemoth, the story of East Asian transformation has been central to any serious analysis of the dynamics and trajectory of the global political economy. Integrated into a coherent, critical narrative, this book examines key political-economic and social dynamics that helped forge the 'miracle' economies of East Asia and continue to drive them forward in the volatile circumstances of our current epoch. Insisting that a discourse of 'transformation' is the most appropriate for understanding contemporary change, this book analyses such issues as the relation between states and markets, the changing nature of economic governance and its relation to inequality, the causes of economic crises and the rise of China and its global consequences. Historically informed and comparative in nature, the book contributes to the analysis of the transformations of Japan, Hong Kong, South Korea, Taiwan, Singapore, Malaysia and China and is the first to cover the ground in one volume. Written by a leading analyst of East Asian and international development, the book uses an open, non-technical language, making it useful as an advanced textbook for East Asian studies, international political economy, development studies and cognate subjects.

Jeffrey Henderson is Leverhulme Research Professor of International Development and Co-Director of the Centre for East Asian Studies in the University of Bristol, UK. His books include *The Globalisation of High Technology Production* (published by Routledge), *States and Development in the Asian Pacific Rim* and *Industrial Transformation in Eastern Europe in the Light of the East Asian Experience*.

East Asian Transformation – relevance of Escher

M.C. Escher's lithograph, 'Convex and Concave' (1955), is used here to symbolise the complex, multi-directional processes associated with on-going economic, political and social transformation; processes that, crucially, have unknown end points. Images in the lithograph can be taken to represent the ladders towards prosperity that East Asian countries have climbed, the fact that their success has been universally heralded, and the negative social consequences that their routes to industrial capitalism have often involved. Escher's inclusion of an African woman hints at the global significance of East Asian transformation, and in particular, at China's engagement with Africa.

EAST ASIAN TRANSFORMATION

On the political economy of dynamism, governance and crisis

Jeffrey Henderson

Routledge
Taylor & Francis Group

LONDON AND NEW YORK

1006562570

First published 2011
by Routledge
2 Park Square, Milton Park, Abingdon, Oxon OX14 4RN

Simultaneously published in the USA and Canada
by Routledge
270 Madison Avenue, New York, NY 10016

Routledge is an imprint of the Taylor & Francis Group, an informa business

© 2011 Jeffrey Henderson

Typeset in Bembo by Swales & Willis Ltd, Exeter, Devon
Printed and bound in Great Britain by TJ International, Padstow, Cornwall

British Library Cataloguing in Publication Data
A catalogue record for this book is available from the British Library

Library of Congress Cataloging in Publication Data
Henderson, J. W. (Jeffrey William)
    The political economy of East Asian development : against the orthodoxy /
    Jeffrey Henderson.
    p. cm.
    Includes bibliographical references and index.
    1. East Asia–Economic policy. 2. East Asia–Economic conditions. I. Title.
    HC460.5.H46 2011
    338.95—dc22
    2010029043

ISBN: 978–0–415–54791–8 (hbk)
ISBN: 978–0–415–54792–5 (pbk)
ISBN: 978–0–203–83313–1 (ebk)

To Ying and Alexander; both, though in different ways, of East Asia.

CONTENTS

FIGURES AND TABLES

Figures

Tables

PREFACE: AN EAST ASIAN JOURNEY

I first entered East Asia on the morning of September 1, 1981. I arrived at Hong Kong's old Kai Tak airport via a Cathay Pacific flight from London. As an escapee from Thatcherism, and facing what was beginning to look like a long period of unemployment thanks to her government's slashing of higher education budgets, I was more than grateful that the University of Hong Kong had offered me a material and intellectual home for the coming years.

Emerging into the wall of people and sound that was a constant feature of the old airport's arrivals hall, we were met by two of my new colleagues. Courtesy of one of the University's limousines, we were whisked off across the Kowloon peninsula. On the way the road cut through a working class housing district. For someone who had never been east of Greece before and had yet to venture into what was then still known as the 'third world' (though lost on most 'western' commentators, by 1981 Hong Kong was already a fully industrialized, though decidedly inegalitarian, society), the sight of these apartment blocks came as a major shock. In the immediately preceding phase of my life I had lived in Birmingham, England, and had been engaged on research that regularly took me to some of that city's public housing estates. By the early 1980s, British public housing – what had been one of the greatest achievements of the welfare state – was already in disarray. With the best of the housing stock being sold off as part of the Thatcher government's drive for 'popular capitalism', much of what was left had suffered from years of under-investment. Add to this the fact that the life-chances of the estates' residents were representative of the social fallout occasioned by de-industrialization, unemployment and the consequences of neoliberal social policies, and Birmingham's contribution to housing the working classes and the poor, were a sorry sight indeed.

Compared with what assaulted our eyes on the way to Hong Kong's harbour crossing, however, Birmingham's public housing estates were veritable palaces. Hong Kong's attempts to house its working class (though what we saw was private, not publicly rented accommodation) really were something else: block after block of tiny apartments, so close together that little natural light could have penetrated them. Once white in colour, the buildings were encrusted with the grime of years of unregulated factory and automobile emissions. The newly washed clothing, strung on poles from the windows, must have been soiled from the sheer filthiness of the air before it was even dry. Driving towards the harbour (the University is on Hong Kong Island), I was reminded of Engels' account of the appalling housing conditions of Manchester's working class in the 1840s (Engels 1892) and of a line from the first analysis of Hong Kong's development I had read before leaving Britain: 'business (there) has been allowed to go on a permanent rampage, 24 hours a day, 365 days a year' (Halliday 1974: 94).

Having survived an uncomfortable first few days in our University-provided apartment (very large, but with no air conditioning in a 35 degree centigrade, 95 per cent humidity, sub-tropical climate; things got much better once air conditioners arrived), I not only enjoyed my new life in Hong Kong, but I prospered.

One's social and intellectual prosperity always depends on whom one meets, engages with and with whom one becomes friends. I was no exception. From the moment I stepped into the University's Sociology department, my new colleague, Daniel Han, became a firm friend. Daniel was my first guide to the peculiarities of Hong Kong culture and society. He taught me how to read the signs (literal and metaphorical) that were essential to navigating the unique time-warped, but frenetic and bizarre, social and spatial construction that was colonial Hong Kong. For this, and much more besides, I remain for ever in Daniel's debt.

My arrival in Hong Kong marked the beginnings of my transition from a 'semi-parochial' British sociologist (though I had been partly educated in California and had written on US race relations and working class militancy) into someone who worked internationally and particularly on East Asia. My first piece of work on the region – on its electronics industries – had been conjured-up in collaboration with a longstanding British friend, Robin Cohen. Though Robin was not an East Asian specialist (though he was a development sociologist) and was unable to see the project through to its conclusion, it was his intellectual stimulation and support that set me firmly on the road to becoming an analyst of East Asian transformation. For this, as for many other things across the years, I owe Robin a deep debt of gratitude.

While working on the emergence of electronics industries in East Asia, I began to pose the wider question: how had the industrialization trick, in general, been pulled there? This was an important question at the time (and remains so because of its implications for industrialization in the contemporary developing world) because the 1980s were witnessing the full flowering of the ideological and political project we now know as neoliberalism. Beginning in the United States and Britain and rolled out across the globe by such agencies as the IMF and the World Bank, the supposed superiority (even moral superiority) of the decisions and actions of private investors responding to market signals had been enshrined, not merely as a common sense 'truth', but as a theology: the private sector as a deity whose every action was to be worshiped.

But there was a major problem with this account when applied to industrialization in East Asia (as it had been since the late 1960s). While it was true that at the corporate level East Asian industrialization was largely a private sector project (though with important state enterprise participation in Taiwan and Singapore; these debates predated the recent industrialization of China with its heavy involvement of state owned enterprises), it was clearly about far more than supposedly free markets. Together with two colleagues at the University of Hong Kong's then Centre of Urban Studies and Urban Planning, Jonathan Schiffer and Sandy Cuthbert, I set about trying to unravel this seeming mystery. With Jonathan taking the lead until he left in 1985 (see Schiffer 1991), we focussed on our own backyard: Hong Kong – the newly industrialized territory that, at first glance, seemed the epitomy of free market development.

For most, a first glance became their last glance, and indeed that was all it took for one of the high priests of neoliberalism, Milton Friedman, to declare that Hong Kong was perhaps *the* free market paradise (Friedman and Friedman 1982). Friedman and his ilk, of course, never examined *how* actual economies functioned in real time (preferring to rely on neoclassical theory's *assumptions* about how economies *in the abstract* were supposed to function), so their pronouncements on that terrain exposed them as ideologues, not the scientists they claimed to be. With one of Friedman's acolytes installed as head of the University's economics department (in 1982), interesting experiences were in store for us, particularly for Jonathan who had originally held half of his appointment in the economics department.

Our conviction that interventionist state policy was an important part of the story of even Hong Kong's development, was substantially reinforced by the work of Manuel Castells. Manuel had joined the Centre as a visiting professor for a couple of months in 1983 and while there, he began the ground-work for what became perhaps the principal account of the role of the state in the development of both Hong Kong and Singapore (Castells *et al.* 1990). To my eternal good fortune it was Manuel who encouraged me more than anyone else (over many years and in a variety of international contexts) to intervene in the wider debates on East Asian industrialization and transformation. For this and much more, I am deeply grateful to him.

Attending to the broader issues of East Asian transformation, however, had to await a new wife, the birth of our son, and relocation from Hong Kong to take first a visiting, and then a permanent appointment, at Manchester.

My first opportunity to research, reflect and write more generally on the political economy of East Asian transformation came from my collaboration with Richard Appelbaum. Rich and I had been friends since my time as a graduate student at the University of California's Santa Barbara campus. By the late 1980s, Rich was becoming bored with the US-oriented urban sociology that had become the principal component of his empirical portfolio and wanted to see and analyse the world in ways other than those afforded by the library, the internet, or by the occasional overseas conference or study tour. In particular, he wanted to work on East Asia.

During a fleeting visit to California in August 1988, he and I devised a scheme that, if successful, would kick start Rich's inauguration into East Asian research. The result was a workshop that we organized in Santa Barbara in 1990 and out of that came a book (Appelbaum and Henderson 1992) that went on to become one of the standard references on the role of the state in East Asian development. For this, for the big fun (including at 'Das Inst') we've had over many years and for our recently renewed collaboration, I am enormously grateful to Rich.

Once firmly established at the University of Manchester, the opportunities for further research and reflection on East Asian transformation proceeded apace. As well as working on the region itself, I had the opportunity to consider the implications ('lessons') of economic development there, for other parts of the world. Between 1992 and 1994, for instance, I worked as an advisor to the British Labour Party politician, Robin Cook. At that time Robin held the Party's Industry and Trade brief ('Shadow Minister' in British parliamentary parlance) and was conscious that after the Thatcherites had finished 'wasting' the country's manufacturing sector and a Labour Government had been returned to office, nothing less than the wholesale reindustrialization of Britain would be necessary. Robin was interested in what the experiences of industrialization in East Asia might have to say for an strategy designed to rebalance the already finance-dominated, asymmetrical, British economy. That's where my advice came in. Had Robin not been removed from an economic brief when the Blair-Brown 'New Labour' axis took control of the Party in 1994, and had gone on, after the election victory in 1997, to achieve the ministerial position he craved – that of Chancellor of the Exchequer (Finance Minister) – it's possible that the British economy would not have been as racked by the finance-induced, structural instability we have today. Robin Cook's premature death in 2005 robbed British parliamentary politics of one of its greatest radical thinkers and humanitarians.

With the historical rupture that occurred in the state-socialist societies of Central-Eastern Europe between 1989 and 1991, additional opportunities arose for me to reflect on the implications of East Asian transformation for other parts of the world. In collaboration with my Manchester colleagues, Richard Whitley and Laszlo Czaban, East Asian experiences formed part of the backdrop for our research on industrial and economic change in Hungary. Richard, in fact, had been responsible for bringing me to Manchester in the first place (specifically to the Manchester Business School) and throughout the 1990s he helped me adapt my interests in economic sociology and political economy to the peculiarly constrained (particularly in terms of teaching) intellectual environment of business schools. Laszlo, also, emerged not only as a close colleague, but as a good friend. He and I collaborated on a related project sponsored by the International Labour Organization, and both he and Richard contributed to a book of comparative essays I edited, on East Asia and Eastern Europe (Henderson 1998). Scholarship benefits enormously if one's associations are with intellectuals as smart as these.

By the beginning of the twenty-first century I had reverted, once more, to the direct study of East Asian economic transformation. A comparative project on global production networks in the development of East Asia and Europe, conducted with Peter Dicken, Martin Hess, Neil Coe, Jennifer Johns and Henry Yeung, allowed me to reprise and develop some of the work I had done on the region's electronics industries in the 1980s. A further comparative project on economic governance, inequality and poverty in South Korea, Malaysia and Hungary, allowed me to take forward some of the theoretical and empirical questions that had been stimulated by my work on the East Asian economic crisis of the late 1990s. In this project, I worked alongside David Hulme and Richard Phillips, as well as with Eun-Mee Kim, Nurul Ainur and Laszlo Andor. With Richard Phillips, I went on to do further research on Malaysia and South Africa that bridged both these projects. I am enormously grateful to all of these colleagues and friends for their intellectual – and social – contributions to my life. In connection with this book, I am particularly grateful to Richard Phillips, as he co-authored with me, the paper that forms the basis of Chapter 6.

In 2005, thanks to a phone call from Raphael Kaplinsky, my interest in the analysis of East Asian transformation was able to add a new dimension. Raphie, John Humphrey and others at the Institute of Development Studies (IDS) at Sussex were in the process of initiating an international research network on what they called the 'Asian Drivers' of the global economy. Raphie kindly invited me to contribute to this initiative. For a number of reasons, I was more than happy to do so. First, it provided me with a vehicle to engage with one on the truly big questions of our contemporary epoch: the rise of China (some in the network are also concerned with India) and its implications for global development; and, second, it allowed me to deepen my credibility in development studies, subsequent to the transfer of my post from the Manchester Business School to Manchester's Institute of Development Policy and Management (now part of the School of Environment and Development).

My involvement in this network with Raphie (who's now at the Open University), John and other IDS colleagues, and with my Manchester colleagues and friends, Khalid Nadvi and Nicola Phillips, initially took the principal form of an application for an Economic and Social Research Council (ESRC) Research Centre on the Asian Drivers and the future of the developing world. While that application was ultimately unsuccessful, the enormous amount of work involved in its preparation (five people for six months), yielded other benefits. For instance, the application proved to be a major stimulus for the ESRC's current research programme on 'Rising Powers, Global Challenges and Social Change' and it led directly to my successful application to the Leverhulme Trust for a 'major fellowship' focussed on China and global development.

As much as anything else, it was my engagement with China and global development that attracted the interest of colleagues at the University of Bristol. Thanks predominantly to the ground work done by my friend of very many years, Ray Forrest, I have now been part of the Centre for East Asian Studies at Bristol for the past two years. I am grateful to my colleagues in the Centre, and particularly to its former and current Directors, Yongjin Zhang and Misa Izuhara respectively, as well as its Manager, Emma Holland, for keeping my non-research commitments as low as I reasonably could have expected.

From the mid-1980s through to the present day, my work on East Asian transformation has been encouraged and facilitated by other colleagues and friends whom I've yet to mention (in contexts that some of them may have now forgotten). These have included, Reg Kwok, Murray Groves, Paul Lubeck, Leslie Sklair, Pang Eng Fong, the late David Drakakis-Smith, Jomo K.S., Terence Gomez, Allen Scott, Harry Dimitriou, Jim Newton, Wong Siu-lun, Maurie Daly, the late Ralph Miliband, Will Hutton, Ha-Joon Chang, John Ritchie, Colin Kirkpatrick, Paul Cook, Tang Wing Shing, Lai On-kwok, Martin Carnoy, Noriko Hama, Robert Wade, Gary Rodan, David Harvey, Kingsley Bolton, Gillian Koh, Peter Nolan, Richard Robison, Meghnad Desai, Ian Holliday and Grahame Thompson. While I am grateful to them all, in the context of this book, Grahame and Ian are worthy of particular mention as it was they who encouraged me to write the early versions of three of the chapters that appear here and facilitated their initial publication.

To all the friends and colleagues mentioned in this Preface, the usual disclaimers apply with regard to blame that may be necessary for any deficiencies evident in the discussions that follow. For these, the fault is entirely mine. I am also grateful to my editor at Routledge, Peter Sowden. He not only encouraged the book's initial conception, but when I fell behind schedule, he took my excuses with good grace.

Across the sometimes difficult years of research, reading and thought that lie behind the discussions the reader is about to apprehend, two people have been fundamental to my life: indeed, to its being. One is my partner, Suet Ying Ho. An academic in her own right, Ying has been a constant source of inspiration, debate, cultural guidance and emotional support. Our son, Alexander, has also been there for me. It is he who reminded me how difficult it is, sometimes, being a young man in contemporary Britain, but how, with the benefit of an education in state schools, it remains possible to both prosper intellectually and continue to respect and enjoy the company of those from class backgrounds other than one's own. Ying and Alexander are thus inextricably linked to who I now am; not merely as an intellectual, but more importantly as a human being. They help me, immeasurably, to live a fortunate life. It is to them that this book is dedicated.

Bristol and Leeds
July, 2010

ACKNOWLEDGEMENTS

Some of the chapters presented here draw on earlier contributions. For the purposes of this book, these have been revised and, in some cases, extensively re-worked and/or deconstructed and re-formed. I am grateful to the editors of the various publications in which they originally appeared for allowing them to be used here.

The details of the original versions are:

'On the role of the state in the economic transformation of East Asia', Chapter 5 of Chris Dixon and David Drakakis-Smith (eds), *Economic and Social Development in Pacific Asia*. London, Routledge, 1993.

'Danger and opportunity in the Asia-Pacific', Chapter 14 of Grahame Thompson (ed.), *Economic Dynamism in the Asia-Pacific*. London, Routledge, 1998.

'Uneven crises: institutional foundations of East Asian economic turmoil', *Economy and Society*, 28(3), 1999.

'Governing growth and inequality: the continuing relevance of strategic economic planning', Chapter 22 of Richard P. Appelbaum and William I. Robinson (eds), *Critical Globalization Studies*. New York, Routledge, 2005.

'Unintended consequences: social policy, state institutions and the "stalling" of the Malaysian industrialisation project', *Economy and Society*, 36(1), 2007 (with Richard Phillips).

'China and global development: towards a Global-Asian Era?', *Contemporary Politics*, 14 (4), 2008.

1

MAKING SENSE OF EAST ASIAN TRANSFORMATION

From the re-emergence of Japan as an industrial power in the 1950s through to the recent rise of China as a potential economic and political behemoth, the story of East Asian development has been central to any serious analysis of the dynamics and trajectory of the global political economy. In the essays that constitute this book, I offer an account of some of the key elements that have helped forge the nature and contours of East Asian development over the past half century or so. These essays were originally written between 1993 and 2008. For presentation here, however, they have been updated and re-written in order to take account of more recent developments and scholarly interventions and to render explicit what was originally only implicit: an underlying narrative coherence.

In essence this narrative coherence and the theorisations integrated within it, revolves around the role of state-market relations (or economic governance) in the forging of the economic dynamism of some – though by no means all – of that part of the Eurasian land mass and its adjacent island states that stretches from Burma in the west to Japan in the east and from China in the north to Indonesia in the south. This focus on state-market relations, with their particular social and institutional sources and attendant politics and policy agendas, marks-out this book as a contribution to a long tradition of political-economic analysis that originated not (or at least not especially) in the classical political economy of Smith, Ricardo or Say (nor in the work of their principal neoclassical revisionists, Jervons, Walras and Marshall), but in the work (at one and the same time related and disparate) of Marx, Weber, Keynes, Schumpeter and Polanyi.[1] Their tradition – that of *critical* political economy – sought explanations not merely for the sources of dynamic capitalism, but for its internal contradictions and its social consequences; for its structural tendency, amongst other things, to degenerate into periodic crises.

For 50 years, the East Asian world-region has been 'home' to some of the world's most dynamic capitalist economies; but as elsewhere, they have been dynamic economies that have threatened to spin out of control, as some of them did spectacularly in the late 1990s and could well do so again in the coming decade. This book offers a series of related explanations for this contradictory dynamism and its consequences. Its focus, however, is not on East Asia as a whole, but on some of its supposed 'miracle' economies – predominantly (though not exclusively) South Korea, Taiwan, Hong Kong, Singapore,[2] Malaysia and China – that until relatively recently were considered part of the 'developing world', though with China still firmly rooted in that category. It is the economic growth and development of these countries, together with Japan, that have been the primary focus for scholarly debate and policy analysis on East Asia. Furthermore, it is their development experiences (with the exception of China's) that have been repackaged along neoliberal lines (as I show in Chapter 2) as ideologically-distorted complements to those of the USA and Britain, and offered-up in advice to the developing world on how to pull the 'rags to riches' trick. In as far as this process is ongoing, in spite of the global financial crisis of the late 2000s and the explanatory-policy failures of neoliberal economic theory that it has exposed, an exposition – and a reminder – of the role of the state in East Asia's dynamic capitalism, continues to be of crucial importance; certainly for many parts of the developing world, but perhaps also for 'radical neoliberal' developed economies – such as Britain – where 'free-market' prescriptions over the last 30 years have produced a dangerously unbalanced, asymmetrical economic structure.[3]

In this introductory chapter I begin by acknowledging the remarkable economic rise, since the 1950s, of the principal countries with which the book will be concerned. Subsequently, I sketch some of the concepts that will help to guide my analysis throughout the book. I then turn to a brief summary of the contents of the various chapters to show how the particular analyses they contain build one on another to presage my general conclusion: that the global political economy, and thus the life experiences of all that depend upon it, may be on the verge of being reconstructed by a new form of globalisation: a 'Global-Asian Era'.

Rags to riches

Puncturing pre-existing myths about the supposed 'miraculous' nature of East Asian economic development from the late 1950s through to the early 1990s, Paul Krugman (1994) has reminded us that there was nothing especially noteworthy in the economic growth of Japan, South Korea and the rest that set them apart, for instance, from the former Soviet Union (USSR). All of them had achieved very high, and broadly similar, growth records as a consequence of mobilising and combining vast quantities of both labour and capital, rather than through productive, technological innovation (ultimately, the only route to sustainable, high value-adding and thus high wage economies). Although Krugman's argument was undoubtedly right, compared with the progress of other developing and industrializing societies prior to the mid-1990s, some of the East Asian countries were unusual.

If we take one relevant index, gross national income (GNI) per capita, extrapolating from the data in Table 1.1 we can see that whereas the proportional increases

TABLE 1.1 Gross national income per capita (current US$) by country, 1965–2008

Country Name	1965	1970	1975	1980	1985	1990	1995	2000	2005	2008
China	100	120	170	190	290	310	530	930	1740	2940
Hong Kong	700	890	2040	4910	6110	11950	23490	26570	28150	31420
Indonesia	—	80	190	430	530	590	1010	590	1250	2010
Japan	890	—	4100	8920	10900	25300	40350	34620	38950	38210
Korea, Rep.	130	260	530	1560	2340	5660	10770	—	16900	21530
Malaysia	320	380	760	1570	1950	2260	4030	3450	5200	6970
Singapore	520	910	2300	4140	6890	11200	23260	22960	27670	34760
Thailand	130	200	320	610	790	1410	2690	1960	2670	2840
Brazil	270	420	970	1890	1570	2540	3740	3870	3970	7350
India	110	110	160	230	300	370	380	450	740	1070
France	2050	—	5560	11040	9640	19130	25190	24450	34940	42250
Germany	—	—	5440	10800	9560	19500	28630	25500	34990	42440
United Kingdom	—	—	3560	7100	8100	15480	19430	25480	38320	45390
United States	3670	—	6840	11140	17070	22080	27910	34410	43570	47580

Source: The World Bank: World Development Indicators http://ddp-ext.worldbank.org/ext/DDPQQ/member.do?method=getMembers&userid=1&queryId=135, (accessed 17 March 2010)

from 1965 to 1995 in Brazil, Thailand and Indonesia (from 1970 in its case) were respectively 1,385, 2,069 and 1,263 per cent (highly respectable growth rates in their own right), in Hong Kong and Singapore, the equivalent respective increases were 3,356 and 4,473 per cent. Though it had (re) industrialized earlier than the others, Japan, between 1965 and 1995, achieved a 4,435 per cent growth in GNI per capita. South Korea, however, was the ultimate star performer on this measure, ramping-up 8,285 per cent – an extraordinary 80-fold increase in GNI per capita – in the same 30 year time frame that India and China were achieving 345 and 530 percentage increases respectively. While China's economic growth took-off after the benefits of economic reform began to be felt – with a 1,547 per cent increase in GNI per capita between 1980 and 2008 – its most appropriate comparator, India, on this measure at least, performed less well, with a modest 465 per cent increase in the same time frame (extrapolated from Table 1.1).

Bringing this measure of economic growth and comparative material well-being through to the present day, it is clear that industrialization and economic transformation have placed not only Japan, but some of the East Asian newly industrialized countries (NICs) at par with the world's longest-standing advanced economies. This is clear not only from the 2008 data presented in Table 1.1, but from other data.[4] On the basis of this same measure (GNI per capita), the world's 20 most developed economies (ranging from Luxembourg to Italy) consist of 15 European countries together with Canada, the USA, Japan, Singapore and Brunei[5] (though from the data presented in Table 1.1, it would also be appropriate to include Hong Kong and South Korea). For further comparative purposes, it seems that Spain, for instance, comes in at twenty-eighth, Argentina at forty-third, South Africa at sixty-eighth, Turkey at seventy-second and Russia at eighty-second on the GNI per capita world league table.

TABLE 1.2 Life expectancy at birth (total years) by country, 1960–2008

Country Name	1960	1965	1970	1975	1980	1985	1990	1995	2000	2005	2008
China	36.32	57.38	61.74	65.06	65.50	66.67	68.25	69.80	71.41	72.62	—
Hong Kong	66.04	67.65	70.95	73.37	74.67	76.43	77.38	78.68	80.88	81.58	—
Indonesia	41.49	44.60	47.92	51.32	54.81	58.61	61.73	64.71	67.53	69.79	—
Japan	67.67	70.20	71.95	75.06	76.09	77.65	78.84	79.54	81.08	81.93	—
Korea, Rep.	54.15	56.68	61.84	63.96	65.80	68.53	71.29	73.39	75.86	78.43	—
Malaysia	54.28	—	61.55	—	66.88	68.88	70.29	71.52	72.65	73.81	—
Singapore	63.68	65.73	67.74	69.89	71.49	72.89	74.34	76.40	78.05	79.99	—
Thailand	54.76	—	59.72	—	66.23	68.77	68.96	68.41	68.26	68.57	68.99
Brazil	54.70	—	58.75	—	62.68	64.61	66.50	68.50	70.29	71.75	72.52
India	42.26	45.77	49.30	52.84	55.71	57.85	59.65	61.21	62.47	64.02	—
France	70.24	71.01	72.01	72.85	74.18	75.25	76.75	77.78	78.91	80.21	—
Germany	69.54	70.17	70.46	71.39	72.63	74.15	75.21	76.42	77.93	78.93	—
United Kingdom	71.13	71.62	71.97	72.72	73.68	74.63	75.88	76.84	77.74	78.95	—
United States	69.77	70.21	70.81	72.60	73.66	74.56	75.21	75.62	77.03	77.74	—

Source: The World Bank: World Development Indicators
http://ddp-ext.worldbank.org/ext/DDPQQ/member.do?method=getMembers&userid=1&queryId=135, (accessed 17 March 2010)

It seems, then, that though the economic growth records of Japan and the East Asian NICs may not have been 'miraculous', they clearly have been far better than those of any other developing countries, both during the period of their transition from 'industrializing' to 'industrialized' countries and through to the present day. But it is not merely in regard to their growth records that they have been superior. This has also been evident on a series of social development indicators.

If we take life expectancy (a key health indicator), for instance, then it is clear from Table 1.2 that while in 1960 Japan, Hong Kong and Singapore had better rates than elsewhere in the region (and far better than India or Brazil), they lagged behind the most advanced industrial economies, such as France, Germany, the UK and the USA. By 2005, however, they had matched and, indeed, outstripped the life expectancy rates in these 'mature' developed countries. What is more, other East Asian countries – China, South Korea and Malaysia, for instance – while starting from a lower base than the others in 1960 (China from a much lower base), by 2005 had life expectancy rates that had begun to approximate those of Western Europe and the USA (see Table 1.2).

If we take another key health indicator, childhood mortality rates, a similar picture is evident. The data in Table 1.3 shows that while starting from a base line in 1960 that was typically lower that those of the advanced industrial countries (particularly true of South Korea), by 2005, Japan, Singapore and Korea had matched or bettered the achievements of France, Britain and the USA. On this index, Malaysia and, particularly, Thailand, had also made substantial progress, far better in their case than, for instance, Indonesia or Brazil.

During their periods of industrialization or re-industrialization, then, Japan and the East Asian NICs seem to have achieved far higher levels of economic and social development than their capitalist equivalents in the developing world.

TABLE 1.3 Mortality rates for children under five years of age (per 1,000 under-5s), 1960–2005

Country Name	1960	1965	1970	1975	1980	1985	1990	1995	2000	2005
China	—	—	118.2	86.5	58.9	46.1	45.4	43.7	36.6	25.4
Hong Kong	—	—	—	—	—	—	—	—	—	—
Indonesia	216	204	172	153	125	109	91	66	48	36
Japan	39.9	24.7	17.7	13.1	9.9	7.4	6.4	5.9	4.5	3.7
Korea, Rep.	127	—	54	—	18	—	9	6.4	5.4	5
Malaysia	113	88	70	55	42	31	22	17	14	12
Singapore	40	—	27	—	13	—	8	—	4.1	2.9
Thailand	148.8	118.6	102.6	82.9	59	42	31	19.7	12.7	8.3
Brazil	176.3	157.3	133.7	109	89.5	73.7	57.9	42.1	31.8	24.2
India	234.1	211.3	190.3	171.5	156.2	136.8	116.6	104.1	91.2	76.9
France	31.6	25.2	21.3	16.2	12.8	10.3	9	6.2	5.5	4.6
Germany	40	—	26	—	16	—	9	6.5	—	4.7
United Kingdom	25.5	22.2	20.8	17.7	14.3	11.2	9.5	7.2	—	6
United States	30.2	27.5	23.8	18.7	15.2	12.9	11.4	9.3	—	7.9

Source: The World Bank: World Development Indicators http://ddp-ext.worldbank.org/ext/DDPQQ/member. do?method=getMembers&userid=1&queryId=135, (accessed 17 March 2010)

Subsequently, they went on to broadly match and sometimes surpass the perform-ance of many of the countries of Western Europe and North America. In addition, these achievements were sometimes forged at the same time as they delivered low levels of income inequality. By the mid-2000s, and on the basis of net income, the gini coefficients for Japan and South Korea, for instance, were 0.32 and 0.31 respectively.[6] While they were some way from matching the world's most egalitar-ian societies in income terms – the European social democracies such as France and Sweden (with gini coefficients of 0.28 and 0.23 respectively) – these data suggest that they are more egalitarian than those developed economies, such as Britain and the United States (with gini coefficients of 0.34 and 0.38 respectively), that in recent years have succumbed most to neoliberal economic and social reform, with its profoundly negative consequences for social equality (see Pontusson 2005 and, more generally, Wilkinson and Pickett 2009).

The 'rags to riches' story in East Asia, underlined briefly by the data presented here, provides the backdrop to the discussions and arguments developed in this book. While the empirical detail of economic dynamism and its contribution to social development will enter the analysis judiciously from now onwards, we need to mark here that these achievements would have been almost inconceivable had the East Asia countries emerged after World War II not as 'plan rational' political economies (see Chapter 3), guided by pro-active states who engaged in strate-gic economic planning, but as *laissez faire* 'market rational' political economies, as orthodox economic scholarship would have us believe. That Japan, South Korea, Taiwan and the others, and China today, are examples of successful economic and social development 'orchestrated' by proactive states, is nothing new in the annals of comparative economic history. Indeed, the world's first and second generation industrial economies, with very few exceptions, were themselves, in part, a prod-uct of strategic economic planning when they were developing countries. Chang (2002), has shown how the 'rags to riches' story in Britain, France, Germany and (particularly) the United States, for instance, was intimately bound-up with indus-trial policies designed to protect infant domestic industries from foreign competi-tion. Most spectacularly, Chang (2002, Table 2.1: 17) shows that from the 1820s to the late 1940s, the US Federal Government protected its domestic manufactur-ing industries from foreign competition with tariffs that averaged from 41 to 45 per cent. This is a crucial part of the 'western' rags to riches story that orthodox economic opinion has conveniently forgotten (or was never taught).

Development, transition or transformation?

In this book I am concerned with explaining the processes of political-economic *transformation* in East Asia and with their consequences both in that world-region and (especially in Chapters 7 and 8) globally. My preference for the term 'trans-formation' rather than the more usual and – at first sight – seemingly similar terms, 'development' or 'transition', has scientific grounds and this needs to be briefly explained.

Conventionally these three terms have been used, separately or interchangeably, to grasp the processes of economic, political and social change, irrespective of scalar considerations.[7] *Development* has been the most extensively used of them. Although this term has long been associated with major disciplinary (e.g. sociology, politics, economics) and interdisciplinary (e.g. development studies and urban planning) arenas of social-scientific and policy analysis, it seems that its use, in the latter at least, has been more 'common sense' than scientific. In English, according to *The Concise Oxford Dictionary*, 'development' refers to a 'gradual unfolding, fuller working out, growth, stage of advancement, more elaborate form' (as well as other meanings inappropriate to social-scientific analysis). As a result, without significant definitional clarification, it seems that the term has multiple, mutually exclusive meanings that render it too imprecise to be useful as an analytic concept for understanding historical change. Notwithstanding this qualification, the term 'development' is used ubiquitously in 'everyday' discourse and consequently it would be difficult to write a book of this sort without employing the term from time to time. As a result, when 'development' is used here, it will be as a synonym for 'transformation'.

Applications of the notion of *transition* to the understanding of change processes has had a long history, for instance, in the political and administrative sciences where it has been used to refer, among other things, to changes in policy regimes and organisational forms subsequent to changes in the governing authority. In historiography – a science more directly relevant to current concerns – the term has been employed, for instance, in reference to the changes in late medieval and early modern Europe that ultimately resulted in the replacement of feudal economic, political and social orders by capitalist ones (as in the work of Hilton 1976 and Holton 1985).

During the 1990s, 'transition' was a term that dominated analytic and media discourses on the changes that were taking place in the former state-socialist countries of Central and Eastern Europe subsequent to the historical rupture that occurred variously in those countries between 1989 and 1991. Pertinent to some of my concerns here, it is a term that is now influencing analyses of changes that are afoot (or not afoot as the case may be) in China, as in the otherwise excellent work of Minxin Pei (2006). As in Central-Eastern Europe, however, so in China. The use of the term 'transition' is beginning to impose particular ways of 'thinking' and 'seeing' the processes of Chinese 'development' which are, as in the earlier European cases (see Henderson 1998: Chapter 1), inappropriate. They are so because as *The Concise Oxford Dictionary* indicates, 'transition' is understood as a 'passage, change, from one place or state or act or set of circumstances to another'. The sense the term conveys, then, is of movement from a known starting point to a *known* end point. Thus while a discourse of transition is a legitimate way of understanding processes of historical change whose consequences and legacies are now settled (as in the transition from feudalism to capitalism in Europe), this is not the case when we are dealing with contemporary processes where we ourselves are living through the period of historical change. In those circumstances – and this is true of most of

East Asia, including China – to adopt a discourse of transition is, in effect, to assume that we can predict the future and allow our predictions (albeit unconsciously) to influence our analyses of the change process. Clearly, this is a methodologically dubious way of proceeding that is likely to lead to implausible analyses and inappropriate policy responses. This is particularly so when our commitment to transition discourses leads us to assume that China, for instance, is – or, more normatively, needs to be – on the road to some 'western' liberal-democratic form of modernity; a proposition advanced by Will Hutton (2007) among others, but a supposed future that has been heavily contested, for instance, by Martin Jacques (2009).

When it comes to the analysis of recent and contemporary history where the processes of change are very much ongoing, it seems that we require a different conceptual lens and with it, a different discourse; one influenced by the notion of *transformation*. In *The Concise Oxford Dictionary* the verb 'to transform' is defined as '[making] (especially considerable) change in the form, outward appearance, character, disposition etc.' of the element in question. While economic, political and social transformation must include changes in content as well as form, it seems clear that, at least in English, the term 'transformation' signals a process with a known starting point, but with an *unknown* (and thus no pre-defined) end point (Henderson 1998: 4–9). Employing a discourse of transformation, then, allows for the possibility of serious – but, crucially, open-ended – reflection on the dynamics and consequences of political-economic change. As such it is a far more appropriate discourse than its competitors for analysing the changes that have been forged in East Asia; from the re-industrialization of Japan and the nascent industrialization of colonial Hong Kong in the early 1950s through to the industrial powerhouse that China has become today.

Things to come

In many ways Chapter 2 sets the tone for the rest of the book. It does so, in part, by suggesting that the contemporary moment in East Asian transformation – and indeed, the global political economy as a whole – is perhaps best depicted as being one of 'crisis'. The notion of crisis first broached in this chapter, and then developed in various ways throughout the book (particularly in chapter 7), however, is not the one evident in European languages with its overwhelmingly pessimistic connotations. Rather, the notion of crisis adopted here is that evident in Chinese. There, it is a more optimistic expression that emphasizes the dialectical relation between 'danger' and 'opportunity'.

Having discussed the utility of viewing East Asian transformation through this particular lens, the chapter turns to an assessment of the ways in which a neoliberal reading of the sources of the region's extraordinary development record has been used as an intellectual (indeed, ideological) justification by the OECD, the IMF, the World Bank and other international agencies, for the national development projects they have recommended to governments across the developing world. Subsequently, the chapter turns to a discussion of the major forms of capitalism that have been evident in East Asia, focussing, *inter alia*, on Japan, South Korea, Taiwan, and most recently, China. The concern here is to link the nature of these forms – influenced as they all have been (though in different ways) by interventionist states – to the international competitiveness of their respective economies and major firms and to the consequences they have had for social development and inequality in particular. The chapter then turns to a discussion of the ways in which some of these forms of capitalism have articulated with the processes of globalization in recent decades before concluding with a brief commentary on the continuing prospects for transformation in the region and the broader global implications of this. In so doing, these latter sections signal some of the implications of the rise of China for the nature of the global political-economic order, an issue that is dealt with in detail in chapters 7 and 8.

The starting point of Chapter 3 is the discussion in the previous chapter of the way in which the East Asian economic 'miracles' of the 1950s onwards have often been communicated, in intellectual and policy discourses alike, as 'free market' success stories. Beginning with a four-fold typology of national political economies, the chapter critically engages with the neoliberal account of East Asian development. It does so by locating Japan, South Korea, Taiwan, China, etc., within the typology along with the US, Britain and a number of European countries ('east' and 'west'). In doing so, the subsequent discussion – which draws the comparisons and contrasts between the various political economies – is facilitated. This discussion recognizes that while all of the national examples are hybrids in relation to the typological categories (China being a particular case in point), all of the East Asian cases approximate more clearly a 'plan rational' form than they do the 'market rational' form as neoliberal economic theory, by implication, would have us believe.

Throughout the discussion in this chapter, and indeed, throughout the book, the real empirical differences between the states and societies in question (including their systems of economic governance) is recognized, as are the social 'dark sides' of their development projects (inequality, repression of opposition, etc., as relevant) during particular phases of their recent past.

Picking up on the previous chapter's discussion of the role of the state in East Asia's economic transformation, Chapter 4 focuses on the period in the late 1990s – typically known as the East Asian 'financial crisis' – that neoliberal commentators considered proof for their belief that state 'interference' in free markets was counterproductive. While the chapter rejects such simplistic readings of the economic reversals that affected a number of East Asian countries at that time (associated, as they were with such notions as 'crony capitalism' and 'moral hazard'), it accepts that there were causes of the 'crisis' that were associated with the institutions of national economic governance in the region. Given variations in the incidence and depth of the reversals, however (as between, say, near economic collapse in Thailand compared with a relatively minor recession in Singapore), the chapter argues that the causes were intimately associated with asymmetrical state capacities to mediate between the respective domestic and international economies. Consequently, in order to explain the causes of economic reversal in, say, Thailand or South Korea, it was necessary to account for the relative absence of reversal in Taiwan and Singapore. Furthermore, the chapter suggests that while many of the internal causes of the economic reversal in Thailand, Malaysia and Hong Kong, for instance, can be traced to real estate speculation encouraged by neoliberal 'light touch' regulation, this was not true of South Korea where different dynamics were at work. Having discussed some of the general issues associated with 'developmental states' in Chapter 3, Chapter 4 is ultimately a discourse on the uneven presence and differing forms of developmental states in East Asia and on their possibilities for effective economic governance in the context of neoliberal globalization.

Chapter 5 takes the general argument of the previous chapter a stage further. While Chapter 4 raises the question of the appropriate forms for national economic governance in an age of neoliberal globalization, this chapter examines a relatively neglected area for work on East Asia and, indeed, the global political economy more generally: the relation of different forms of economic governance to the incidence of inequality and poverty.

The chapter proceeds by sketching two essential building blocks in the argument: the relation of economic growth to inequality and of economic governance to the growth record. It then turns to an examination of the globalization-governance-inequality/poverty matrix in two of the East Asian countries most affected by economic reversal in the late 1990s: South Korea and Malaysia. Assessing their contrasting experiences, the chapter shows that in an age of neoliberal globalization, the maintenance of state capacities for strategic economic planning seems to be essential if economic growth and development is to be achieved and sustained with low levels of social inequality.

Continuing with the theme of appropriate forms of economic governance, but expanding it to include attention to the economic implications of social policy, Chapter 6 looks at some of the growing problems for the continuation of Malaysia's industrialization project. Against the backdrop of the rise of China as a major competitor in the markets for manufactured commodities on which Malaysia (and other recently industrialized economies) depend, this chapter examines some of the consequences for industrial development of the Malaysian government's redistribution and migration policies.

The chapter argues that while the former has been central to social harmony in Malaysia's multi-racial society, taken together with the country's immigration policies, it has constrained the movement of domestic companies into the higher valued-added operations that are necessary for achieving the knowledge and technology-intensive forms of industrial development that are essential for sustaining Malaysia's prosperity. Partly as a consequence of these laudable, but now inappropriate government priorities, key manufacturing sectors – such as electronics – have remained locked into low to medium technology operations. With the emergence of China as a low-cost, but increasingly innovative manufacturing powerhouse, this is a dangerous situation for a country's principal economic sector to be in.

While the book engages, in a number of its earlier chapters, with the re-emergence of China as a global economic and political power, it does so as part of the general discussion. In Chapter 7, however, I turn directly to the implications of China's transformation for the global political economy. Recognising that the emergence of China as an economic and political 'driver' of the global economy is becoming one of the defining moments of world history, the chapter argues that its dynamism and international expansion are on the verge of creating a 'critical disruption' in the global order that has pertained for over 60 years. The chapter explores this proposition by focussing on aspects of China's 'global footprint' in terms of its economic and political actions and their geo-political consequences, showing why these are likely to be markedly different from what has gone before.

Focussing particularly on China's economic-political relations with other parts of the developing (including the newly industrializing) world, the chapter sketches a series of vectors – trade, aid, human rights and energy security – along which its impacts are being registered. Returning to the theme of 'crisis', broached in Chapter 2, the chapter argues that, at least for these vectors, the rise of China is providing opportunities as well as dangers for national development projects. In this latter sense, part of the discussion in this chapter links to that in Chapter 6 on the constraints that China is posing for the deepening of Malaysia's (and other Southeast Asian countries') industrialization project.

In concluding the book, Chapter 8 provides an alternative to a mere summary of its core themes and arguments. Instead it projects some of those arguments into the future. Specifically, and drawing on the discussion in Chapter 7, it speculates about the implications of China's rise for the nature of the global order. In so doing it presents as a 'working hypothesis', a proposition that we may be on the verge of a 'Global-Asian Era'; a new global political-economic order that is likely to be dramatically different from the current 'Anglo-American Era'. While the chapter recognises that a 'western style' crisis in China is a possibility that could delay or even deflect the emergence of a Global-Asian Era, it ends by briefly sketching some of the wider implications of a China/Asian driven global order.

2

DANGER AND OPPORTUNITY IN THE TRANSFORMATION PROCESS

Political-economic transformations on the scale that has been wrought in East Asia since the 1950s, are always fraught with huge difficulties and risk. At the end of the twenty-first century's first decade, however, there seems to be widespread agreement among academic, media and political commentators alike, that our current epoch is one of turbulence and uncertainty unprecedented, perhaps, since the end of World War II. In such periods, the concept of crisis is often invoked as a means of grasping and expressing our predicament. The multifaceted and dynamic crisis we now confront, however, should not be understood in the largely negative, medical sense, evident in European languages: a decisive moment in a potentially terminal illness. Rather, it needs to be understood in the more optimistic sense evident in Chinese.

In Chinese, the term for 'crisis' combines two symbols: *wei*, meaning 'danger' and *ji*, 'opportunity'.[1] This dialectical conception of crisis, coming as it does from Asia's most important indigenous language, helps us to grasp the condition of contemporary East Asian transformation and, indeed, that of the global political economy more generally.

Beginning in Japan in the early 1990s and emerging in other parts of East Asia by the end of that decade, the region has indeed been in crisis in the Chinese sense of the term. Economic and social development have been profoundly uneven in the region, both within its major countries (China particularly so) and from one country to another (Japan and Singapore, for instance, compared to Indonesia or The Philippines), compounding pre-existing tendencies towards socio-political fragmentation.[2] Economic development has also brought with it untold environmental degredation, of which travellers to even one of the region's most advanced territories – Hong Kong – become immediately aware. Additionally, and attempts to develop institutions for regional governance such as ASEAN and ASEAN + 3 notwithstanding (see, for instance, Thompson 1998: Chapters 7 and 13, Ba 2003), the processes now afoot are leading not only to cut-throat economic competition in the region,[3] but potentially, to geo-political conflict as well.[4] When we add to these issues and more, the impact of the global economic recession that began in 2008, then the foreseeable future of the East Asian region is clearly one that is fraught with danger.

But at one and the same time, the recent past and the contemporary period have been periods of opportunity. In little more than a generation, hundreds of millions of people across the region have been lifted out of abject poverty, most spectacularly in China, and some of these are now on their way to enjoying the sort of prosperity that has been known in North America and Western Europe for some time. Similar processes to those that have underlain such achievements continue to transform the lives of hundreds of millions more in the region. While workers (inevitably under capitalism), women and some ethnic minority groups (such as Tibetans and Uighurs in China and Koreans in Japan) have been obliged to bear the negative consequences of development more than others, it seems clear that ongoing economic transformation in East Asia continues to promise a scale of generalized prosperity unknown in human history.

It is this interface between danger and opportunity that now sets the parameters for ongoing transformation in the region. In this chapter I seek to explore the economic possibilities inherent in East Asian transformation, identify their limitations and evaluate some of their implications for other parts of the world economy. In so doing, I use this chapter to 'set the tone' for the discussions that follow in subsequent chapters.

The chapter begins by assessing the significance of the East Asian 'miracle' as an intellectual – and, indeed, in neoliberal discourse, an ideological – construct. It then turns to a discussion of the major forms of capitalism that compose the region's political economies and to some of the processes of globalization that connect them to the world economy more generally. It subsequently assesses the prospects for continued economic transformation in the region and its broader political implications, before concluding with a brief comment on the challenge that East Asia represents.

East Asian economic 'miracles' as intellectual and ideological constructs

A consideration of the significance of East Asian 'models' of economic progress for growth and transformation elsewhere in the world takes us straight to the heart of the central issue of how the economic 'miracles' there came about. It does so because it throws into high relief determinants of economic development and performance that have been popularized, in various combinations, in academic and policy debate. While these include such things as the historical contexts and conjunctures out of which the transformative processes in the region emerged; the role of foreign aid (military and civil, and mainly from the USA) in the context of the Cold War; the subsequent benefits of foreign direct investment in terms of transfers of knowledge, technology and skills; the significance of a regionally unique 'economic culture' rooted in Confucianism; the existence of repressive labour systems that have ensured supplies of cheap labour (cheap, that is, in previous decades in South Korea, Taiwan, Singapore, etc., but still centrally important in China, Vietnam, etc., today); the importance of free markets; and the role of state policy and influence. As I and many others have interrogated the significance of these determinants elsewhere (for instance, Appelbaum and Henderson1992, Amsden 1989, Wade 1990, Woo-Cumings 1999, Castells 2000b: Chapter 4, Chang 2003), with two exceptions, I do not propose to traverse the same ground here. These exceptions – markets, states and their inter-relation – do warrant further attention as it is these determinants that continue to form the major intellectual legacies of the region for countries that are currently in the throes of economic transformation; not only, for instance, from South Africa to Russia, or from Romania to Brazil, but for Britain and other advanced industrial countries that have been badly damaged by the excesses of neoliberal, or 'market ideological' capitalism (see Chapter 3).[5]

Markets

The rapid economic transformation of Japan from the 1950s and the 'first generation' East Asian NICs – Hong Kong, Taiwan, South Korea and Singapore – from the 1960s, came as a surprise to radical development analysts schooled in the various traditions of dependency theory as that had been developed by Baran (1957), Frank (1969) and others. This work implicitly denied the possibility of development in East Asia because of it was imbricated (along with Latin America, Africa, etc.) in the neo-imperialist structure of the world economy and inter-state system.[6] It did not come as a surprise, however, to economists imbued with the neoclassical paradigm. Since the work of Jacob Viner (1953) and that of Peter Bauer and Basil Yamey (1957), neoclassical analysts had become convinced that the blockages to development in what was then widely known as the 'Third World' were largely self-imposed. They were seen as the products of 'distortions' in the markets for labour, capital, natural resources, technology and so on that arose from endogenous cultural forms and social practices, but particularly from the 'interference' (and usually corruption) of the national (and sometimes the provincial or local) state. It was argued that the reason why Japan had become one of the world's most successful economies and why the East Asian NICs (at that time almost alone amongst the societies of the developing world) had moved decisively in the direction of high productivity-high wage economies, was because they had been relatively free from market distortions. In particular, it was suggested that unlike many other developing, and indeed developed economies (France and Britain being examples at that time), their respective states had either not intervened to distort markets, or if they had intervened, they had done so to correct pre-existing market distortions. Either way, their economies had been exposed rapidly to world-market competition, partly through export-oriented strategies, and as a consequence domestic prices (for labour, capital, etc.) were a reflection of international conditions. Having got relative prices 'right', the positive influence of 'market forces' were maximized, and the near double-digit growth rates typical of the period from the 1960s to the 1990s, achieved.

From this latter perspective, the experience of economic transformation in East Asia seemed to vindicate the premises of neoclassical economic theory and Japan and the East Asian NICs came to be seen – together with Thatcherite Britain, and to a lesser extent Chile (subsequent to the military coup in 1973) – as the world's most significant empirical supports of the truth claims of neoclassical theorizing. In such circumstances it was not long before this particular version of economic transformation in East Asia became enshrined as a major ideological support for the 'structural adjustment' policies of the International Monetary Fund (IMF), the World Bank and similar international economic agencies, as they attempted to influence the state-economy relation in the developing world, and more recently in the former state-socialist societies of Eastern Europe.[7]

The first attempt to use the East Asian experience to legitimate neoclassical propositions came in the 1960s, in a series of OECD-sponsored studies of developing economies. Taiwan was the East Asian 'representative' in this research programme, and in the book summarizing the results of that work (Little *et al.* 1970) it was used as a benchmark of what could be achieved if autarkic development strategies associated with import-substitution industrialization (the norm in the developing world at the time) were abandoned in favour of liberalized, relatively open domestic economies whose growth was predicated on a full engagement in international trade via export-oriented strategies.

In addition to projecting the Taiwanese experience as a model for the rest of the developing world, interestingly this work set the tone as to how that experience (and those of the East Asian NICs generally) came to be explained in more sophisticated neoclassical pronouncements from the 1970s onwards. While insisting that Taiwan's export success was the result of a multiplicity of factors, Little *et al.* acknowledged that 'among these the economic policies followed by the Government were certainly important' (1970: 256). Unfortunately, the only government policies they discussed were the ones directed towards the liberalization of the domestic economy, the enhancement of markets and export promotion. Proscriptive economic planning, interventionist policies such as the selective protection of domestic markets, extensive state ownership of upstream industries and banks – all evident in Taiwan at that time (Wade 1990) were buried under the words 'various other measures were adopted as well' (Little *et al.* 1970: 255). Twenty years later, it seemed that the position of orthodox economics on East Asia had barely progressed. In spite of volumes of non-neoclassical scholarship to the contrary, the eminent Johns Hopkins University/World Bank economist, Bela Balassa, still felt able to comment that 'It would appear . . . that the success of the Taiwanese economy cannot be attributed to planning' (Balassa 1991: 103).

Drawing on the work of Little, Balassa and others, the influence of neoclassical theorizing as the principal underpinning for the policy prescriptions of the major international economic agencies proceeded apace. Particularly important in this sense were developments in the World Bank, which by 1981, with the publication of the 'Berg Report' on Sub-Saharan Africa (World Bank 1981), had become 'captured' by the market-enhancing/minimalist state conception of the route to efficient, dynamic economies. Two years later, the Bank's *World Development Report* (World Bank 1983) embodied what had become its prevailing wisdom: namely that 'the *universal* application of neoclassical economic theory holds the key to economic efficiency' (former World Bank official quoted by Hayter and Watson 1985: 140 – my emphasis).

While there were other important intellectual monuments along the World Bank's 'road to Damascus' that need not detain us here, that same year (1983) one of the more ideologically committed of neoclassical economists, Deepak Lal, underlined the significance of his view of the East Asian experience. In the context of an attack on the very idea that developing economies require forms of theorization distinct from other economies (and hence their own specialization, 'development economics') he contrasted the structure and performance of the South Korean and Taiwanese economies with that of India. While the Indian government since independence (1947) had pursued an autarkic development strategy based on ISI and domestic market protection, which he considered responsible, through to the 1980s, for India's economic stagnation, South Korea had flourished, he suggested, as a consequence of Government policies that had ensured 'virtually free markets' (Lal 1983: 87–90). Unfortunately for Lal, 'virtually free' hid such a vast armoury of market constraining policies relating to technology access, corporate finance, speculative investment, foreign investment and many more (see among others, Woo 1991, Chang 1994 and Kim, E.M. 1997) that Nigel Harris felt able to comment that South Korean economic success has been:

> just as much a triumph of state capitalism as [were] the achievements of the first Five Year Plans in the Soviet Union or the People's Republic of China.
> (Harris 1987: 145)

Although Lal's was possibly an extreme position (as was Harris's from a different point on the ideological spectrum), it was symptomatic of the way the East Asian experience, reconstructed to fit neoclassical preconceptions, had become an ideological battering ram to wield against the defences of governments around the world who thought that a modicum of economic planning, and (sometimes) a commitment to redistribution and a welfare state, were the best ways of pursuing growth (with equity). In the case of the World Bank and the IMF, 'structural adjustment' policies based on the supposedly universal principles of neoclassical reasoning continued to be foisted on the developing world and, for a while, the former state-socialist societies of Eastern Europe. This continued in spite of the fact that, as a consequence of Japanese pressure, the World Bank was forced to reconsider the role of the state in economic growth and transformation.

By the late 1980s, the Japanese Government had become the second largest contributor (after the USA) to World Bank funds and was becoming increasingly irritated that its own development experience – so much associated with the state's 'administrative guidance' – was effectively being denied in the policy advice (backed by leverage) which the Bank was offering to governments of the developing world. The consequence of Japanese pressure was the Bank's reassessment of the East Asian route to industrial capitalism (the study was also financed by the Japanese Government) which culminated in its report, *The East Asian Miracle* (World Bank 1993). As Wade (1996) shows, the report was a contradictory mishmash negotiated out of the political need of the Bank to accommodate the Japanese Government's legitimate interests, on the one hand, and its firm conviction that it should hold to the neoclassical 'structural adjustment' line on the other. Though the publication of *The East Asian Miracle* was a source of surprise, if not excitement, in academic and policy circles, there is little evidence that it had much effect on World Bank – or IMF – advice and funding decisions.

Whatever one's assessment of the various orthodox accounts of economic growth and performance in East Asia, the spectacular rise of China as an economic powerhouse has posed explanatory difficulties for those economists and international agencies who continue to be wedded to the neoclassical paradigm. Indeed, with the exception of a few contributions that are staggering in their ideologically audacious 'economy with the truth' (see, for instance, Cheung 1986: 65–79) and a number of more measured interventions (for example, Sachs and Woo 1994), neoclassical commentary on the macro level transformation of the Chinese economy since the early 1980s has been somewhat muted. This is perhaps not surprising given that in the lexicon of neoclassical theory it is supposed to be impossible for an economy to grow at the double-digit rates of the Chinese economy when the state still controls many of its 'commanding heights', where markets are still only partly responsible for resource allocation, where selective domestic market protection continues through to the present day, and where the development of property rights and the rule of law are recent and still insecure phenomena. In short, the state – in its national, provincial and local forms – remains central to economic progress in China (Wang 2009), and it is impossible to conceive of a plausible and empirically adequate explanation of Chinese development over the past 25 years without recognizing this fact.

States

If the perceived role of free markets in East Asian transformation has been appropriated by academic, political and policy interests for their own ends, then alternative explanations of economic expansion in the region have been used by others as a basis for policies to improve prospects in the developing world and elsewhere. Various conceptions of the role of the state in East Asian transformation are outlined in Chapter 3 and I have no wish to pre-empt that discussion here. It is important to note, however, that whatever position on the issue is adopted, the assertion of the *necessity* of a proactive state for development purposes in the region (and thus strategic economic planning) remains *at least* of enormous symbolic significance when viewed from the perspective of other countries and world-regions seeking pathways to prosperity.

As I have indicated earlier, many parts of the developing world continue to be under considerable economic and political pressure to liberalize and deregulate their economies and reduce welfare expenditure, etc. In many developing and developed countries (amongst the latter, Britain being perhaps the classic case in point) essentially neoliberal policy agendas continue to be the order of the day, in spite of the considerable evidence that they fuelled the economic crises in Mexico in the early 1980s, East Asia in the late 1990s (see Chapter 4), Argentina in 2001 (among others) and most spectacularly, the global economic reversal that emerged in 2008. It is in such places that the theory and practice of the economically proactive state, informed by East Asian experiences through to the mid-1990s (and in some cases beyond), comes as an intellectual breath of fresh air.

In many cases analysts have gone further than mere assertion of a proactive role for the state and have attempted to specify the circumstances under which particular institutional frameworks and policy initiatives drawn from East Asian experiences may be worthy of attention in other contexts. I briefly review some of these arguments later.

In spite of a rising tide of 'state friendly' analyses of East Asian transformation from 1977 onwards,[8] it was Robert Wade, in his now classic, *Governing the Market* (Wade 1990), who was the first to begin to think through the implications of his version of this perspective for developing and other industrializing countries. While this is not the place to summarize his observations, it is worth noting that in addition to calling, for instance, for a central role for manufacturing industry in state policy thinking, and its need to be privileged in an investment structure which ensures tight regulation of finance capital,[9] Wade considered a centralized authoritarian state to have the best prospects of developing the institutions necessary for 'governing the market' in the initial stages of industrialization. For him these institutions needed to be in place before political democratization ensued, otherwise the tensions and conflicts typical of democracies were likely to engulf the economic bureaucracy, destroying the autonomy which Wade sees as necessary to effective economic management in the context of rapid industrialization.

In the 1990s and early 2000s, other contributions sought to use various 'state friendly' analyses of East Asian development to argue for a reorientation of transformation strategies in Eastern Europe. These were generally of two sorts. The first extrapolated from the assumption that the principal points of commonality between the two regions have been in the institutional legacies of state socialism. Consequently, it was argued that the most appropriate comparisons were to be made between the territories of the former Soviet Union on the one hand and China (and to a lesser extent Vietnam) on the other. Bolstered by arguments about the decisive role of central and local state institutions in recent Chinese industrialization (see, for instance, Qian and Weingast 1997, Nee and Su 1998), such contributions generally emphasized that the state orchestrated form of industrialization pursued by China (itself influenced by Japanese, South Korean and Taiwanese experiences) has produced far superior economic performance, with greater generalized prosperity, than the more market-centred forms typical of Russia and elsewhere in Eastern Europe (see, for instance, Nolan 1995, Lo and Radice 1998).

Other contributions, however, insisted that aspects of the experiences of capitalist East Asia were relevant to Eastern European circumstances more generally. Thornton (1995), for instance, recommended that Eastern European countries should adopt some of the institutional arrangements and management techniques of the Japanese economic bureaucracy, though without using a distorted version of its practices as an excuse to avoid dismantling state enterprises and heavy handed state direction of industry. Vartiainen (1995), on the other hand, argued that Eastern European countries had much that is positive to learn from the experience of state-guided economic development, not only of South Korea (prior to 1993) and Taiwan, but also of Austria and Finland.

The most developed arguments in this vein, however, came from Alice Amsden and her colleagues (1994) and some of the contributors to the volume edited by Henderson (1998). In the former case, Amsden *et al.* (1994: 49) argued that 'all successful industrialization experiences have rested on state intervention' (an argument endorsed, extended and deepened by Chang's work on the now developed economies – including the USA – when they were themselves developing economies; Chang 2002, 2007a). They used the experiences of South Korea and Taiwan, in particular, to argue that the former state-socialist economies of Eastern Europe required state co-ordination in order to be transformed into effective, high performing capitalist ones. In the latter case, a number of contributors argued that while East Asian experiences of industrialization and transformation did not constitute panaceas for Eastern Europe, they contained pointers – for instance in the state-business relation, the nature of the regulatory regimes and the institutional capacity of the economic bureaucracy – as to what types of initiative might be useful for building economic dynamism in the region.

With the hindsight of the late 2000s, we now know that such advice either never reached the respective Central-Eastern European governments, or if it did it was either ignored or squashed in the drive to 'sign-up' to the European Union's particular brand of economic neoliberalism. Only in Slovenia, it seems, was advice of this sort taken seriously, and then only by implication, as intellectuals and economic planners there probably drew more on Austrian than East Asian developmental models (cf. Whitley 1999: Chapter 8).

Whatever the relation of the state to economic performance in East Asia in the past, this relation has changed, at least in Japan and the NICs though less so, of course, in China. While this matter will be pursued in chapters 4 and 5, at this point we need to turn to other, more general questions, which have influenced the political-economic past and will continue to influence the future of the East Asian region.

Globalization and forms of capitalism

Raising the issue of the relation of states and markets to economic transformation in the East Asian region leads directly to a number of other issues. These include: the extent to which the economies of the region embody particular forms of capitalism that are distinct from those evident in Europe, North America and elsewhere, and which have differing implications for economic performance; the extent to which these distinctions are being eroded as a consequence of the integration of the region's economies into the wider global economy; and the nature of the competitive challenge posed by the region's economies and their constituent business organizations. In what follows in this section I assess the nature and significance of these issues, both in their own right and as a prelude to the penultimate section. Here, and in that section, I return to the dialectic of danger and opportunity – the dimensions of crisis – with which I began the chapter.

Competing capitalisms

Competition in the world economy involves not merely the drive of firms for greater market share, or the struggle of workers across the globe for jobs, better standards of living and better working conditions. Competition also involves a clash of different – in some cases radically different – versions of capitalism. With the advantage of hindsight, and with more than 130 years of mature (internationally competitive) industrial capitalism behind us, we now know that the core of capitalist economic systems (the elements they have in common) is more restricted than earlier thought. Indeed, for Gary Runciman, it amounts to no more than:

> a mode of production in which formally free labour is recruited for regular employment by ongoing enterprises competing in the market for profit.
>
> (Runciman 1995: 33)

Around that core has been constructed a variety of institutionally variant forms of capitalism which incorporate sometimes vastly different forms of corporate and economic governance, different investment priorities and relations between finance and industrial capital, different capacities for and orientations to state economic planning, different welfare regimes, etc.

Even within East Asia itself, as Richard Whitley (1992) has shown, the institutional bases for different national capitalisms vary dramatically, as does the nature of business organization and managerial priorities and styles, as say between the large 'collectivist' Japanese corporation which seeks to incorporate many employees into the lower levels of its decision-making structures, and the autocratic, family-controlled companies typical of Taiwan, Hong Kong and parts of China's economy, for whom employees are mere labour power, to be used, exploited, and discarded as necessary. In order to develop some sense of the significance of these various forms of capitalism in the region, and of their international implications, I begin by advancing a provisional typology of these and other significant forms elsewhere in the world economy.[10] This typology attempts to grasp the national capitalisms as they existed at the end of the twentieth century, while appreciating the changes that have taken place since then, particularly in the case of South Korea since its economic upheaval in 1997–98 (see Pirie 2007) and the continuing evolution of the Chinese economy. Whether the global economic reversal of the late 2000s will result in significant changes in the nature of US, British and other European capitalisms, at the time of writing (late 2009), remains an open question.

While this is not the place to unpack these categories in any detail, a few brief comments need to be made in order to be able to comprehend their methodological bases and to distinguish East Asian forms from each other and from those of other world-regions.

Two general points are needed in order to explain the distinctions made in Table 2.1. First, the terms used to designate the various forms are meant to emphasize the primary sources of institutional power responsible for economic and corporate governance. Thus, in the case of 'shareholder capitalism' (Britain), economic sovereignty rests almost exclusively in property owners who are disengaged from the firms they own and trade their assets on the stock market in the interests of maximizing short-term profits from their investments. Firms raise their funds largely through stock market flotations, and they are managed predominantly in the interests of short-term profitability rather than market growth or competition on the basis of technological development. Thus the structure of the economy evolves in an *ad hoc*, unplanned fashion, with little (or at best, irregular) input from industrial policy. Economic nationalism is barely part of the collective psyche and, as a consequence, nearly everything is available for sale to almost any prospective buyer. In the terms developed in Chapter 3, state-business relations tend to approximate a 'market ideological' form.

The notion of 'managerial capitalism' (USA), on the other hand highlights the significance of managerial co-ordination in the context – unlike Britain – of firms that have been very large vertically and horizontally integrated organizations. While corporate finance is again largely capital-market generated, regulatory mechanisms through to the early 1980s ensured that shareholders were more engaged (committed, loyal) with the companies concerned than their British counterparts. While

TABLE 2.1 Major forms of capitalism in the late twentieth century

Form	Representative economy
Shareholder capitalism	Britain
Managerial capitalism	USA
Co-ordinated managerial capitalism	Germany
Collective capitalism	Japan
State-directed capitalism	South Korea
Co-ordinated proprietorial capitalism	Taiwan
Market Neo-Stalinism	China

financial deregulation during the Regan administration and beyond has tended to propel the US form of capitalism towards the British polarity, developments in the wake of the 2008 financial crisis may have begun to tip the scales in the opposite direction. In any case, economic nationalism remains a much more significant feature of US capitalism than is currently true of Britain.

In the case of 'co-ordinated managerial capitalism' (Germany), professionalized management in the context of large, integrated companies has also been significant, but with four major differences. Networks of small and medium-sized firms (*mittelstand*) subcontracting to the large firms have been central to the form of capitalism that has evolved since 1945; corporate finance is largely through bank credit in arrangements whereby the banks become committed to the long-term growth (rather than short-term profitability) of the companies concerned; worker representatives are formally incorporated into the governance systems of larger companies; and the state – central and local – plays a more proactive role in economic co-ordination and in encouraging socially integrative institutions which influence worker-management relations, and society at large. Germany and other continental European economies, together with Japan, represent what might additionally be termed 'stakeholder capitalism' (cf. Hutton 2002: Chapter 8).

Japan, though often seen as the prototypical form of East Asian capitalism, is very different from the other East Asian cases. In its case, the notion of 'collective capitalism' addresses the significance of social and institutional integration to economic and corporate governance. Employee integration and systematic consultation is achieved within the large corporation (but hardly exists in the important and very large small and medium-sized enterprise sector), while inter-firm integration is achieved across the *keiretsu* network. The 'collective' nature of Japanese capitalism is enhanced by the committed involvement of banks via a system where corporate finance is raised largely through bank loans rather than the stock market, and, importantly, by a proactive state that has sought to orchestrate the structure of the economy and the trajectory of development (Dore 2000: Parts I and II).

Drawing heavily on Japanese practices prior to the World War II, 'state-directed capitalism' emerged in South Korea from the early 1960s. Central to this form has been a partnership between an authoritarian – and until the late 1980s, militarized – state, and big business (the *chaebol*), wherein the state, for much of the period, has been the senior partner. Once again, corporate finance has been largely provided by bank loans, but under circumstances where the state tightly controlled access. Additionally, the state has been heavily involved in technology acquisition, market protection and economic planning more generally (Woo 1991, Chang 1994). The political process began to be democratized in the late 1980s and aftermath of the country's economic reversal in the late 1990s (explored in Chapter 4) has undoubtedly led to a neoliberalisation of South Korea's economic governance, but it remains a matter of debate as to how significant this development has been for the nature and dynamics of South Korean capitalism (cf. Pirie 2007; Woo 2007).

Similarly influenced by Japanese practices, but also by the economic planning techniques of the Nationalist Chinese Government in the 1930s, Taiwan has developed a form of capitalism since the late 1940s where economic co-ordination is also partly a state function. Depicted as 'Leninist' by Taiwan's eminent sociologist, H.H. Michael Hsiao (1995), the Taiwanese government engaged in many of the 'market-leading' activities typical of the Japanese economy and other NICs of East Asia, but additionally it encouraged a substantial state (or the dominant political party – the Kuomintang) owned industrial sector in upstream processing industries, banking aerospace, etc. Taiwanese capitalism is characterized by a large, small and medium-sized enterprise (SME) sector, though a few larger companies have emerged from it (of which the best known ones include Tatung, Acer, Mitac and Evergreen). It is the SMEs that have been largely responsible for the country's export performance. Such companies are generally family-owned (hence 'proprietorial'), organizationally bounded by kinship networks and embedded in complex production networks, nationally and internationally and in the latter case particularly with Chinese firms.

The term 'Market Neo-Stalinism' refers to an emergent form of capitalism of which the People's Republic of China is the principal representative (though Vietnam could also be located within this form). As a set of institutional arrangements that are very much in transformation (between state socialism and some form of capitalism), the defining characteristic is the continuing decisive economic role of an authoritarian, 'Neo-Stalinist' state in a context where resource allocation has been partly marketized, and the economy partially globalized.

The second general point concerns the historical limits to these various forms of capitalism. The institutions and social arrangements that constitute these capitalisms have in some cases evolved over considerable periods of time (particularly in Britain, but also in the USA), but often have been the product of deliberate 'institutional engineering' on the part of the respective states subsequent to historical ruptures such as defeat in war (Germany and Japan), military coups or acquisitions (South Korea and Taiwan), or changes in political élites (China). Whatever the historical sources of these capitalisms, their characteristic institutional arrangements have supported improvements in economic performance and prosperity for varying periods of time (though some better than others: for example, Germany *vis-à-vis* Britain).

As with all products of human consciousness and action, however, there are inevitably limits to the effectivity of these arrangements. In the case of Britain, it has been argued that the long-term decline of the economy can be traced to the inappropriateness of the country's institutions subsequent to the intensification of international competition from the late nineteenth century onwards. As for the USA, while 'managerial capitalism' has been responsible for the highest level of productivity the world has known, the relative decline in its international competitiveness in recent decades has been linked, in part to the nature of its economic institutions. In both cases, the 'financialisation' of the global economy since the 1980s (Glyn 2006), with the City of London and Wall Street at its heart, has deflected investment in the productive bases of both economies, but especially in the Britain case. Similarly, the Japanese recession since the early 1990s has been traced in part to the rigidities of the *keiretsu* and 'permanent employment' systems, which some regard as being inappropriate in a 'globalized' competitive environment where all high cost producers, including Japan, are under increased pressure from low cost producers elsewhere in Asia.

Whatever the nature and significance of the historical limits of the different forms of capitalism, changes are clearly under way, including in the East Asian region. The sources of change are in some cases endogenous, as in the case of China where the nature of uneven development is producing serious social dislocation (see later), but in all cases are partly exogenous and associated with various dimensions of globalization. It is to that issue, and its implications for East Asia, that I now turn.

Economic fusion

This is not the place to present an overview and critique of the various meanings of globalization. That has been done effectively enough by Hirst and Thompson (1999) and Held *et al.* (1999) among others, and has been the focus of an extraordinary empirical and analytic synthesis by Manuel Castells (2000a, 2000b, 2003). What I propose to do here is to pick-up on Castells' (2000a) insistence that the 'glue', if not the defining characteristic, of globalization is increasingly the multifaceted nature of social, economic and political networks and the dynamics and implications of the processes of networking. It is clear that globally organized business networks are decisive for the economic present and future of the East Asian region. To anticipate my argument, however, these networks are not necessarily entirely positive in their implications. As we shall see, their logic and dynamics are responsible for compounding the processes of uneven development and thus the economic basis for fragmentation (and hence conflict) in East Asia, as they are elsewhere.

A useful conceptual device which helps us gain analytic purchase on most, if not all, national and international business networks is the notion of 'global production networks', which has been developed by Henderson, Dicken and their colleagues (e.g. Henderson *et al.* 2002a, Coe *et al.* 2004) from the earlier work by US sociologist, Gary Gereffi and his collaborators (see, for instance, Gereffi and Korzeniewicz, 1994, Gereffi and Kaplinsky 2001; see also, Gereffi *et al.* 2005, Bair 2005, 2008). In this approach, a global production network (GPN) is conceived as:

> the nexus of interconnected functions and operations through which goods and services are produced, distributed and consumed . . . Such networks not only integrate firms (and parts of firms) into structures which blur traditional organizational boundaries – through the development of diverse forms of equity and non-equity relationships – but also integrate national economies (or parts of such economies) in ways which have enormous implications for their well-being. At the same time, the precise nature and articulation of firm-centred production networks are deeply influenced by the concrete

socio-political contexts within which they are embedded. The process is especially complex because while the latter are essentially territorially specific . . . the production networks themselves are not.

(Henderson et al. 2002a: 445–46)

From the perspective of economic development, in East Asia as elsewhere, of vital concern is not merely where and how much value is created within the GPN, but how much of it is captured in a particular location. GPNs link different sets of raw materials, labour, skills, technology and managerial inputs across geographic space and each of these, in principle have different 'gearings' to value creation. They also link different types of firms embedded in different social and institutional contexts: that is, different forms of capitalism, and these different forms have different 'gearings' in terms of their capacity to capture value. Central to the former is the nature of corporate power, how it is distributed and whether and how it can be enhanced within the GPN. Central to the latter is institutional power (states, trade unions, etc.), how it varies in particular countries or sub-national territories, and the extent to which it can be brought to bear on the firms and subsidiaries in the GPNs at those locations, in order to capture a significant proportion of the value generated there.

The consequence of this is that the ability of 'lead firm' (transnational corporations – TNCs – for instance) subsidiaries, or firms subcontracted to them (be they foreign or domestically owned) constituting particular nodes in the GPNs, to contribute to the development and prosperity of economies of which they are a part, is profoundly asymmetrical (Henderson 1994). In the case of the production, marketing and distribution of manufactured goods such as garments, footwear, personal computers, some consumer electronics, furniture and metal products (such as bicycles), the bulk of the value is added – and captured – not in the manufacturing stages (now performed overwhelmingly in the developing world, including East Asian countries such as China, Vietnam, Cambodia, Thailand and Indonesia), but at the stages of 'branding' (the company owning the brand name) and marketing, activities still controlled overwhelmingly by firms from the advanced industrial economies of the USA, Japan and the European Union, but with an increasing presence of firms from the newly industrialized countries of East Asia and South Korea in particular.

On the latter point, it is clear that East Asia's economic dynamism has been as much a product of the national and international activities of domestically-owned firms as it has of direct investment by foreign (non-east Asian) TNCs (see, for instance, Lakhera 2008 on Japanese firms). It has been estimated, for instance, that foreign-owned firms, at the turn of the twenty-first century, were responsible for only about one per cent of GDP in Japan and about 15 and 25 per cent respectively in South Korea and Taiwan (Thompson 1998: Chapter 8). Similarly, while Japanese companies were the East Asian pioneers in the globalization of manufacturing activities (to North America, Europe, elsewhere in Asia, South America, etc.), they have been followed more recently by companies from South Korea (e.g. Samsung,

Hyundai and LG) and Taiwan (e.g. Acer and Mitac). As part of this process, South Korean and Taiwanese companies – particularly in electronic products – are now among the principal sources of new foreign direct investment (FDI) into Southeast Asia (see, for instance, Chen 1998; Phillips and Henderson 2009), and are significant players in regard to FDI flows into China (see Kim and Mah 2006).

Though the economic integration in the region that is being forged by East Asian and non-regional (particularly US) TNCs is important, not least because of the developmental consequences of the divisions of labour that are being established as a result of the GPNs that bind the region's productive bases, it is the fractious (as well as the integrative) consequences of the GPNs that may prove as significant in the longer term. In the case of Malaysia, for instance, the changing global architecture of electronics GPNs has helped to lock that country's key manufacturing industry–electronics – into a relatively low value-added, low wage growth regime. In the context of economic transformation in China and the export competitiveness associated with it, the consequence, arguably, has been the 'stalling' of Malaysia's industrialization project (Phillips and Henderson 2009; see also Chapter 6). Serious social consequences potentially flow from this for Malaysia and other East Asian countries confronted by Chinese export competition.[11]

Economic fission

As I have hinted earlier, globalization connects not only firms, markets and populations internationally, it also connects the differing organizational structures and economic, social and political priorities that constitute the different forms of capitalism. In connecting these different forms, global business is able to exploit the variations in wages, labour-management relations and state welfare and regulatory regimes that the various capitalisms embody. To what extent, then, do the various forms of capitalism in East Asia that have been connected and projected outwards to other parts of the world economy by the processes of globalization constitute challenges to the more developed – and with the rise of China, the less developed (see Chapter 6) – economies of East Asia and beyond?

The principal basis of the export economies of China, South Korea, Taiwan, Singapore, Malaysia and Thailand is manufactured commodities. These manufactures largely consist (depending on the country in question) of consumer electronic products, personal computers, semiconductors and other computer components and peripherals, automobiles, auto components and other metal products. In addition, the coastal provinces of China, and increasing, Vietnam, Cambodia and other parts of Southeast Asia, are the world's largest producers and exporters of textiles, garments, shoes and toys. As such, the former export profile brings Korean, and to a lesser extent Taiwanese (and probably in the future, Chinese) firms – for they, other than Japanese firms, have the major brand-names from the region – into competition less with US or EU firms,[12] than with their Japanese counterparts.

The competitive threat of some of the East Asian economies for Japan, however, is based on more than the nature of the products that the various economies manufacture and export. Underlying their product foci are virulent forms of economic nationalism (particularly true for China and South Korea). In recent decades the principal object of this economic nationalism has been to 'catch up with and overtake' the USA, but Japan also has been an object of attention. Fuelled as it is by animosity that goes back at least to the dawn of Japan's colonial expansion (from 1895) and exacerbated by the sometimes brutal experiences of Japanese domination before and during the World War II, the competitive threat posed by 'Greater China' (China in particular, but for current purposes including Taiwan) and Korea to the Japanese economy should not be underestimated. Given the difficulties of developing effective international institutions for economic co-operation and governance in East Asia (see, for instance, Higgott 1998, Staples 2008), the competitive dynamics emerging within the region could become a major cause for concern in the next few years.

Compared with any other form of capitalism in East Asia – and indeed with many of those evident in Western Europe (Britain in particular) and North America – the Japanese form has been exemplary. While its negative features are well known (rigidly gender-segmented and discriminatory labour markets, high stress levels generated by the nature of work and life, the relative underdevelopment of the welfare regime, etc.), the productive capacities embodied in its corporate structures and the socially integrative nature of its corporate governance systems are among the best in the world.

The contraction of world markets for manufactured commodities during the 1980s, early 1990s and late 2000s, coupled with increased competition, the rising value of the yen (in the earlier periods) and increasing labour costs, placed severe strain on the Japanese form of capitalism. Specifically, the 'permanent employment' contract (covering around 30 per cent of the workforce of large companies by the 1990s) has had the effect of transforming labour costs – which in non-Japanese companies are flexible costs – into fixed costs. While in previous recessions the flexibility for cost cutting by major companies had been found by pushing the consequences of recession out into the subcontracting chain of the *keiretsu* (that is on to smaller firms whose workers are often female and do not have the protection afforded to their counterparts in the major companies), this has not been possible to the same extent in recent times (since the relative stagnation of the Japanese economy from the early 1990s). Additionally, while the institutional relationships between firms in a given *keiretsu* have been advantageous to innovation and product quality, they have tended also to become rigidities in periods of recession where they have restricted the capacities of major companies to force down the cost of supplies.[13]

The response of some of the more prominent companies, such as Nissan and Hitachi, to such rigidities has been to chip away at the 'permanent employment' contract and to disengage from their long-term relations with even some of their primary subcontractors, replacing these with forms of interaction that approximate more strictly market transactions. Though some commentators have argued that the processes of (neoliberal) globalization will ultimately require the institutional reconstruction of the Japanese economy along Anglo-American lines, there is little evidence, as yet, that convergence of this sort is underway (Whitley 1999).

In the longer term, the principal competitive threat to Japan – as well as to the USA – may well be China. In 2002, China replaced the USA as the principal exporter to Japan and by 2008, for instance, Japan was running a negative trade balance with China of 2.9 trillion yen (about $35 billion),[14] though this imbalance has been relatively stable, at least since 2004. On the other hand, while the USA continues to run a substantial negative trade balance with Japan, averaging more than US$72 billion between 2006 and 2009, its principal imbalance is now overwhelmingly with China. In 2009, for instance, this amounted to nearly $227 billion, though the deepest imbalance so far was in 2008 when it reached $268 billion (and the annual average between 2006 and 2009, was nearly $247 billion).[15] While it is important to adopt a critical perspective on trade data such as these (not least because China's exports – unlike those of Japan – in large part represent value that predominantly flows to foreign-owned companies[16]), it seems clear that state industrial policy is designed, as much as anything, to move the Chinese economy into higher value-added operations. There are pockets of evidence that suggest that this strategy is beginning to bear fruit (such as developments in nanotechnology; see Appelbaum *et al.* 2006, Appelbaum and Parker 2007) and if these transmute into generalized upgrading successes across a majority of industrial sectors, then China's ability to decisively transform the global economic-political order, may be on the cards. Rather than pursue this discussion here, however (as it is reprised in various ways in Chapter 8), it may be useful to broach a number of general observations, not merely on the Chinese political economy, but on the future prospects for continued transformation in East Asia.

Prospects

While future decades promise significant opportunities for further economic growth, social development and prosperity in the East Asian region, they also threaten to see the maturation of a number of emerging dangers for many societies there, whose significance can already be discerned. While these dangers certainly include impending environmental disaster in some parts of the region (with devastating water shortages already evident in some parts of China, for instance: see Watts 2010), it is some of the more strictly economic problems of development, and their possible geo-political consequences, that I wish to address here. Specifically I wish to engage with two issues: the first concerns the question of whether there are structural limitations on the prospects for future transformation in the region; the second broaches the nature of Chinese transformation and its consequences for China itself and the region more generally.

Limits to transformation?

All products of collective social action have temporal limits. Consequently it can be reasonably assumed that somehow and at some point, this will be true for East Asian economic transformation as it has evolved over the past half-century or so. While it is possible to imagine that, ultimately, the limits to transformation might be posed by environmental, economic or geo-political catastrophe (or a combination of the three), to speculate on the possibilities for the emergence of those limits, would take us way beyond the bounds of the discussions developed in this book. Consequently in this section, I focus on three dynamics that may pose structural limitations for the nature of economic transformation in the region. The first two are concerned with the institutional architecture of economic globalization within which the productive activities of the East Asian region are enmeshed. The third is concerned with the way in which the productive and exporting capacities of the Chinese economy, in itself may be posing limits for transformation elsewhere in the region.

For many scholars who have contemplated the future of economic transformation in East Asia, the 'flying geese' model of development has often been invoked to help explain the processes involved (see, for instance, Thompson 1998: Chapter 2, 10; Staples 2008). First proposed by the Japanese economist, Kaname Akamatsu, in the 1930s to explain the alternating periods of free trade and protectionism that seemed to characterize the trajectories of economic development, the subsequent argument has focussed on how some of the other economies of East Asia have followed, one after the other, Japan's lead; often, as a consequence of mobilizing foreign technologies and investment, including by Japanese companies themselves (Akamatsu 1962, Kojima 2000, Hayter and Edgington 2004) More specifically, it was suggested that just as Japan first combined cheap but relatively skilled labour with foreign technologies to produce low value-added commodities (garments, cheap electronic products, etc.) for export, and then moved on to produce more capital-intensive, higher value-added products which were associated with a deepening of indigenous technological and innovative capabilities, shedding the former in the process, so the other economies in the region in wave after wave (first Hong Kong, South Korea, Taiwan, Singapore; then Malaysia and Thailand; now China and Vietnam) have been able to replicate the process. The implication of the model is that while Japanese industry may well stay at the front of the flight of geese by means of its capacity to move into ever more innovative and higher value-added processes and products, the other economies, in its wake, may still be able to achieve the first rank as industrial economies.

In order to reach – and maintain – 'big league' status as an economic power, a society must be able to generate industries whose leading companies can move beyond factor-led competitiveness (for example, low labour costs) to a position where they can institutionalize innovation. Additionally, however, the value-added associated with innovative processes and products needs to be captured within the domestic economy if it is to have a significant effect on economic and social development and generalized prosperity.[17]

In a widely cited article, Bernard and Ravenhill (1995) deliver what appears to be a crushing blow to the 'flying geese' model. Arguing against the state-centric notion of development that underpins the model, they suggest that the evolution of a regional division of labour in manufacturing industries in the Asia-Pacific region (for that is what the model implies) has effectively locked the first and second generation NICs into an intermediate role. As a productive economy, only Singapore seems, subsequent to the mid-1990s, to have escaped from this role. Though the dynamics may be changing (with Taiwan, in particular, showing evidence of innovation across a number of manufacturing industries: see Choung 1998) it seems that even the lead firms in economies such as South Korea, Taiwan and Malaysia remain heavily dependent on technological inputs and innovation from Japanese companies on the one hand, and access to the US, EU – and increasingly Chinese – markets on the other.

In spite of optimistic work to the contrary (for instance, Hobday, 1995, Thompson 1998: Chapter 10), innovation in indigenous companies (as opposed to foreign-owned TNC subsidiaries) in the NICs and second generation NICs continues to be limited (see, for instance, Yusuf 2003: Chapter 4). Additionally, the continuing dependence of some of the region's firms – including some of the largest Korean and Taiwanese companies – on 'original equipment manufacturing' (OEM) strategies,[18] restricts their ability to generate and capture the highest value-added. In principle, the latter position can only be achieved where companies are able to evolve from being OEMs into becoming 'own design' (ODM) and ultimately 'own brand' (OBM) manufacturers in their own right (as have the leading Japanese electronics and automobile companies since the 1960s). Some of the Korean *chaebol* (Samsung and LG, for instance), have now achieved this position as a consequence, in part, of becoming sufficiently cash rich to undertake the huge investments necessary to establish, maintain and enhance their own brand names. For Taiwanese, Singaporean and Malaysian companies, however, this has not yet been possible (in spite of the relative visibility of Taiwanese companies such as Acer and Mitac). Part of the reason for this may be cultural-historical. As Whitley suggests (in Thompson 1998: Chapter 9), the nature of the 'overseas Chinese' business system – of which Taiwan is representative – circumscribes managerial inclinations to expand companies beyond a size that can be controlled from within kin and *guanxi* networks. As a consequence, such companies may well be highly profitable, but they are unlikely to generate the huge investment surpluses necessary for them to become global leaders with instantly recognizable brand names in their respective industries.

Irrespective of whether East Asian firms perform OEM roles or not, the architecture of the global production networks (GPNs) in which they are enmeshed, and the changes in those architectures over time, have very significant consequences for their ability to upgrade their technologies and products and thus contribute to the development of higher value-adding, high wage economies. The nature of the GPNs that span East Asia, in other words, could well pose limits for continued transformation and development.

One example where the limits of transformation may have already been reached – in part because of GPN architectures – arises in Malaysia where upgrading in its electronics industry (by far the country's most important) seems to stalling, if not stalled. While there are also endogenous reasons why this is happening, associated with the nature of Malaysian political economy and social formation (explored in Chapter 6), it seems that the rise and relative dominance of largely US-owned 'contract electronics manufacturers' (CEMs) as lead companies organizing the GPNs into which large sections of Malaysian electronics manufacturing is absorbed, has resulted, in itself, in the emergence of exogenous structural constraints on upgrading.

Phillips and Henderson (2009) argue that the GPNs into which Malaysian electronics companies were initially absorbed (from roughly the early 1970s to the mid-1990s) were dominated by US lead firms (such as Intel) in semiconductors and other electronic components. The nature of the business model of such companies, they suggest, together with their tendency to localize the senior management of their subsidiaries, resulted in the structural space (and sometimes lead company encouragement and assistance) for local companies to upgrade and thus re-position themselves in higher value-added roles within the respective GPNs. In more recent years, the rise of CEMs to GPN dominance, seems largely to have closed down that former structural space. CEMs not only manufacture products for brand name companies, but they provide 'total package' business services including purchasing of components and other supplies, logistics and sometimes marketing. They operate as consolidated global supply chain managers, leaving the lead firms (brand name holders, such as Apple) free to concentrate on product innovation (where most value is added and captured). They operate on far tighter operating margins than other electronics companies (less than 3 per cent of revenues in 2000) with very high economies of scale and, as a consequence, tend to be savage cutters, both with regard to supply and wage costs (Phillips and Henderson 2009: 47–55). Within this model there tends to be little room for local suppliers (expect where very low value products are concerned) and almost none for local companies whom, with assistance, could over time become suppliers of higher value-added supplies or services.

The third dynamic that may be imposing limits to transformation in East Asia is internal to the region itself and arises from the explosion of China's competitive capabilities as an exporter of manufactured commodities. The issue is not merely a matter of the fact that China has manufacturing capacities on a scale that are unprecedented historically, or even that it is also a very low cost producer, but that it is able to combine both of these with a significant innovative potential. Additionally, its global significance as a manufacturing economy has meant that new flows of foreign investment that might otherwise have gone to Thailand, Malaysia or elsewhere in the region, to support the production of (say) electronics components, peripherals or for performing sub-assembly operations (e.g. printed circuit boards) are beginning to relocate to China so as to be nearer the sites of final product assembly and what in some industries are beginning to be significant industrial clusters partly composed of Chinese owned companies (as, for instance, in auto components in Shanghai: see Depner and Bathelt 2003).

It is as a consequence of developments such as these that a number of scholars have predicted that the emergence of China as a manufacturing powerhouse could have significant, negative consequences for the continued deepening of the industrialization projects elsewhere in East Asia. Lall and Albaladejo (2004), for instance, argue that China's growing competitive edge in some manufacturing industries (electronics, automobiles and other forms of mechanical engineering, for instance) is likely not only to put the industrialization projects of countries such as Thailand and Malaysia at risk, but those of 'medium technology' producers in the region also. Given that the latter includes South Korea's automobile industry – namely one that already has a significant international presence – demonstrates the sorts of dangers that China's industrialization is beginning to pose for continued economic transformation in East Asia.

Work by Yusuf (2008) and Yusuf and Nabeshima (2009) looks closely at the consequences of China's export competitiveness for continued growth and development in Malaysia and Thailand. Among other things, they show that not only there is a considerable overlap in the sorts of commodities exported by all three countries (they are, in other words, direct competitors), but that China's exports have been growing faster than those of Thailand and Malaysia, and from a far larger base. Additionally they point to the growing evidence that firms in China are upgrading their products and processes faster than those in Thailand and Malaysia and are moving more rapidly into technology intensive and higher value-added areas. The Thai and Malaysian economies, on the other hand, remain more focussed on lower value-added resource based, processing and assembly industries.

In this context, one of Yusuf's scenarios for the future of Southeast Asian economies (by which he predominantly means Thailand and Malaysia) makes depressing reading. He suggests that:

> there is a risk that the current industrial development of Malaysia and Thailand could stagnate and atrophy and growth eventually slow to a crawl. Unable to upgrade existing activities and to diversify, the S.E. Asian countries are undercut by lower cost producers . . . Southeast Asian economies that are forced into this situation would slide down the food chain, and have to compete in resource based low tech industries. . . . There is in addition, a risk of S.E. Asia being reduced to a backwater not only because of the rise of China but more so because of a failure to climb up the innovation value chain. . . . to complement manufacturing capability with innovation capability.
>
> (Yusuf 2008: 35)

While the endogenous dynamics of the possible stagnation of the Malaysian economy, and thus of how that country may be reaching the limits of its transformation, are discussed in Chapter 6, and the wider impact of China's export competitiveness is taken up in Chapter 7, at this point a few preliminary comments on China's own transformation may be in order.

The China conundrum

With over 1.3 billion people, China is the world's most populous country. Over the last decade or so, the Chinese economy has registered annual GDP growth rates sometimes in excess of 13 per cent per annum. If these growth rates continue, China will displace the USA as the world's largest economy sometime in the next 20 years.

Becoming the world's largest economy will undoubtedly be a source for even more glaring headlines in the media and more concerned muttering in the corridors of power in Washington, London, Brussels and perhaps, Tokyo. Becoming the largest economy, however, will have nothing to say about the much more fundamental question for the vast majority of the Chinese population: the absence of generalized prosperity. The reality is that the data on GDP growth (and per capita growth), obscures the fact that China has an economy and society that exhibits massive disparities and gross inequalities. While China's most dynamic coastal provinces (such as Guangdong, Fujian, Jiangsu and the Shanghai region), for instance, have been racking up growth rates of over 20 per cent per annum, some of the interior and western provinces have economic and social conditions that seem to have barely changed in decades. China, in other words, may become the dominant economic power of the twenty-first century, and by so doing release millions more people into prosperity and consumerism, but if it does, it will have been via a process of economic development that will have been one the most uneven the world has ever known.

Herein lies a conundrum composed of at least three related parts. Will China indeed become the greatest of the world's economic powerhouses? If it does, will that be associated with political liberalization and with China's development as a positive force for progress and prosperity globally? Or will China, under the strains of uneven development, fragment or even implode as a unified state, as did the Soviet Union in 1991. While it is beyond the scope of this chapter and book to explore these questions in detail, a number of points can be made.

The contemporary Chinese version of capitalism, what I termed earlier, 'Market Neo-Stalinism', is a contradictory, hybrid set of elements, probably unlike any other in the world. In terms of its corporate base, the Chinese economy can be subdivided into seven components: the state sector; the military sector; the local state sector; the foreign-invested joint-venture sector; the indigenous private sector; peasant agriculture; and the informal sector. While these are related to each other in important ways (not least through transfers of value), they embody their own logics of development, priorities and vested interests. As a consequence, while currently locked into a dynamic whole, there are, within and between them, sources of tension and potential conflict that under certain circumstances could disrupt the national economy as a functioning system.

The *state sector* consists largely of central and provincial state-owned enterprises (SOEs) involved in steel, petroleum and gas, chemicals, heavy engineering, shipbuilding, textiles, banking, etc. Additionally, state trading companies operate internationally, and together with the overseas divisions of the Bank of China, are involved in currency and other forms of financial speculation. Subsequent to the 1997 Congress of the Chinese Communist Party, privatization of some state assets has taken place, but unlike the chaotic, disruptive, capitalist 'fire sale' that occurred in the former Soviet Union and in other state socialist countries of Central and Eastern Europe, in China the privatization process has been closely regulated ensuring the state's (in its various forms) continuing control over assets and, to some extent strategy, while allowing the SOEs to operate, in some ways, as 'normal' market oriented companies. In some cases – steel is an example – productivity has been dramatically improved and reasonable levels of profitability are now probably being achieved (Nolan 2001). Importantly, in terms of the globalization of China's corporate base, SOEs are by far the most important, particularly with regard to energy (e.g. Sinopec, China National Offshore Oil Corporation), minerals extraction and construction (e.g. China Metallurgical Group, China Railway Engineering Corporation).

Though formally responsible to the political apparatus of the central Party and state, the *military sector* – the economic arm of the People's Liberation Army (PLA) – constitutes an arena of economic power in its own right. While direct military involvement in the production of weapons, uniforms, etc., is not unknown in developing countries, what is unusual about the economic operations of the PLA is that it now has its own subsidiaries involved in the manufacture and export of an array of products, from toys to textile machinery and medical equipment to foodstuffs (frozen fish, for instance). A prominent example of such diversification is Poly Technologies. Still partly controlled by the PLA (along with other state agencies), it continues to produce military equipment (and was involved in the attempted illegal export of arms to Zimbabwe in 2008), but now has divisions involved in real estate speculation (including in Hong Kong), civil engineering and in the import and sales of luxury cars (Ferrari and Maserati).[19]

A distinctive element of China's economic transformation compared with transformations in the former state socialist societies of Central and Eastern Europe is the presence of a large *local state/local Party sector* that in some parts of the country (for instance, Jiangsu Province) used to consist of 'township and village enterprises'(TVEs). As the name suggests, these enterprises were largely a rural phenomenon and were developed to help alleviate rural underemployment, improve prosperity and as a consequence help anchor the peasantry on the land. Invested in by local governments, individuals and groups, they constituted a form of local corporatism, and became one of the most dynamic sectors of the Chinese economy. They were a major source of subcontracted manufacturing operations which linked them to firms in Hong Kong and Taiwan, and via these 'overseas Chinese' business networks to companies in the USA, Europe and elsewhere (Hsing 1998). Though the TVEs have now largely transmuted into more orthodox companies, they still involve participation by local Party officials who have become entrepreneur-capitalists while retaining their roles as central actors in the lowest levels of the Communist Party's organizational structure (Wang 2009).

Not withstanding the TVEs and their successors, local state and Party officials are often imbricated in entrepreneurial activities. For instance, as cities have expanded to encompass rural areas on their fringes, peasants, encouraged and organized by local Party officials have sometimes sold their collective land use rights to the city authorities and/or real estate developers and used the proceeds to turn the village committees into real estate speculators. In so doing, they have created an 'urban village' phenomenon that now houses perhaps 50 per cent of China's 200 million plus migrant population.[20]

Another significant contributor to China's economic dynamism has been the growth of *foreign invested* companies in which foreign and domestic interests have collaborated in manufacturing (for example, garments, electronic products, phar-maceuticals, cars, steel, glass, aerospace) real estate development and services (for example, tourism and retailing). These typically have been joint-ventures and have included some between major multinationals (for example, Volkswagen, Unile-ver, Honda, Samsung, etc.) and state or private Chinese interests. The vast major-ity of the foreign companies (some of which now involve 100 per cent foreign equity holding), have been between 'overseas' (non-mainland or Southeast Asian) Chinese companies, particularly from Taiwan, Hong Kong and Singapore. Indeed, by the late 1980s it was estimated that Hong Kong companies remained respon-sible for perhaps 60 per cent of all 'foreign' direct investment in China. Though this proportion undoubtedly has declined, Hong Kong companies remain very significant players, particularly in real estate speculation (cf. Chapter 4). Taiwanese companies, on the other hand, have been much more significant for the productive basis of the economy. They have tended to focus on the use of China as a low cost manufacturing base, particularly for the assembly of electronic products, and local-ized industrial clusters are now emerging to supply and support the Taiwanese and other foreign operations (Yang and Hsia 2011).

Paralleling the growth of local state and foreign operations has been an explosion of *domestically-owned private* companies. Numbering in their millions, many of the original entrepreneurs emerged from the ranks of the PLA. While these companies are often small, family-run businesses, engaged in such activities as manufacturing, construction, retailing, etc., some of them have grown to a significant size and have become the economic basis for a burgeoning capitalist class. While many of these companies are oriented towards the domestic market, significant numbers of them are involved in subcontracting relations with foreign invested companies (in gar-ments, toys, consumer electronics, automobiles, for instance) and as a consequence are integrated into the global economy via the particular production networks con-stituted in these industries. A very small number of these companies are beginning to become international players in their own right, with their own brand names. Subsequent to its purchase of IBM's personal computer division in 2005, the Hong Kong based computer company, Lenovo, has become the best known of these, though the Qingdao based white goods manufacturer, Haier (a privatized, former state owned company) and the Shenzhen headquartered telecommunications company, Huawei, are also emerging as significant operations.

Agriculture continues to be the primary basis for the livelihood of about 60 per cent of China's population. Though the productivity of the land adjacent to the major urban centres has increased dramatically as a result of the relaxation of state controls, agricultural production in more remote areas has stagnated. As a consequence, rural poverty continues to be widespread and this has helped to set in train waves of rural-urban migration on a scale (about 15 to 20 per cent of the current national population) that is probably historically unprecedented. Given the state's inability to control internal population movements, with migration has come an explosion of urban underemployment and – as during the current global overaccumulation crisis (Hung 2008) – rising unemployment. Numbering possibly 250 million by 2015[21] these migrants live on the margins of society. They tend be employed in the most menial, low paid and dangerous jobs (on construction sites or in factories using toxic production processes). Additionally, as welfare benefits have been tied to the official place of residence or to the employer (where the latter is a state-owned enterprise), the migrants often find themselves among the most degraded and exploited of Chinese society.

The *informal sector* (or 'grey' economy) is a significant feature of China's Market Neo-Stalinism (as it is of other developing countries). Although it is impossible to estimate the number of people who are active in the informal sector or the size of the sector's contribution to GDP, it seems likely that proportionally, in both senses, China's informal sector is amongst the largest in the world. Informal sector operations range from 'skin trade' activities such as begging to home working (for instance, women sewing garments in their own homes), to small manufacturing or construction businesses, to petty crime, to organized criminal gangs ('triads') engaged in running prostitution, drugs, smuggling and money laundering.[22] In the latter case, the triads have globally-organized networks and are believed to be responsible for handling a significant proportion of the world's illegal drug trafficking.

As can be inferred from these comments on the nature of Market Neo-Stalinism, the Chinese political economy is cut-through with multiple contradictions and has generated very high levels of income inequality (with a gini co-efficient of 0.44 in 2004; Chen 2007: 109) and burgeoning crime and corruption. It is also a political economy that is cut-through with intense inter and intra-Provincial rivalry to attract, for instance, foreign investment and high status infrastructural projects such as international airports (compounding structural tendencies to overaccumulation in manufactured commodities and real estate, etc.) As a consequence of all these elements and more, Market Neo-Stalinism is a form of capitalism that is not only decidedly in transformation, but structurally, is potentially highly unstable. The question, of course, is what type of economy and polity is likely to emerge from the transformation process?

There seem to be at least three general scenarios of relevance here. The first is that the tensions of uneven development and the social (largely class, but sometimes ethnically based) conflict that it is engendering, will threaten the survival of the central state. This has happened periodically in Chinese history, particularly in the context of weakened dynastic rule accompanied by desperate inequality and poverty (such as during the Taiping rebellion of 1850–64). On previous occasions, society and state degenerated under the control of provincial or locally-based warlords. While a modern version of 'warlordism' cannot be taken as a serious prospect in the twenty-first century, under the social and political stresses of growing overaccumulation and, possibly, financial crises (in the 'western' sense of that term), temporary fragmentation of the unified state and, with it, the Communist Party, could be a possibility. Were this to occur, then presumably some of the interior, western and poorer provinces of the country could collapse into a form of 'bandit capitalism', similar to some of the territories of the former Soviet Union. Those provinces that already have high degrees of economic and *de facto* political autonomy, and for some time have been thoroughly imbricated in global production networks and the world economy in general (for instance, Guangdong, the Hong Kong SAR, Fujian, Jiangsu, Shanghai, etc.) would presumably develop their relative autonomy to its logical conclusion and become significant powers in their own right.[23]

The second scenario suggests that the unity of the central state will remain intact. With the continuation of the economic reform process, deepening marketization and engagement with the global economy, the Communist Party's principal legitimation for its rule – its ability to deliver rising affluence to the growing middle class – will survive. Coupled with a continuation of its ability to compromise with key elements of the emerging class structure (including a revitalization of welfare benefits) and engage in the selective repression of 'dissident' groups, the smartest Communist Party the world has ever known will be able to keep the spectre of wholesale political reform at bay. As a consequence, Market Neo-Stalinism will continue to mutate into a more thoroughly capitalist, but still authoritarian, economic and political form, approximating, perhaps, that of South Korea between the early 1960s and late 1980s. This is a scenario that most analysts consider likely to choke-off China's continued economic development (see, for instance, Pei 2006, Hutton 2007, Shirk 2007), but it is one that is not only realistic (see, for instance, Jacques 2009), but might eventually come to prove that Market Neo-Stalinism is the best 'shell' for continued capitalist development in China for some decades to come.[24]

The third scenario suggests that while the unity of the central state will remain intact, the deepening of capitalist social relations and the class forces that are now being released will result in a successful struggle for political reform and democratization. While reform is unlikely to result in a version of the liberal-democratic state form beloved of much 'western' political philosophy and of US commentators in particular (cf. Hutton and Desai 2007, Jacques 2009), China could take a similar path to modernization and democracy as have South Korea and Taiwan, for instance, since the late 1980s, or, indeed, emerge with a polity that compares more closely to authoritarian 'democracies' such as those of Singapore, Malaysia, or Russia.

As the social sciences, for methodological reasons, cannot predict the future, we are unable to say which of these scenarios is likely to come to fruition. What we can say, however, is that the resolution of the question of Market Neo-Stalinism and its continued transformation, is fundamental not only to the future of China, but to that of the East Asian region and the global political economy in general.

Conclusion: opportunity and danger

The societies and economies that compose the East Asian region have come a very long way in a much shorter time frame than their European and North American counterparts when they were industrializing and subsequently became industrialized countries. The bulk of that journey, at least since the end of the World War II, has been overwhelmingly positive for humanity and prosperity, the horrors of the Korean and Vietnamese Wars, other conflagrations, China's 'great leap forward' (of the late 1950s) and so on, notwithstanding. But the East Asian region (and with it, the global political economy) is now, very much, at a critical turning point. Even if one rejects the hype and triumphalism associated with the notion of an 'Asian Century' (as, for instance, in Mahbubani 2008), or the idea of a possible 'Global-Asian Era' as an emergent form of globalization (see Chapter 8), it is still clear that East Asia will prove to be one of the keys to what the twenty-first century holds for us all. On the one hand it is quite possible that the human ingenuity that the East Asian region possesses in abundance, will be further released and channelled in ways that will benefit humankind globally. On the other, the contradictions of its economic and political transformation, and the international resistance that its economic prowess and growing geo-political muscle may yet engender, could help to deepen the new age of barbarism that neoliberalism seems to have unleashed on the globe.

In a nutshell, these are the sorts of possibilities that are embedded within the dialectics of danger and opportunity that constitute the contemporary human condition, in East Asia as much as elsewhere. They are amongst the possibilities that the following chapters explore, beginning, in Chapter 3, with a conceptualized discourse on the state in the transformation process.

3
STATES AND TRANSFORMATION

Over 40 years ago Ralph Dahrendorf drew a distinction between two types of rationality that had begun to infuse industrial society. 'Market rationality', he suggested, was based on the assumption that 'a smoothly functioning market is in fact to the greatest advantage of the greatest number'. As regards the state, it resulted in a 'politically passive . . . hands-off attitude in matters of legislation and decision-making'. 'Plan rationality', in contrast, he suggested, 'has as its dominant feature precisely the setting of substantive social norms. Planners determine in advance who does what and who gets what' (Dahrendorf 1968: 219). While it is clear that Dahrendorf treated market and plan rationality as ideal-type constructs, it is also clear that he regarded the capitalist political economies of North America and Western Europe as the closest approximations to the former and the state socialist political economies of the USSR and Eastern Europe, to the latter.

Dahrendorf's conceptual distinction, and their empirical affiliations, were developed at a time when liberal European intellectuals, such as he, still harboured a residue of optimism about soviet-type societies and when the industrializing societies of Asia, with the partial exception of Japan, were but a blur on the consciousness of most 'western' scholars. He can thus be forgiven, perhaps, for not drawing a further distinction between the rational intent of market and plan rational political economies and the empirical consequences of their 'rationality-in-action'. Given the benefit of hindsight, were we to draw this distinction today, then the inequities, and irrationalities, of both types of political economy would become clear. We would be forced to recognize that whatever its contribution to the expansion of GDP, improved living standards, the eradication of poverty and the construction of relatively egalitarian social arrangements, the Leninist project – and particularly its Stalinist derivatives – was ultimately a failure. Additionally we would have to take cognizance of the fact that 'market rationality' has itself engendered significant 'deformations' over the last 30 years or so. Driven by economic and social policies that were originally legitimated via the tenets of neoclassical economic theory (and subsequently subsumed by the broad political project that is neoliberalism), these 'deformations' have been responsible for the destruction of the livelihoods (and sometimes the lives) of hundreds of millions of people from Britain to the United States, from Australia to Eastern Europe and from Africa to Latin America (among a vast literature see, Chang and Grabel 2004, Harvey 2005, Henderson 2010).

To construct a typology of the world's political economies adequate to the task of reflecting the realities of the first decade of the twenty-first century, considerable refinement and supplementation of Dahrendorf's proposal would be necessary. This would be so not simply because of the aforementioned historical transformations, but also because it would have to take into account the experience of Japan and the other industrialized countries of East Asia, as well as China, which have developed neither market rational nor plan rational political economies as Dahrendorf understood them. As will become clear as the chapter unfolds, these societies, while definitely not socialist (China being the principal, but highly ambiguous exception) are very much a product of state planning and influence; and while they are definitely capitalist, they cannot be easily equated with the market-based societies of Western Europe and North America.

I begin by elaborating a typology of national political economies designed to grasp empirical variations as they can be seen to exist in the contemporary period. Japan, China and other East Asian countries are located within the typology so as to allow us to draw, more effectively, the comparisons and contrasts between them and other political economies. As part of this process I argue that it is these societies that now need to be grasped as the best examples of plan rational political economies. Subsequently, I turn to a justification of why these societies should be understood primarily as examples of state-orchestrated economic transformation. Picking-up on part of the discussion in Chapter 2, this section involves a critical assessment of other claims to the determination of East Asian transformation, and in particular those advanced by economists working from within the neoclassical paradigm. It also involves an attempt to be sensitive to the real empirical differences between the societies in question, as well as attending to the 'dark sides' of their developmental dialectics. Finally, I advance some hypotheses as to why the East Asian route to the modern world should have involved such a decisive role for state policy and influence.

Conceptualizing national political economies

Following the lead of Chalmers Johnson (1982:18–26), I suggested earlier that the concept of plan rationality is now more suitable for the analysis of Japan and some other East Asian political economies than it is for the small number of societies that are still fundamentally state socialist. For Johnson, the state socialist societies that existed in the early 1980s were more appropriately conceptualized as 'plan ideological' political economies. However, if we are to distinguish between sets of political economies in which the activities of the state have been decisive to their economic and social fortunes, then logically we need to interrogate the empirical referents of market rationality in order to identify whether conceptual distinctions need to be made among the political economies that might otherwise be grouped together under that rubric. I suggest that the rise and application of neoliberal economic and social policies from the 1980s through to the present day, necessitates a further conceptual distinction. I propose, therefore, to distinguish between market rational political economies on the one hand, and 'market ideological' ones on the other.

We can define *market rational* political economies as those in which the state sets the parameters (legal and otherwise) in which private companies operate. While the state certainly regulates the economy in various ways (and what state does not?), investment, production and distributional decisions are mainly the preserve of private companies and their actions. If disciplined at all, they are largely disciplined by the market, though in exceptional circumstances – such as the financial crisis of 2008 – states may be forced to take disciplinary action themselves.[1] Such exceptions notwithstanding, decisions on whether a given technology is utilized, whether a particular product is developed or a market penetrated, is substantially the sovereign concern of the company itself.

A *plan rational* political economy is one in which state regulation is supplemented by state direction of the economy. Here national economic goals are identified and the state operates to encourage or cajole companies to act in accordance with these goals. While the economy is largely and usually overwhelmingly in private hands and companies engage in competitive relations with one another and are disciplined by the market, the state also intervenes to discipline companies, where necessary, in order to achieve national goals. Unlike in market rational political economies, where state discipline is an exceptional procedure, in plan rational political economies, it is a normal part of economic policy. Should an industry deemed essential to economic growth not exist, then in plan rational political economies, the state may well induce it. A plan rational political economy is one in which the state is likely to intervene deliberately to get 'relative prices wrong' (Amsden 1989: 139–55) should this be necessary for national economic advancement. A plan rational political economy, then, is one in which economic ministries and planners recognize, at least implicitly, that there is no simple or direct relationship between corporate profits and national economic health; one, in other words, in which transformation is orchestrated by a capitalist 'developmental state' (Johnson 1982, Wade 1990, Appelbaum and Henderson 1992, Evans 1995, 2008, Woo-Cumings 1999).

While there are some similarities between plan rational and plan ideological political economies, especially in terms of the state's setting of national economic goals, their differences are of greater significance. In *plan ideological* political economies the state owns and controls most, if not all, economic assets. Resource allocations, investment decisions and sometimes price setting, are generally a state rather than a corporate or market function. Furthermore the state, at least officially, has as a central concern the redistribution of wealth and income. Most importantly for our purposes, however, empirical evidence that particular policies are failing to meet their aims, tends to be disregarded. Ideological dogma, rather than scientific analysis or pragmatism, dominates policy choices and applications.

A *market ideological* political economy is one that seeks to revert essentially to the state-civil society relation that pertained during the epoch of competitive capitalism; namely one in which the state merely 'allocates' those resources and responsibilities that have traditionally been under its control, rather than 'producing' resources that during the epoch of monopoly capitalism have been historically under-provided by private capital (Offe 1975). Such a political economy has an important element in common with a plan ideological political economy, and this, in fact, is its defining characteristic. In a market ideological political economy, policy formulation and implementation is relatively impermeable to argument and to empirical evidence which contradicts its basic values. Policies arise, then, from ideological dogma, usually legitimated intellectually by neoclassical economic theory, which reifies – indeed deifies – 'the market.' A market ideological political economy, then, is one that is fundamentally neoliberal in orientation and practice (cf. Henderson 2010)

As with Dahrendorf's original constructs, those proposed here should be regarded as ideal-types. Actually existing political economies are always combinations of elements of two or more of these ideal-types; always to a greater or lesser extent, hybrids. The point is where the balance lies. Which of the ideal-types, in other words, best characterizes a given society in a particular historical moment in terms of its state-economy relation.

On the basis of these conceptual distinctions, it is now possible to represent, diagrammatically and provisionally, state-economy relations for the political economies in question. For the sake of comparison, a number of other industrial and industrializing societies are included as is a sense of their possible developmental trajectories over the next few years.

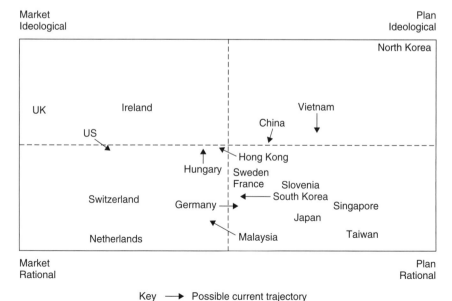

FIGURE 3.1 National political economies, circa 2000–2005

Although the contents of Figure 3.1 should be regarded as no more than a heuristic approximation, if for current purposes we define 'success' as sustained growth with significant levels of social equity, then they serve to indicate that many of the world's recently most successful political economies can be located in, or close to, the plan rational 'quadrant' (implied, for East Asia, in the work by Evans and Rauch 1999 and Henderson *et al.* 2007). The principal exception here is China. Though sustained economic growth there is undoubted, it is currently only an emergent plan rational political economy and remains a long way from the fully industrialized societies that the others have become. In particular, it has a far worse record on social equity than any of the political economies grouped in the plan rational quadrant in Figure 3.1. Recent calculations by Chen (2007, Table 5.3–1: 109), for instance, suggest that in 2004 China had a national gini coefficient of 0.442, indicating not only very high income inequality, but according to Chen, an increase in inequality of 146 per cent since the onset of economic reform in 1978. It is for these reasons that China cannot yet be considered as a quintessential case of plan rational economic transformation and, consequently, its experience does not figure in the following discussion. Additionally, it would go far beyond the scope of this chapter to try to justify the positioning for all the cases represented in Figure 3.1.[2] Consequently, the next section presents a justification for why Japan and the other now fully industrialized countries of East Asia, in spite of the many important differences between them, should be regarded as plan rational political economies.

Forging plan rationalism in East Asia

In discussing the components of plan rationalism in this section, I do so in a way that abstracts them, methodologically, from their historical and empirical relation with the other determinants of East Asian economic transformation. I do not intend by this to imply that the nature of the state, its policy instruments and implementations should be the sole focus of those who seek to unlock the mysteries – or the myths – of economic transformation in the region. However, as I indicated in Chapter 2, the issue of free markets or 'unfettered enterprise' as the key determinant of transformation, made most of the running in attempts to explain the East Asian economic 'miracle', and continues to exercise its ideological grip in many scientific and government circles across the world, in spite of the legitimation crisis that should now confront it in the wake of the 2008 global financial turmoil. As a result, and though broached in Chapter 2, it is necessary here to pay further attention to this account. The following discussion, and the critique of neoclassical development theory that it will involve, will lead naturally into our argument about the significance of state initiatives for East Asian economic transformation.

Free market explanations

An interesting fact about orthodox (neoclassical) commentary on the East Asian transformation process, was that the bulk of it originally came from Western economists who, as Chalmers Johnson (1988) pointed out, hardly ever studied the empirics of the Japanese or East Asian economies. From the vaunted heights of their 'imperial science' (Stigler 1984) they were sufficiently confident merely to extrapolate from their conceptual tool-kit without the need to befuddle their minds with the often awkward detail of the empirical world. The mere suggestion that state industrial policy, for instance, could have made a positive contribution to economic growth in East Asia, was ruled out, *a priori*.[3] Even when economists indigenous to the region engaged in empirical investigations, similar explanatory problems were evident. For instance, one of the region's then leading economists, Edward Chen (1979: 41) argued when talking of Japan, South Korea, Taiwan, Hong Kong and Singapore, that '. . . state intervention was largely absent. What the state provided was simply a suitable environment for the entrepreneurs to perform their function.' More recently, even some economists from mainland China (Chen is from Hong Kong) have resisted the idea that state intervention – at least in the form of strategic industrial planning – has been central to the story. Justin Lin (now chief economist at the World Bank), for instance, has argued that growth would have been faster in the developing world had governments there focussed on the improvement of 'endowments' (education, etc.) rather than on direct attempts to orchestrate industrialization (Lin 2003, 2005).

The essence of the neoclassical account of rapid economic growth in East Asia was that these countries 'enjoyed' political regimes that allowed the efficiencies derived from market-based resource allocations to be maximized (Balassa 1981). East Asian governments (that is, those of Japan and the 'first generation' NICs), it was argued, either never intervened in normal (private) market allocation functions or if they did, they progressively 'liberalized' their economies prior to the initial periods of rapid economic growth associated with export-oriented industrialization (e.g. between 1958 and 1962 in the case of Taiwan, and from the early 1960s in the case of South Korea). Either way, state-induced market distortions were kept to a minimum and as a consequence markets worked more efficiently than in other developing societies.

Robert Wade (1990: 23–24), however, pointed to a secondary theme within the neoclassical literature that gave credence to a modicum of state intervention. Here it was argued that at the aggregate level, East Asian governments successfully balanced domestic market protection with export-promotion policies. The overall effect, supposedly, was the neutralization of one set of state-induced market distortions by another. The influential work of business economist, Michael Porter (1990), would appear to fit into this second category insofar as it engages with the Japanese and Korean experiences. While Porter (1990: 88) allows a 'proper role' for govern-ment 'as a catalyst and challenger; . . . to encourage – or even push – companies to raise their aspirations and move to higher levels of competitive performance', it is clear from his chapters on Japan and Korea that he has no real conception of how state industrial policy and influence (not to mention, at key moments, state equity-holding) have been at the heart of corporate success in both cases. For Porter the state's role, at most, was an important contingency, but ultimately not central or decisive to the stories of Japanese and Korean economic growth.[4] As Wade (1990) argues, in spite of allowing explanatory space for state intervention, 'simulated free market' theorists, as he calls them (and Porter would probably be amongst the more creative), have little interest in analysing the empirics of state intervention, as they identify as their primary determinants of economic growth, open markets, unfettered enterprise, the nature of the trade regime, and for those such as Porter, intense competition among domestic firms.

Twenty years ago it was perhaps understandable that neoclassical economists could make these sorts of claims about East Asian development, and get away with it; to claim, in effect, that Japan and the rest really were examples – perhaps supreme examples – of market rational political economies. At a time when many of the social sciences had been lurching from one intellectual crisis to another, under the hegemony of the neoclassical paradigm, economics had evolved into the least introspective of them. In spite of the current global recession and the financial debacle that initiated it,[5] most mainstream economists continue to countenance few lingering doubts about their common project or how it should be accomplished. They inhabit a realm of methodological and theoretical certainty out of which can be distilled supposedly universalistic models from which flow policy prescriptions that are good for all times and all places. That these policy prescriptions have helped to devastate the daily lives of hundreds of millions of people across the globe from the initial neoliberal experiments in New York City and Chile in the 1970s (Harvey 2005) through to Britain or Ireland today, is a matter of serious concern to which I shall return later. For the moment, however, it is important to mark the fact that for over 30 years there has been a significant body of scholarship and empirical investigation that, had it been read and taken seriously by mainstream economists, might, at the very least, have resulted in pause for critical reflection.

Indeed, as early as the late 1970s, the orthodox claim to a monopoly on truthful knowledge on East Asian growth and development had already begun to be punctured. The earliest sustained alternatives to the neoclassical explanation that I am aware of came in Frances Moulder's (1977) world-systems inspired book on the historical antecedents of post-war Japanese (and Chinese) development, a book chapter on the Japanese Ministry of International Trade and Industry (MITI) by Chalmers Johnson (1977) and a paper on *etatisme* in Taiwanese development by Alice Amsden (1979). In the 1980s, however, the challenges to the economic orthodoxy began to mount. The seminal contribution was Johnson's book on MITI (1982), though Michio Morishima's (1982) historical-cultural analysis of Japanese development was also significant, not least because he had already by then been appointed to a chair in the economics department at the London School of Economics and Political Science, a department not exactly renowned for its sceptical orientation to the neoclassical paradigm. These were followed by Linda Lim's (1983) path-breaking paper on Singapore, and further contributions on Taiwan by Amsden (1985) and Gold (1986). The book by Harris (1987) and the collections edited by Deyo (1987), White (1988) and Appelbaum and Henderson (1992), provided more general interventions, while the most sustained engagements with the neoclassical accounts of economic transformation in the 'first generation' NICs came with the books by Amsden (1989) on South Korea, Castells *et al.* (1990) on Hong Kong and Singapore, Rodan (1989) on Singapore, and particularly Wade (1990) on Taiwan and the 'first generation' NICs more generally. During the 1990s, important contributions came from Jonathan Schiffer (1991), who helped to demolish even the Hong Kong support for the neoclassical account, while Jung-en Woo (1991), Ha-Joon Chang (1994) and Eun Mee Kim (1997) respectively laid bare the significance of targeted finance and industrial policy more generally, to South Korean dynamism. Additionally, the work of Jomo and his collaborators (e.g. Jomo 2007) helped to make the case for the role of federal and local industrial policy in the making of one of the more recent East Asian success stories: Malaysia.

These contributions and many others of their ilk (such as those that dealt more widely with the 'developmental state', e.g. Haggard 1990 and Evans 1995) exposed how partial and often misguided neoclassical explanations of East Asian economic growth and development were. Some of them were even written by *bona fide* economists (for instance, Morishima, Lim, Schiffer, Chang and Jomo), but ones who were open to heterodox ideas which put them beyond the scientific pale as far as the orthodoxy was concerned. Collectively, what this work underlined was that the vast majority of neoclassical research and scholarship on East Asian transformation, failed the tests of empirical adequacy and analytic plausibility, the only ones that can be considered credible in the social sciences where 'facts' cannot, in themselves, be used to adjudicate the truth claims of explanations that arise from within competing intellectual paradigms (Sayer 1984). While it would be interesting to speculate on why neoclassical economists did not bother to read the sort of analyses indicated earlier (or if they did, why they must have dismissed them as unworthy of serious consideration), it seems clear that part of the explanation must lie, on the one hand, in the nature of the epistemological and methodological foundations of neoclassical economics (see, for instance, Hutchinson 1994 and Fullbrook 2004) and in the other, in the intellectual and social pressures within major economics departments, particularly since the early 1970s, for researchers to conform to the neoclassical paradigm.

On this latter point, Chalmers Johnson has argued that there are (or at least were) systematic attempts in the economics departments of US universities to persuade colleagues against the empirical study of the Japanese and similar economies. He suggests that:

> Members of the senior economics faculty prefer to study theory; they warn members of their departments, particularly those who do not have tenure, not to undertake applied or comparative research since it might reveal the large number of anomalies that have developed in American-oriented theory.
>
> (Johnson 1988: 79)

Business economist, Neil Kay, locates the source of the general problem in the nature of the contemporary economics curriculum. In a particularly robust tone, he argues that:

mainstream economics has continued to be a fertile source of sterile theo-
ries. . . . It represents an intellectual tragedy of the first order. The waste of
potential academic talent, the premature hardening of cerebral arteries bred
by repetitive neoclassical modelling, and the filtering out of bright, deviant
students who regard neoclassical theory as irrelevant or unrealistic, all these
factors perpetuate the neoclassical paradigm as the basic framework for economic analysis. The process starts with the first year economics textbooks;
once the *tabula rasa* of beginning students has been filled in with neoclassical theory and IS/LM macromodels, it creates a deterministic equilibrium
mental set by which future analysis is judged, accommodated, or rejected.
Irrevocable damage is done in the first few terms of economics teaching
experienced by a new student. Once started the process is depressingly self-
perpetuating; the individual intent on pursuing a career as an economist has
to be bright enough to understand the abstract ramifications of neoclassical
theory and dumb enough to have faith in them.

(Kay 1984: 187–88)

Clearly this is not the appropriate context in which to pursue further this particular
line of investigation, though it is one that could significantly illuminate why it is
that so many 'poor policies' have been allowed to damage the developing world
in recent decades (see Chang 2007a). From here on, this chapter has a different
project: to identify and justify the common thread that runs through the analyses of
East Asian transformation cited earlier. Namely, that the rapid economic growth of
Japan, Hong Kong, South Korea, Taiwan and Singapore, would have been inconceivable if they had emerged as market rational political economies, as neoclassical
accounts, in effect, would have us believe, rather than as plan rational political
economies that they were and, generally, remain.

Elements of plan rational political economies

In this section I propose to abstract from the historical evolution of the state-
economy relation in East Asia in order to identify both the common features of that
relation in the various cases, and the unique aspects that have been significant to
one or perhaps two cases, but not to the others. Though this procedure risks doing
an injustice to the rich empirical detail and specificities of the various aspects of the
state-economy relation in each country, it has the advantage of allowing us to identify quickly the commonalties and dissimilarities associated with the construction of
plan rational political economies in the region.

   An additional point that needs to be made is that little time will be spent here
embedding the state-economy relation in each case in their relevant historical contexts. This is not to say that I accord little determinate significant to, say, the experience of Japanese colonialism or US military and civil aid for the development
experiences of South Korea and Taiwan, or to booming world markets from the
1950s to early 1970s for the rapid export-oriented industrialization in the NICs as a
whole. Indeed I accept completely Braudel's methodological premise that:

> the present . . . [is] in large measure the prisoner of a past that obstinately survives, and the past with its rules, its differences and its similarities, [is] the indispensable key to any serious understanding of the present.
>
> (Braudel 1984: 20)

The point is simply that the task of historical contextualization of the evolution of the state-economy relation in East Asia would take us far beyond the scope of this chapter and, in any case, these issues have been addressed extensively elsewhere (e.g. Moulder 1977, Cumings 1987, So and Chiu 1995, Arrighi 1996, Arrighi *et al.* 2003)

In what follows I mark the economic processes on which state policy or influence in East Asia was brought to bear at particular historical moments when the course of growth and development, or often state-defined national economic goals, required it. In what follows the focus is predominantly on those countries and territories that were the first, after Japan, to industrialize: South Korea, Taiwan, Hong Kong and Singapore.

State equity

Development strategies have often involved a role for the state as an industrial entrepreneur. In addition to the obvious cases of Russia and other parts of the former USSR through to the early 1990s and China through to the present day, many western European countries (for instance, Britain and France) built their post World War II prosperity partly on the basis of state equity holding. Although this was not as significant a feature of the political economies of Japan and most of the NICs as it was for these cases, it was a significant feature of Taiwan's development (Wade 1990) and was used by a number of the region's governments as a means of inducing particular industrial sectors or of ensuring a steady supply, at stable prices, of commodities essential to the growth of their domestic economies. Only Hong Kong among these East Asian cases did not use state equity-holding (the exception was land) as part of a general development strategy.

Thus in the case of Taiwan, Amsden (1985: 91) reports that in 1952, 57 per cent of both industrial production and manufacturing output were accounted for by state enterprises. Although by the early 1980s the share of such companies in manufacturing production had fallen to less than 20 per cent, through the 1980s state companies remained dominant in the production of heavy machinery, steel, aluminium, shipbuilding, petroleum, synthetics, fertilizers, general engineering, and for a time, semiconductors. By 1981, 16 per cent of Taiwan's GDP was still accounted for by state-owned companies. While privatization – including of the banks – began in 1996, the former state-owned enterprises (SOEs) remained tightly regulated, with the government maintaining a controlling stake (average 35 per cent of equity and 60 per cent of board members) in 18 of them (Chang 2007b, Box 3: 11).

In South Korea, subsequent to the military coup which brought the Park regime to power in 1961, the state took the leading role in the production of petrochemicals, synthetics, cement and steel (Amsden 1989). Of particular note in the country's steel industry is the Pohang Iron and Steel Company (POSCO), established by the Korean government (against World Bank advice and consequently a refusal of funds to support its establishment) in 1968. Remaining state owned until privatized in 2000, by the mid-1980s it had become the world's most productive steel company and remained so until the late 1990s. Today, it is the fourth largest steel company in the world. (Chang 2007b, Box 2:10–11). Additionally, the banking sector in South Korea (as in Taiwan) was overwhelming state owned until the early 1990s (see later and Chapter 4).

In Singapore, as in South Korea and Taiwan, the state also acted as the industrial entrepreneur in some sectors. The Government (via its sovereign wealth company, Temasek Holdings) continues to have significant equity participation in such sectors as air transportation (e.g. Singapore Airlines, with currently a 54 per cent stake), petrochemicals, ship-repairing, shipping, engineering, construction and banking (Lim 1983; Castells *et al.* 1990: 182–84). Overall, as recently as 2001, 22 per cent of Singapore's GDP was accounted for by fully, or partially (minimum 20 per cent equity), state owned companies (Chang 2007b, Box 1: 9)

In the case of the NICs, if they drew on any foreign models for state equity participation and its relation to economic transformation, they were not those of western Europe, Russia or China (with the exception of Taiwan where nationalist China, prior to 1949, did constitute something of a model), but it was probably Japan. Initially devoid of a capitalist class capable of driving the industrialization process, the Japanese state, subsequent to the Meiji Restoration of 1867–68, acted as the industrial capitalist, setting up its own companies in steel, shipbuilding, engineering, fertilizers, railways and banking. In the 1880s and 1890s, the state effectively created Japan's industrial capitalist class when it privatized many of these companies, thus orchestrating the emergence of *zaibatsu* (family-owned conglomerates) such as Mitsubishi, Mitsui and Sumitomo (Moulder 1977, Morishima 1982).

Inducing industries

In addition to establishing new industries by means of equity-holding, some East Asian states also induced new industrial sectors by means of encouragement, involving financial subsidies, or, indeed, the direction of private companies to invest in new product areas consistent with government industrial strategies. Some of the best examples of this occurred in South Korea (for rich detail and theoretical reflection, see Amsden 1989, Chang 1994 and Kim, E.M. 1997). Supported by subsidized credit delivered by state-owed banks (Woo 1991) and benefiting from a protected domestic market and a variety of technical assistance acquired from Britain and Japan (Amsden 1989: 269–90), Hyundai Heavy Industries, now one of the world's largest shipbuilding companies, was created on government instructions (by the Hyundai *chaebol*) in the early 1970s. Similarly, semiconductor production by Samsung, Goldstar (now LG) and Hyundai was induced as a result of state planning and support, the latter including the identification and funding of the acquisition of foreign technologies and technical assistance, heavily subsidized research and development (R&D) and a protected domestic market (Amsden 1989, Henderson 1989: 65–67). As a consequence, South Korean companies (particularly Samsung), have for 20 years, been the world's largest producers of semiconductor memory devices.

In addition, the reorganization of corporate structures in the interests of economies of scale and scope, on occasion has also been subject to state direction. Again South Korea provides one of the best examples. In the early 1980s, as a result of duplicate investment and over-capacity, Hyundai and Daewoo were directed by the Government's Economic Planning Board to transfer to each other their respective production capacities in power plant equipment and passenger cars, creating effective monopolies in those sectors for the companies concerned (Koo and Kim 1992: 141).

Protecting domestic markets

The North East Asian political economies (Japan, South Korea and Taiwan), at various moments in their past, protected their domestic markets from foreign imports. While in earlier periods, market protection was associated with import substitution industrialization (ISI) strategies, such as in Taiwan in the 1950s, more recently with the liberalization of the international trade regime associated initially with the General Agreement on Tariffs and Trade (GATT) and then the World Trade Organization (WTO), domestic market protection became more selective. Often (and, again Taiwan is a good example here), protection was afforded to those products areas where the government sought to build domestic capacity. However, domestic markets were liberalized where government economic planners did not seek to build domestic capacity, where imported components and technologies were needed to build domestic capacity in a particular product, or where the country concerned already had an internationally competitive industry (such as, by the 1980s, certain machine tools in Taiwan's case; Amsden 1985, Wade 1990). Similarly South Korea, learning from the earlier Japanese experience of market protection, used this device to build domestic capacity in, for instance, ships and automobiles in the 1970s and 1980s. With regard to the latter, from the early 1970s to the mid-1980s, only Korean built cars (be they Korean or foreign brands) were seen on the country's roads (Amsden 1990). Undoubtedly learning from Korean and Japanese practices, the Malaysian government, when seeking to develop its 'national car' industry (Proton), nurtured it behind high tariff barriers. From the sale of its first cars in the mid-1980s, through to 2006 (when it became subject to WTO and ASEAN agreements), Proton's domestic market has protected it from foreign imports with escalating tariffs of 140 to 300 per cent (Chee 2003, Arnold 2005).

Subsidized capital

A common feature of the North East Asian political economies is that their banks where either state-owned, as in South Korea and Taiwan (through to the late 1980s early 1990s), or where private, as in Japan, they were subject to tight regulation by the central bank. In the cases of Korea and Taiwan, state control over the banking system was has been coupled with restrictions on companies raising capital by stock flotations, or from foreign sources. The consequence of this was that major corporate expansions – developing capacity in new commodities, opening-up new markets, etc. – were funded by loans from state or stringently regulated banks. For projects initiated or approved by state agencies, loans were often delivered at interest rates far below those prevailing in domestic or international money-markets (Amsden 1989; Wade 1990; Woo 1991). In the case of South Korea the control of domestic credit and the mediation of foreign credit by the Economic Planning Board and the Bank of Korea (the central bank), meant that the state, until the liberalization of banking in the early 1990s (see Chapter 4) had almost complete control over access to investment capital. Given that the *chaebol* (conglomerates) had been financially structured since the 1960s to ensure high debt/low equity ratios (sometimes giving debt–equity ratios of 5:1), most of them, through to the onset of the country's financial crisis in the late 1990s, were technically bankrupt at any particular moment. This resulted in a high level of dependency on state controlled finance and this was regularly used to ensure that the *chaebol* followed state economic directives and continued to offer political support to the governing regime (Woo 1991). When in 1979 the Yolsan *chaebol* failed in its latter obligations, the Park regime blocked further credit, the company collapsed and its assets were distributed to more compliant *chaebol* (Cumings 1987: 74).

Performance standards

Delivering subsidized capital to private companies seeking to expand or re-orient their operations is nothing new in the annals of state-business relations. This much has been done by many European governments and the EU, for instance – in the form of special development grants, depreciation allowances, start-up costs (often under the auspices of 'regional aid') – for a considerable period of time. What was different about the North East Asian cases, however, is that there, the state required recipients of subsidized capital to meet certain performance standards. One such measure of corporate performance was the requirement to export a proportion of output within a specified period of receiving the subsidy. In the case of South Korea since the late 1960s, companies in receipt of subsidized capital were required to export a minimum of 25 per cent of output, even where the product – for instance paper – was hardly a prime candidate for export potential (Amsden 1989, 1990). Subjecting companies to performance standards in these ways, helped to minimize the possibility that subsidies would result in speculative, non-productive investments or indeed, corruption.

Regulation of speculation

An important feature of the financial systems of South Korea, Taiwan and Singapore (though not Hong Kong) was that they were all, in various ways, able to limit the flows (inward and outward) of speculative investments and hence avoid many of the negativities associated with 'casino capitalism' (see Chapter 4). This was not simply a matter of controls on the movement of capital (although that did happen, particularly in case of Korea: see later), but rather, in part, it was a reflex of the fact that the major business corporations were funded through bank credit. As with many of the features of plan rationalism in the Northeast Asian economies, Japan was, once more, something of a model. There, the Tokyo stock market was constrained (relative to the size of the Japanese economy as a whole) as a result, in part, of the limited recourse to capital markets to fund corporate investment (Whitley 1992, Dore 2000).[6] In Korea, the Seoul stock market remained relatively underdeveloped until well into the 1990s because it was almost irrelevant to investment finance for the *chaebol*. As indicated earlier, they were funded overwhelmingly through loans from state-owned banks. Constraints on stock market growth typically has the indirect effect of ensuring the flow of domestic investment into productive activities in the real (that is, non-financial) economy. However, in Korea, capital controls have been necessary, in part, to check the possibilities for corruption and misuse of funds that could otherwise have arisen with the large flows of subsidized capital to the *chaebol*. One such control in Korea was a law, dating from the early 1960s, that forbade the export of funds in excess of the equivalent of US$ 1million, without government permission, on pain of penalties ranging from ten years imprisonment to death (Amsden 1990: 22).

Price controls

In some cases state agencies have intervened to control prices of particular commodities on the domestic market. This was done either to discourage exploitation in cases of monopolistic supply – as in South Korea – and/or was used to contain prices of basic foodstuffs and hence help deflect upward pressure on wages. In the Korean case, the government until well into the 1980s controlled the rents for (privately owned) working class housing (Kim W. J. 1997) and for some foodstuffs (Amsden 1989, 1990). Hong Kong, however, was probably the best example of the latter. There, the then colonial government, from the 1950s to the 1980s, organized (in collusion with the government of the adjacent Chinese Province of Guangdong) what was in effect a cartel to control the price of rice, vegetables, chicken and pork (Schiffer 1991).

Land, labour and collective consumption

With the exceptions indicated earlier, Hong Kong and Singaporean plan rationalism was not associated with the policy instruments of the Northeast Asian political economies. Their governments did not control credit or directly subsidize capital, they did not induce new industries, nor did they seek to discipline business (except on occasion, in Singapore's case, speculators). This is not to suggest, however, that Hong Kong and Singapore were more market rational than plan rational political economies. On the contrary, they used public assets as important budgetary tools, and they provided significant welfare sectors which subsidized the wage and helped to socially stabilize potentially volatile populations.

In the case of Hong Kong, state ownership of land, which continues to be allocated to real estate developers on a leasehold basis at market rates, has meant in recent decades that about a third of government revenues have been generated by this means,[7] thus allowing the state to engage in massive welfare expenditure while maintaining low levels of corporate and personal taxation. Central to its welfare expenditures has been the provision of a heavily subsidized public housing system which by the early 1990s housed about 45 per cent of the population, and hence about 85 per cent of the working class. For a supposed free market paradise, the Hong Kong government (British colonial until 1997, now a Special Administrative Region – SAR – of China) has intervened substantially in two of the factors of production – land and labour – to the benefit of export competitiveness (via subsidized wages), capital accumulation and its own coffers (Castells *et al.* 1990: Part I; Schiffer 1991).

In Singapore, the Central Provident Fund (CPF) has played a similar role to that of land in Hong Kong. Compulsory employer and employee contributions have resulted in an enforced form of saving that by the 1980s had amassed such a considerable sum that it is was used by the Government as a significant budgetary asset (for instance, as collateral against government borrowing). In some ways the existence of the CPF has been a fulcrum of state economic policy. It has helped fund Asia's most extensive welfare state, which includes the world's largest public, and subsidized ownership, housing system;[8] it has allowed the state a high degree of financial stability; and in the mid-1980s, to take the historically unique step for any government, of forcing up labour costs (by increasing employer contributions). This initiative was a deliberate attempt by the government to pressure manufacturing companies (largely foreign owned) to investment in more technology intensive, higher value-added forms of production (Lim 1983; Castells *et al.* 1990: Part II).

Labour containment and repression

Central to the plan rational project in East Asia has been the containment and sometimes the direct repression of popular, oppositional forces, particularly organized labour (Deyo 1989, Castells 1992). Beginning with Japan in the late 1940s and early 1950s, where socialist-inspired trade unions were neutralized to be replaced by more compliant company unions, through to the imprisonment of supposedly 'Marxist' social workers in Singapore in 1987, East Asian governments have consistently operated to exclude popular participation in economic and political decision-making from the development agenda.

Throughout the period analysed here, only The Philippines has evolved (since the end of US colonialism in 1946) a liberal-democratic polity, but even in its case, it was host to the dictatorial Marcos regime between 1965 and 1986 and has been burdened with incompetent, corrupt autocracies ever since. Taiwan and

South Korea began to democratize in the late 1980s and Taiwan, in particular, seems to have successfully institutionalized a liberal-democratic politics. Prior to these recent developments, however, repression has been direct and brutal (and in some parts of the region – Burma and China in particular – remains so today). In South Korea, for instance, responsibility for labour relations, from the late 1940s through to the 1980s, lay not with a government ministry, but with the police and the Korean Central Intelligence Agency (Cumings 1987). In some instances these agencies responded to opposition (largely from students and workers) with murder and assassination, as during the infamous Kwangju uprising of 1980, when perhaps two to three thousand people were killed. During the 1980s, new trade unions emerged in South Korea and Taiwan and they formed a large part of the bedrock on which the subsequent democratization of both polities was forged (Asia Monitor Resources Center 1988; Ho 1990).

Plan rationalism's social and political costs

This list of elements that have composed the plan rational project in the various East Asian political economies clearly indicates that there has been far more to their success than can be encompassed by even the more sophisticated, 'simulated free market' (Wade 1990) versions of neoclassical theory. Given the substantial body of scholarship referred to earlier, it is now patently transparent that neoclassical accounts have simply ignored a substantial part of the empirical record on East Asian economic transformation. In short, such accounts appear to have been, at best, barely partially right and to a large extent they have been wrong.

Before moving to examine the reasons why East Asian states have operated in the ways that they have, it is important to mark that there has been (and there remains) a number of 'dark sides' of their transformation projects. Whereas plan rationality in Western Europe (see Figure 2.1) has been tempered by victories in working and living conditions and welfare provision won through decades of working class, women's and other popular struggles, the benefits of such struggles, except in a small number of cases, do not appear to have been a significant feature of the East Asian route to the modern industrial world.

As I have already indicated, while the East Asian societies under discussion have at various moments been the sites of popular mobilization (South Korea and Taiwan in the 1980s, for instance), these, in general, have not ensured the emergence of liberal-representative-democratic state forms. Even in Japan, which Johnson (1982) categorized as 'soft authoritarian', one party rule (by the centre-right, Liberal Democratic Party-LDP) has persisted for all but three short periods (1993, 1994 and 2009 onwards) since its foundation in 1955. Only in Taiwan (and, to some extent, The Philippines since the overthrow of the Marcos regime in 1986), with its governing shifts between the Nationalist Party (Kuo Min Tang – KMT) and the Democratic Progress Party (DPP), has there been an approximation of the political processes typical of Western Europe or North America. The presence of 'Western' political processes should not, however, be taken as the benchmark of 'good governance' in East Asia, or indeed elsewhere. Arguably more important is that the region's governing regimes – be they in their 'soft' or 'hard' authoritarian forms – have delivered genuine improvements to the living standards of their populations, including dramatic reductions in poverty and, for significant periods, less income inequality than even some of their European counterparts (Castells 1992).[9] While this is an issue with which I shall engage more directly in Chapter 8, we need to mark here that East Asian transformation has brought with it working and living conditions that, in some cases, seem particularly oppressive.

Even with regard to Japan, one of the 'downsides' of re-industrialization and transformation has been long working weeks.[10] The OECD (2009) reports that in 1970 the average Japanese work year was 2,243 hours. Twenty years later, in 1990, the average had fallen by a little over 200 hours (9 per cent), to 2,031. By contrast, the average German work year in 1970 was 1,969 hours which by 1990 had fallen by nearly 400 hours (20 per cent) to 1,580. The comparable figures for those same years for Britain were 1,943 and 1,771 hours (9 per cent); for the USA, 1,898 and 1,827 (4 per cent); for Spain 2,040 and 1741 (15 per cent); for France, 2,011 and 1,702 (15 per cent); and for Canada, 1,915 and 1,776 hours (7 per cent). Subsequent to 1990, the average work year in Japan continued to fall towards some of the other advanced industrial society norms, but the reductions involved were probably a function of the economic stagnation – and thus rising part-time employment – that its economy has experienced for much of the last 20 years, rather than a consequence of negotiated reductions or state regulation.[11] Thus in 2007, Japan's average working year was 1,785 hours compared with 1,794 in the USA, 1,736 in Canada, 1,670 in Britain, 1,635 in Spain, 1,533 in France and 1,433 in Germany (OECD 2009). Given these reductions, Japanese employees still seem to work nearly 200 hours a year more than their counterparts in the European advanced industrial countries (where the average in 2007 was 1,599 hours a year).[12]

This work schedule, coupled with the general tensions and pressures of life in Japanese cities, has resulted in extraordinary increases in stress–related health problems such as high blood pressure and nervous disorders. Between 1955 and 1985, for instance, the incidence of such problems increased from 38 per thousand people to 145 per thousand. Over the years, Japanese business has preferred to respond to such high levels of stress-related illness by offering commodified 'pseudo-solutions' such as special kinds of chewing gum, meditation chambers and 'refresh capsules' which allow immersion in the sounds of 'murmuring brooks, singing birds and gently breaking waves' (McCormack 1991: 122–23).

Working hours and related health problems in Taiwan, Hong Kong and possibly, Singapore, were – and probably still are – much worse than in Japan. In Hong Kong, for instance, by the late 1980s, a 56 hour working week with seven days paid holiday a year, was the norm. South Korea, however, of all the East Asian industrialized societies, and in relation to the OECD countries (the world's most economically developed ones) in general, is a significant outlier. For instance, OECD (2009) data suggests that in 2007, South Korea's average working year was still a very high 2,316 hours. As such it was over 500 hours (24 per cent) higher than Japan's, over 300 hours (14 per cent) higher than the OECD's next 'worst' performer, Hungary, and an astounding 924 hours (40 per cent) higher than its 'best' performer, The Netherlands. Given South Korea's level of economic development (with 39 per cent of its GDP from manufacturing in 2008 and with a GDP per capita of US$27,700 in 2009 – the same as New Zealand's[13]), these data suggest that its workers continue to be subject to levels of exploitation – technically and socially – that are unprecedented in the industrialized world.

So, while the plan rational project in East Asia has been enormously successful in creating rapid economic growth and delivering substantial material benefits for the population, in the case of some of the region's industrialized countries and territories – and particularly China today – it has brought with it working experiences (and often conditions) that are far more negative than those that now exist in other industrial and industrializing societies. It has also brought with it centralized, autocratic, and sometimes authoritarian and repressive state forms.

It seems clear that the development model pioneered by Japan and reproduced via a number of mediations by the NICs, involved, as central components, autocratic or authoritarian states, irrespective of whether they were democratic in form, as they were in Singapore and Japan and more recently in Taiwan and Korea. In all of these cases, the state was able to develop a high degree of autonomy from economic interests and from civil society more generally. In Japan this was achieved as a consequence of the Meiji Restoration of 1867–68 when a putsch allowed the formation of a new state that was then able to draw clear of the landowning-based constraints of the Shogunates and subsequently itself induce an industrial capitalist class which became its principal social base (Moulder 1977; Morishima 1982). In Korea and Taiwan, state autonomy was partly a result of the elimination of the large landowning classes, first by the Japanese during the colonial period (1895–1945 in Taiwan; 1910–45 in Korea), and subsequently by the land reforms organized by the United States administration and the Rhee regime in South Korea and the Chiang regime in Taiwan, both during the 1950s. Additionally in South Korea, the state was militarized subsequent to the Park-led coup of 1961; and in Taiwan the Kuomintang government, which occupied the island in the 1940s, not only held it under marshal law (until 1988) but was an ethnically (though not racially) alien regime. This contributed to its isolation from indigenous social forces to which it otherwise might have needed to respond (Koo and Kim 1992; Amsden 1979, 1985). In the case of Hong Kong, no land-owning class of any significance predated British occupation in 1941 and the colonial regime's encouragement of commerce and subsequently industry, created a capitalist class that generally saw its interests as consistent with those of the colonial regime. The racially alien and colonial character of the regime contributed to its isolation from internal political pressure. When Singapore was expelled from the Malaysian Federation in 1965, the People's Action Party (PAP) government, as with Hong Kong's colonial regime, had no land-owning class of significance capable of constraining or derailing its activities. While an indigenous commercial class existed as a consequence of the country's entrepôt function, industrial capitalism was not an indigenous phenomenon, but rather became a product of foreign direct investment. While the transnational corporations that invested in Singapore clearly had an interest in political stability and in state policies that did not disrupt their activities, they were not concerned with the internal political and economic dynamics of the country in the way that an indigenous industrial capitalist class would have been.

I have already argued that a *sin qua non* of the plan rational project in East Asia has been the neutralization of working class and popular forces generally, by a combination of repression, fragmentation (such as in Hong Kong) and incorporation. This, coupled with the elimination or incorporation of the landowning and capitalist classes, has ensured that, perhaps unique in the developing world at that time (or in much of it today) the East Asian NICs, and Japan before them, developed political economies in which their respective states had high levels of structural autonomy. Such levels of autonomy would have been inconceivable had their routes to the modern world been forged by popular struggles from which democratic state forms could have arisen as in the 'classic' cases of France, England and the United States (Moore 1966). History, then, provided initially Japan, and subsequently Taiwan, Korea, Hong Kong and Singapore also, with the structural space in which authoritarian states were able to shoulder the responsibility for development. Without this room for manoeuvre, it is difficult to imagine how big business could have been disciplined in the way of a Japan or a Korea; or how, in the case of Hong Kong, companies could have been 'allowed to go on a permanent rampage, 24 hours a day, 365 days a year' (Halliday 1974: 94).

Why plan rational political economies?

Lying behind my discussion thus far has been an important question: why should East Asian states have engaged in plan rational development strategies rather than leaving economic growth to the market as their Western advisors from the US Government and various international agencies advocated? The answer here seems to be associated with their very autonomy from powerful economic interests and popular forces. While the structural autonomy that East Asian states enjoyed was certainly 'embedded' in the sense of Evans' (1995) theoretical elaboration of the relation of national states to the institutional contexts of which they are a part, central to the ability of those states to build dynamic political economies was a state-business relation where in some cases, the state was the senior partner. The downside of this structural autonomy, however, was that these states – particularly Korea, Taiwan, Hong Kong and Singapore – were confronted with particular legitimation problems which derived precisely from their relative lack of integration with their respective civil societies.

There was, in addition, a crucial exogenous factor that compounded the endogenously derived legitimation problems that the respective regimes confronted. The East Asian states in question were in many ways products of the Cold War.

They were formed (in the Hong Kong case re-formed after the Japanese occupation of 1941–45) in a geo-political context where they were the front line in the US-dominated struggle to contain the spread of 'communism' and as such, for ideological reasons, had to be built as showcases for capitalism in the developing world. Furthermore, they were societies that had either been devastated by war (as in the cases of Japan and South Korea), or had been subject to the upheavals and social transformation associated with massive and rapid immigration (Taiwan, but particularly Hong Kong), or, as with Singapore, had been cast adrift (in 1965) as a largely Chinese enclave in a hostile Malaysian/Indonesian sea. Under such circumstances the consent, if not the positive support of their respective civil societies was essential, and it was secured by processes that Castells (1992) has termed, 'the political economy of survival'.

The survival of the respective regimes, while secured in part by the control, fragmentation and sometimes repression of popular forces, ultimately depended on the ways in which they were able to legitimate their rule. The key to legitimation in all cases seems to have been the delivery of rapid economic growth and with it, rising living standards. This is not to say that the delivery of national economic health is not important to the legitimation of all regimes, democratic or authoritarian, but it is to say that the East Asian states were confronted with legitimation problems that were highly problematic precisely because they arose from the articulation of processes derived from world-system factors – particularly inter-state rivalry – with those that emerged from the contradictory moments of their formation as states. As such, economic development could not be left entirely to the hit and miss of market forces. East state, drawing on their different histories and traditions, inevitably went about the task of building legitimation through economic growth in different ways. With Japan as the standard bearer, South Korea and Taiwan went about the task by neutralizing labour and 'guiding' the strategies of the corporate sector in the interests of national economic goals. In both these cases the regimes accomplished their tasks partly by an application of what are often regarded as 'socialist' planning mechanisms: five-year plans in which specific sectors were targeted for development depending on the plan in question (agriculture, heavy industry, information technology industries, etc.).[14] Hong Kong and Singapore, on the other hand, acted not on companies directly, but indirectly through labour (and in the case of Hong Kong, land) markets, and in so doing invested substantially in welfare, and particularly public housing systems. In the case of Hong Kong where the personal security of an immigrant population could not be delivered through citizenship of a sovereign state, entrance into the public housing system became its functional equivalent and hence a central mechanism through which the colonial regime established its legitimacy (Castells *et al.* 1990: Part I).

The emergence of plan rational development strategies in East Asia was not, then, a product of pragmatic experimentation, nor was it a product of any particular ideological conjuncture in which the various states were created, given that those states sought essentially autocratic routes to the retention of that political power.

Conclusion

While it is clear that the economic transformation of Japan, Korea, Taiwan, Hong Kong and Singapore can only be fully grasped by focusing on the articulation of historically and regionally specific world-system factors with internal processes unique to the particular countries themselves, it is also clear that in any attempt to weight the significance of the various determinants, the efficient working of supposedly free markets cannot be privileged over the others. Indeed I have argued that if any such privilege is to be accorded, it has to be to strategic economic planning and the policy formation and implementation associated with it. If this is the case then at least two further questions are raised. First, given that each state went about building plan rational political economies in different ways, using different historically and culturally-derived resources, what are the particular specificities of each case such that they still had sufficient in common to deliver broadly similar economic outcomes? Second, to what extent did the particular versions of plan rationality that served these economies well, at least through to the late 1990s, have significance in the future? While the second question is addressed in Chapter 4, a brief comment on the first can be made here.

With regard to this question, I can address only one of many issues here. While I have argued for the commonalities associated with East Asian plan rationalism, I have also indicated that the region's route to the modern world has involved national variations in the state-economy relation. One of these variations has been in the form that business organization has taken. In the cases of Japan and South Korea, their economies have been organized on the basis of concentrated ownership and control by diversified conglomerates. While similar organizations have a presence in the Taiwanese economy, its dynamism has been more associated with small- and medium-scale firms embedded in extensive subcontracting works. The role of such firms and networks also were pronounced in the case of Hong Kong. While in all these four cases domestic capital has predominated, in the case of Singapore, economic success has been forged from the relation of the state with large-scale transnational capital (Rodan 1989). While the form of business organization itself, then, may have had important implications for the specificity of state-economy relations in each case, it seems likely, as I argued in Chapter 2, that the nature of the institutional matrix – the historically constructed cultural, organizational, financial and political crucible – from which paths to industrial capitalism in each case emerged, has been the key to the matter. While the institutional matrices associated with the various forms of capitalism tend to 'privilege' one or more institutions more than others in the determination of the particular form of capitalism, it seems clear that in the East Asian cases, the state, in its various mediations, has played the principal determinant role.

While various versions of plan rationality have been at the basis of East Asian economic success, it is not clear that these same versions, or indeed plan rationality in general, will continue to hold sway in the future. Indeed, for a period in the late 1990s, the foundations of plan rationality were shaken by first financial, and then generalized economic crisis. It is to that issue and its analysis that I now turn.

4

ECONOMIC CRISES AND GOVERNANCE FAILURES

In 1997 a number of East Asian countries were enveloped in an economic crisis (in the 'western', not 'Chinese' sense of that term) that, with hindsight, can be seen as both a prelude to, and a major warning of, the more dangerous crisis that engulfed the world ten years later.[1] As with all such crises, the East Asian one led to bankruptcies, collapsed currency values, falls in gross domestic product (GDP) and dramatic declines in the living standards of swathes of working and middle class people in those economies that were most deeply affected. As such, it set back over 30 years of robust economic and social development in the region, here and there was accompanied by riot, destruction and death and – on a positive note – provided the backdrop for the overthrow of the Suharto dictatorship in Indonesia.[2]

Globally, the East Asian crisis contributed to a rapid decline in the confidence of portfolio investors in 'emerging' markets (that is, poor countries), triggered stock market and currency collapse in parts of Latin America, and most spectacularly in Russia. Additionally, the relative evaporation of East Asian markets for manufactured commodities that followed the crisis compounded the pre-existing global saturation of product markets and thus in some cases resulted in the withdrawal of foreign direct investment (FDI) and plant closure, including in some of the advanced industrial economies.[3] As important as these consequences, the crisis damaged the ideological significance of the various East Asian 'models' of economic development, representing, as they did, some of the principal – and most effective – capitalist alternatives to Anglo-American 'free-market' arrangements.

At the time of the crisis and since then, there have been two predominant – and usually mutually exclusive – accounts of the origins of East Asia's economic turmoil in the late 1990s. The first of these, from neoliberal economists, signalled that some of them had finally discovered that the state, after all, had played a significant role in the region's economic transformation. However, their interpretation of that role was almost entirely negative. The source of the region's problems, we were told, was that state 'interference' with markets had led to corruption, or in technical parlance, 'moral hazard', that had damaged the 'efficient' functioning of the relevant countries' financial systems (see Chang 2000 and Glyn 2006 for critical discussions of this account). In effect, this account identified the source of the region's problems within the internal institutional operations of the affected countries themselves, without reference to the external, global and regulatory context, within which their financial systems operated.

The second account emerged from more critical voices that saw the preceding (since the early 1980s) deregulation of international financial flows, associated as it was with the globalization of neoliberal ideology and the power of what Wade and Veneroso (1998a) termed the 'Wall Street-Treasury-IMF Complex' as the principal backdrop for economic collapse in the region. Among the better known analyses in this vein were those by Wade and Veneroso (1998a, 1998b) Wade (1998), Haggard (2000) and Stiglitz (2002). In this chapter, I build on this latter account, but predominantly seek to re-focus attention on the causes of the crisis that derived not from 'moral hazard', but from failures of economic governance that were indeed internal to the countries concerned.

An important premise lies behind the analysis presented here. This is that the macroeconomic processes associated with the neoliberal globalization of the time, such as the deregulation of capital markets and the pegging of East Asian currencies to the US dollar, though centrally important, were still only partially responsible for economic turmoil in the region. While not disputing the intellectual power and geopolitical significance of the arguments that focused on the global processes involved, the analysis developed here suggests that to a significant extent the sources of crisis were internal to the national political economies concerned, but crucially, there were important differences in each case. These differences were intimately connected with the institutional capacities of the respective national states to mediate between the international and their domestic economies, and with how and why these capacities changed over time. Consequently, this analysis offers not merely an explanation of why the crisis developed in Thailand, Malaysia, Indonesia, South Korea and other countries, and took the particular forms that it did, but also why it was not particularly significant in Taiwan or Singapore (with the exception of limited currency devaluations). To anticipate the chapter's conclusion, the crisis tells us a great deal not only about the unfettering of international finance capital and the liberalization of domestic capital markets, but also – and as importantly – about the asymmetrical presence of the developmental state (and thus plan rationalism) in the region, and the nature of its evolution and condition by the late 1990s. At the level of the national political economies involved, the crisis was clearly not a monadic phenomenon, generated by the same causes and for which there were formulaic solutions relevant in each case (prescribed, predictably, by neoliberal economic theory and imposed by the IMF on Korea and Indonesia for instance), but with uneven crises whose resolution depended on the political economy in question.

I begin with the observation that the symptoms of the crisis, as these began to emerge from mid-1997, were not the same in all the affected economies. In

Thailand, Malaysia and Indonesia panic took hold when banks, other financial institutions and property development companies began to collapse. Almost all of the companies affected had become financially overexposed as a consequence of their lending, or their mediation of portfolio investment, which in both cases were designed to support speculative investments in stock, but particularly in property markets (*Financial Times,* 12–16 January 1998, Bello 1998, Jomo 1998, Daly and Logan 1998). In Korea, however, the symptoms took a very different form. There the problem was not with companies overexposed as a result of speculative activities on property markets, etc., but rather with major industrial conglomerates (*chaebol*) who had massively overborrowed from foreign and domestic banks to support their competitive struggles against one another (Chang 1998). In my view these differences were not coincidental, but rather were a direct consequence of the structural evolution of the respective political economies in earlier periods. Much of what follows in this chapter constitutes an attempt to explore the nature of the structural differences in the various political economies that gave rise to the different symptoms of crisis.

In the next section I turn to the incidence of crisis in Thailand, Malaysia and Indonesia. Though the crisis there was deeper than in Hong Kong, I argue that there were correspondences between all four political economies. Specifically they had all evolved with structurally weak economies in large part because their respective states had allowed investment to flow into unproductive activities in general and property market speculation in particular. In the subsequent section, I turn to South Korea. Drawing predominantly on Chang's work (Chang 1998, Chang *et al.* 1998), I argue that part of the problem there was the evaporation of the state's ability to control the relation between international sources of capital and the vast concentrations of private economic power (at the time, unprecedented in the capitalist world) that were (and are) the *chaebol*. In the penultimate section I switch the analytic focus to Taiwan and Singapore. In their cases I try to show why they largely escaped the ravages of crisis, and what their escape tells us about the crises that enveloped other countries in the region. In the conclusion I summarize the core of my argument and briefly reflect on the implications of the East Asian crises of the late 1990s for national economic governance more generally.

Property markets and the construction of weak economies: Southeast Asia and Hong Kong

Some accounts of the crisis implied, at the time, that the real (that is, non-financial) economies of all the countries in question were relatively strong prior to the onset of investor panic (e.g. Wade 1998, Wade and Veneroso 1998a). The variations in the symptoms of crisis, however, pointed to an alternative story. That alternative, elaborated here, questions the structural robustness of some – though not all – of the real economies concerned. In the first instance it focuses on the role of property markets in some of the cases, and in the second it explores the viability of other bases for growth and prosperity in the region, associated with the nature and development of manufacturing industry and related services. It is to the elements of that alternative account that I now turn.

As the events briefly summarized earlier indicate, an important difference in the sources and manifestations of economic crisis in East Asia was the fact that property (and stock) market speculation was central to the story in Thailand, Malaysia, Indonesia and Hong Kong, but not (or not particularly) in Korea nor in the non-crisis economies, Taiwan and Singapore. Two questions arise from this observation: why should these differences have been apparent; and what is the relation between property market investment and economic development? I begin with the second issue.

Perils of portfolio investment

Any attempt to grasp the relation of property markets to economic development first needs to address the sources of property finance. Bank credit and portfolio investments traditionally have been among the most important sources, in both developed and developing worlds, with portfolio investment in recent decades being particularly significant. As we see later, however, FDI also seems to have been an important component of property investment in at least one of the Southeast Asian economies. Before moving to discuss portfolio investment in property markets we need to pose the broader question about the relation of portfolio investment to economic development.

By the late 1980s, in an attempt to encourage developing countries to take advantage of the huge quantities of mobile capital then available through pension and investment funds in the industrial economies, many mainstream economists, together with those associated with an influential report from the United Nations University's World Institute for Development Economics Research (WIDER 1990) argued that developing countries should liberalize their financial markets and encourage foreign portfolio investment. By that time, and often under pressure from IMF/World Bank 'structural adjustment' programmes and the US and other governments, many developing countries in any case had already begun to privatize state companies, creating expanded opportunities for portfolio investment flows. The liberalization of capital markets was also probably seen, in some cases, as a way of shifting state reliance on bank and other credit, onto the private sector, and thus as a way of circumventing the crippling foreign indebtedness that had bedevilled national development projects in previous decades. In encouraging portfolio investment flows, the question that does not appear to have been asked by the WIDER group, the Bretton Woods institutions, mainstream economists, and some (but by no means all) of the developing country governments themselves, was whether there was indeed a *positive* connection between portfolio investment and industrialization. Had this supposed connection been problematized (though the weight of orthodox economic opinion was against such a possibility), then the speculative character and short-term horizons invariably associated with portfolio investment and stock market activity might have been seen as inimical to the long-term capital commitments necessary for 'late' industrialization. As Singh and Weisse recognized, in an important critique of the relation between stock markets, portfolio investment and robust development:

> A long-term investment horizon and *patient finance* are central in late industrialization, which is above all a long process of institutional and technological adaptation and learning
>
> (Singh and Weisse 1998: 616 – my emphasis).

As patience is not a well-known virtue of portfolio investors – unless they are disciplined (of which more later) – a further question arises as to whether portfolio investment (and stock market speculation) is indeed a useful supplement to other sources of capital that can be mobilized in the interests of industrialization and development (or at worst, is just a harmless money-making activity). After an analysis of the development record in India, Mexico, and other developing economies, Singh and Weisse emphatically conclude that:

> unfettered financial liberalisation, and specifically. . . . . stock market development and portfolio capital inflows, are unlikely to help developing countries in achieving speedier industrialization and faster long-term economic growth.
>
> (Singh and Weisse 1998: 618)

Property market speculation

If Singh and Weisse are right, and portfolio investment in general has indeed been problematic for development, then the predilection of portfolio investment to flow into property markets – given their significance in the incidence of crisis in Southeast Asia – requires particular attention. Though data on portfolio investment by sector is hard to access for most East Asian economies, useful data does exist for Thailand. From all we know of region's economic development through to the

TABLE 4.1 Thailand: portfolio investment (net) by sector, 1995–97 (Baht, millions★)

	1995	(%)	1996	(%)	1997	(%)
Manufacturing	15,086	(32.0)	19,850	(32.9)	53,947	(47.8)
Finance	643	(1.4)	1,823	(3.0)	3,643	(3.2)
Trade	10,716	(22.7)	14,551	(24.1)	33,361	(29.6)
Property	19,376	(41.0)	20,334	(33.7)	9,081	(8.0)
Others★★	1,371	(2.9)	3,791	(6.3)	12,800	(11.4)
Totals	47,192	(100.0)	60,349	(100.0)	112,832	(100.0)

Source: Economic Research Department, Bank of Thailand
★ Rounded figures and proportions
★★ Mining and quarrying, agriculture, services, etc.

mid-1990s, Thailand, in this case, can be taken as a reasonable proxy for the other Southeast Asian economies that were engulfed by crisis.

In the years immediately preceding the onset of crisis, the Thai data suggest that property constituted the single most important venue for portfolio investment, attracting a little over 37 per cent of the total for 1995 and 1996. Only with the onset of crisis in 1997 was property overtaken by manufacturing as the principal focus for portfolio investment, when investor interest in the former collapsed (Table 4.1). What is additionally interesting about the Thai case, however, is that substantial quantities of FDI also flowed into property over the same period. Table 4.2 indicates that net flows of FDI into the property sector in Thailand exceeded portfolio flows into property, and indeed FDI flows into manufacturing, in both 1995 and 1996 with an average of around 40 per cent of the total for both years. As with portfolio investment, FDI flows into property collapsed in 1997, but continued to flow into manufacturing.

What then was driving the spectacular expansion of the property sector in Southeast Asia such that even supposedly 'patient' and thus non-speculative capital – FDI – was sucked in, in huge quantities? There are at least four elements to an adequate response. In the second and subsequent elements, we begin to answer the other question posed earlier: the sources of national differences in property market speculation. Before we get there, however, there is a general macroeconomic issue which demands attention.

Over 30 years ago, David Harvey (1978) elaborated a scheme to explain the periodic rush of investment funds into particular cities. He argued that structural tendencies to overaccumulation in the primary circuit of capital (largely manufacturing and related services) were periodically relieved by investment switches into either or both of the secondary and tertiary circuits of capital. The secondary circuit resulted in the development of the urban fabric necessary to sustain accumulation in the primary circuit (office blocks, housing, hotels, transport facilities, etc.) whereas the tertiary circuit reproduced the knowledge base necessary for new rounds of accumulation in the primary circuit (education, R&D, etc.). Banks, investment houses and other financial institutions were primarily responsible for mediating the

TABLE 4.2 Thailand: foreign direct investment (net) by sector, 1995–97 (Baht, millions*)

	1995	(%)	1996	(%)	1997	(%)
Manufacturing	14,114	(28.3)	17,942	(31.2)	44,652	(38.0)
Finance	643	(1.9)	1,823	(3.2)	24,559	(20.9)
Trade	11,112	(22.3)	13,798	(24.0)	28,440	(24.2)
Property	22,152	(44.4)	20,836	(36.2)	8,755	(7.4)
Others**	1,867	(3.7)	3,073	(5.3)	11,146	(9.5)
Totals	49,888	(100.6)	57,472	(99.9)	117,552	(100.0)

Source: Economic Research Department, Bank of Thailand

* Rounded figures and proportions

** Mining and quarrying, agriculture, services, etc.

switch of investment into the secondary circuit,[4] whereas the state was particularly important for mediating switches into the tertiary circuit. While we now know – most importantly from Robert Brenner's work (Brenner 2003) – that overproduction and declining aggregate profits in the 'primary circuit' were at the root of the 'long downturn' in the world economy since the early 1970s, part of Harvey's genius was to suggest that just as there were tendencies to overaccumulation in the primary circuit, so too were there in the secondary (and, in theory, the tertiary) circuit. When these tendencies resulted in crises, the classic symptoms of overcapacity in the 'built environment' occurred: empty office and luxury housing blocks, too many hotel rooms, increasingly desperate discounting of prices, rentals, etc. Eventually – should the 'switching crisis' be prolonged – the collapse of asset prices, followed by bankruptcies of property development companies, lending banks, etc., and rising unemployment, became inevitable. As we have seen already, all these symptoms were evident in the Southeast Asian economies (Thailand, Malaysia, and Indonesia) and in Hong Kong, prior to the onset of generalized crisis in the former cases and are evident, once again (2008 onwards), in the current global crisis.[5] But they were not anywhere near as evident in Taiwan and Singapore in the late 1990s, nor even in one of the key crisis economies at that time: Korea (see *Financial Times*, 12–16 January, 1998; Chang 1998, Jomo 1998). For an explanation as to why these differences should have been evident, we need to investigate meso and micro level phenomena and this brings us to our second and third elements.

Social agents, political elites and corruption

Whatever the undoubted merits of Harvey's theory of 'switching crises' (see also Harvey 1982), his scheme implies that investor preferences tend to privilege the primary circuit. While this is usually the case for FDI (though note the aforementioned important exceptions), it clearly does not hold for portfolio investment. In order to investigate the processes in train here, we need to move to a lower level of abstraction and focus on the social agents involved in the drama. At this point we reach the second element in our analysis. There are two matters here that require exploration. The first concerns the sources of investment flows into the property sector, and what the nature of these sources might tell us about some of the interests, externally and domestically, that were directing investment in Thailand and Malaysia, etc. Given that the sources of much of the investment were external to the political economies in question, and recognizing that there seems to have been no reduction in domestic savings, the question arises as to why there should have been a reliance on foreign savings as a primary source of investment. Explaining this and related matters leads to the second concern: the interests of the political elites in each case.

As with portfolio investment by sector, portfolio investment by country of origin is also difficult to access, though in this case data from Thailand can be supplemented by Malaysian data. Tables 4.3 and 4.4 indicate, respectively, the country sources of net portfolio investment in Thailand and portfolio receipts in Malaysia.

TABLE 4.3 Thailand: portfolio investment (net) by country source, 1995–97 (Baht, millions*)

	1995	(%)	1996	(%)	1997	(%)
Japan	12,455	(26.4)	16,065	(26.6)	45,438	(40.3)
Hong Kong	6,343	(13.4)	4,536	(7.5)	12,429	(11.0)
Taiwan	2,580	(5.5)	3,384	(5.6)	3,937	(3.5)
Singapore	3,444	(7.2)	5,339	(8.8)	9,401	(8.3)
China	−22	—	98	(0.2)	−224	(−0.2)
Korea (South)	310	(0.6)	481	(0.8)	920	(0.8)
Malaysia	338	(0.7)	474	(0.8)	385	(0.3)
Indonesia	296	(0.6)	249	(0.4)	200	(0.2)
Philippines	15	—	52	—	291	(0.2)
France	1,413	(3.0)	709	(1.2)	775	(0.7)
Germany	953	(2.0)	685	(1.1)	−517	(−0.4)
Netherlands	2,159	(4.6)	554	(0.9)	3,367	(3.0)
Switzerland	392	(0.8)	1,322	(2.2)	3,463	(3.1)
UK	967	(2.0)	1,661	(2.7)	5,537	(4.9)
Belgium	−2,466	(−5.2)	1,360	(2.2)	65	—
USA	6,332	(13.4)	12,324	(20.4)	22,431	(19.9)
Australia	676	(1.4)	858	(1.4)	3,736	(3.3)
Canada	15	—	28	—	55	—
Others	10,992	(23.3)	10,170	(16.8)	1,142	(1.0)
Totals	47,192	(99.7)	60,349	(99.6)	112,832	(99.9)

Source: Economic Research Department, Bank of Thailand

* Rounded figures and proportions

With regard to Thailand, Japan was the single most important source of net portfolio investment in the two years preceding the onset of crisis, and in the first crisis year (1997) itself, with an average of around 31 per cent of the total across the three years. The USA was the second most important source with an average of nearly 18 per cent of the three-year total. Interestingly, however, Hong Kong and Singapore provided the next most important sources, with an average of nearly 11 and about 8 per cent of the three-year total respectively. Taken together over the 1995–97 period, they displaced the USA as Thailand's second most important source of net portfolio investment (Table 4.3).

A better gauge of the significance of the various sources of portfolio investment than net data, is the details of receipts (inward flows). These data are available for Malaysia. As with Thailand, Malaysia, for current purposes, can be regarded as a reasonable proxy for the other crisis economies of Southeast Asia in the late 1990s.

From the data in Table 4.4 it is clear that between 1995 and 1997, by far the most important sources of portfolio investment flowing into the Malaysian economy were from Singapore and Hong Kong, with averages of nearly 49 and

TABLE 4.4 Malaysia: portfolio investment (receipts) by country source, 1995–7 (Ringgit, millions*)

	1995	(%)	1996	(%)	1997	(%)
Japan	1,233	(1.1)	717	(0.5)	1,212	(0.8)
Hong Kong	24,109	(22.6)	41,699	(28.8)	38,264	(25.7)
Taiwan	524	(0.5)	908	(0.6)	105	—
Singapore	52,154	(49.0)	70,198	(48.4)	72,298	(48.6)
China	—	—	17	—	170	(0.1)
Brunei	74	—	105	—	109	—
Germany	302	(0.3)	400	(0.3)	297	(0.2)
Netherlands	91	—	209	(0.1)	182	(0.1)
Switzerland	465	(0.4)	992	(0.7)	143	(0.1)
UK	12,304	(11.6)	17,656	(12.2)	19,805	(13.3)
Belgium	246	(0.2)	1,526	(1.0)	2,174	(1.5)
Luxembourg	557	(0.5)	948	(0.6)	719	(0.5)
USA	13,778	(12.9)	8,870	(6.1)	10,512	(7.1)
Australia	469	(0.5)	473	(0.3)	448	(0.3)
Canada	53	—	115	—	156	(0.1)
Others	524	(0.5)	908	(0.6)	1,190	(0.8)
Totals	106,414	(100.1)	144,933	(100.2)	148,784	(99.2)

Source: Cash BOP Reporting System, Bank Negara Malaysia
* Rounded figures and proportions

26 per cent respectively of the three year total. Taken together, then, Hong Kong and Singapore were responsible for a staggering three-quarters of all portfolio investment flowing into Malaysia during this period. Bearing in mind that financial institutions in Hong Kong and Singapore – given that they are respectively the second and third most important financial centres in Asia – in part must have served as intermediaries in transactions originating elsewhere and that some of the funds flowing from Hong Kong would have originated in China, what are we to make of these data?

In all three Southeast Asian economies and in Hong Kong, investment switches into the secondary circuit were certainly associated intimately with the activities of foreign (and particularly Japanese) banks, as other work on the crisis has shown (e.g. Bello 1998, Wade 1998). However, the prominence of Hong Kong and Singapore in the data assembled in Tables 4.3 and 4.4, suggests also that they have been associated with a subsidiary, though important agent: 'Overseas Chinese' companies mobilizing their business networks in the region.

Arising out of the 'neo-modernization' paradigm in development studies (especially Berger 1986) and initially obsessed by the supposedly cultural determinants of Chinese business acumen,[6] commentary on the business networks of the Overseas

Chinese has been something of a growth industry for the past 20 years (e.g. Wong 1988, Redding 1990 and more critically, Yoshihara 1988, Seagrave 1996, Hodder 1996, Gomez 1998, Yeung 1999, Gomez and Hsiao 2003). Around 29, 10 and 3 per cent of the populations of Malaysia, Thailand and Indonesia respectively are of Chinese origin. In proportional terms (unless we include Taiwan) the principal concentrations are in Hong Kong and Singapore with around 98 and 77 per cent respectively. While the vast majority of these populations are working class, or are engaged in small-scale manufacturing and commercial operations, they contain within them the branches of large trading, banking, hotel and real estate conglomerates that span the region and beyond. In many cases they have close business relationships with national and local political elites and in any case tend to dominate the domestic economies of the respective countries. Thus in terms of market capitalization, ethnic Chinese interests, by the mid-1990s, were estimated to control 61 per cent of share capital in Malaysia and 81, 73 and 81 per cent of listed companies in Thailand, Indonesia and Singapore respectively (East Asia Analytical Unit 1995: 40–41, 49, 69, 74). Furthermore, the data assembled by Yeung (1999, Table 1) suggests that the principal concentrations of Overseas Chinese companies in Asia, in terms of total assets (1994), were in Hong Kong (US\$173 billion), with Thailand, Singapore and Taiwan some way behind (US\$89–95 billion in each case). Given that Taiwan, since the demise of Hong Kong's manufacturing sector, now hosts far greater concentrations of Overseas Chinese capital in manufacturing than any of the others, Yeung's data, 'mapped' with the data in Tables 4.3 and 4.4, supports the widespread contention that Hong Kong and Singapore are the fulcra of the Overseas Chinese business empires.

Though it is widely assumed that some of the Overseas Chinese conglomerates have triad connections and are involved in the laundering of drug money (Seagrave 1996, Part 2), it is clear that of all their business activities (with the sole exception of Taiwanese companies) they have a predilection for real estate development and property market speculation. While it is argued that the reasons for these preferences derive from the historical experience of the Chinese as vulnerable – and sometimes persecuted – migrants in other societies (hence their reluctance to ensnare their resources in long-term business commitments such as manufacturing), case studies of major Hong Kong and Southeast Asian Chinese business families undertaken for the Australian Government (East Asia Analytical Unit 1995) confirm the significance of property development in their corporate portfolios. Additionally, Ko and Redding's (1998) analysis supports the conclusion that large Overseas Chinese companies in Hong Kong have a strong preference for property market activities. Their data indicate that of all the companies listed on the Hong Kong Stock Exchange during the period 1975 to 1995, an average of 35–40 per cent of them were engaged in property development and rentals. Additionally of the 112 firms with a second business interest, 60 per cent of them had these businesses in real estate. Furthermore, where manufacturing was the primary business interest, and subsequent diversification took place, that diversification was overwhelmingly into property market activities but interestingly, in the light of the argument developed later, not vice versa (Ko and Redding 1998). In the case of Thailand, Pasuk and Baker (1997: 163) note that as the real estate market took off after 1987, most of the funds were domestically generated, but Hong Kong was the most important foreign source. Some of the principal beneficiaries, however, were Sino-Thai families. These included the Karnchanapas family who were originally from Hong Kong and became the most aggressive players in the real estate boom of the period. By the early 1990s they were estimated to have become the wealthiest business family in Thailand (Pasuk and Baker 1997: 163).

What the Southeast Asian economies – and that of Hong Kong – seem to have been confronted with, then, was a strong propensity of mobile capital – partly worked through the regional networks of Overseas Chinese conglomerates – to flood into essentially unproductive economic activities. The consequence of this was that tendencies towards the construction of weak economies in the region were compounded. While I address the nature of these tendencies in the following section, the question that arises here is why were these conglomerates (together with Japanese and other financial institutions) not subject to investment 'discipline' by the respective national states, as they clearly were in Taiwan and Singapore (of which more later). In my view the answer is closely connected with the relative absence of an institutional capacity and competence capable of influencing the sectoral trajectory of inward and domestic investment flows. As such it is connected to matters of political interest and will.

As indicated earlier, in the then contemporary debates on the sources of the East Asian crisis, academic and media commentators alike paid considerable attention to political-economic corruption or 'crony capitalism' (or moral hazard). While some work to which I am otherwise sympathetic (e.g. Wade 1998) tended to dismiss such arguments in order to place the blame squarely on international finance capital and the neoliberal regime of global economic governance under which it operates, such rejections were premature. While political-economic corruption is certainly endemic in East Asia[7] – with the major exception of Singapore and still, possibly, Hong Kong – it has had asymmetrical consequences for development in the region and contributed to the uneven nature of the 1990s crisis.

At a minimum, a distinction needs to be made between, on the one hand, political elites and regimes that favour particular firms and business interests as a means simultaneously to *both* personal financial gain *and* industrialization and development and on the other those for whom financial gain is the *primary* interest and development a *secondary* or indeed unintended consequence. I term the former, 'developmental corruption' and the latter, 'acquisitive corruption'. While political-economic corruption in Korea and Taiwan (and Japan in an earlier period) clearly has had the characteristics of the 'developmental' form, that has not been the case in the Southeast Asian economies, though in varying degrees and with varying effects.

The recent economic development of Thailand, Malaysia and Indonesia has been attended, in general terms, with acquisitive corruption: namely with the blatant and largely unproductive rent-seeking of their political elites (Gomez and Jomo 1997,

Hewison 1997, Robison 1997). This has had two consequences for the respective political economies. First, these elites, both on their own and as a result of their association with Overseas Chinese business interests have encouraged the flow of domestic and foreign investment into speculative activities, such as stock markets and particularly real estate as the data in Tables 4.3 and 4.4 confirm. A corollary to this is that these elites have had little interest (material or otherwise) in developing the regulatory mechanisms necessary to divert investment into productive activities such as manufacturing and related services (for these tend not to deliver high returns in the short term). While significant manufacturing sectors have emerged in Malaysia, and to a lesser extent Thailand, this has been largely a consequence of FDI from Japan and the USA and more recently from Taiwan (Lim and Pang 1991, Rasiah 1995, Phillips and Henderson 2009). Domestically owned manufacturing continues to be under-represented.

There are two riders to this argument about the rent-seeking activities of domestic political elites. The first of these concerns Malaysia. The drive to industrialization there, since 1971, has been led by state-sponsored FDI. While the use of foreign investment may have been partly a consequence of the Malay-dominated Government's desire to avoid the further enhancement of Malaysian Chinese economic power (Jesudason 1989), industrialization – at least until the 1970s – was a product of a relatively coherent industrial strategy (the 'New Economic Policy'). Uniquely in the annals of Asian industrialization, it was also a strategy that involved a conscious attempt to redistribute wealth as a necessary component of economic development. While redistribution involved such things as employment quotas for *Bumiputeras* (Malays and other 'indigenous' peoples), part of it involved the creation of state and UMNO (the principal governing party) holding companies, the most significant of which – HICOM (Heavy Industries Corporation of Malaysia) – has been responsible for major joint-venture operations in steel, automobiles (Proton) etc. While these operations have been relatively unsuccessful, they continue to be heavily dependent on foreign inputs, and to some extent are institutional contexts for acquisitive corruption, they have been representative of a serious attempt by the state to channel investment into productive activities and thus to build a robust industrial economy. Although this strategy has now begun to falter (see Chapter 6), it has helped provide Malaysia with a fully-fledged industrial economy. More than that, Malaysia has become the first 'Muslim-majority' country to have industrialized.

The second rider concerns Hong Kong. While the colonial and current SAR (Special Administrative Region) governments' failings as political-economic regimes cannot be traced to acquisitive corruption, and while they have clearly subsidized the reproduction of labour power, wage costs, and thus accumulation (see Chapter 3), they have not been involved in any of the attempts – typical of their Northeast Asian neighbours – to direct investment into productive activities. There have been three consequences of this. First, the domestically-owned small to medium sized firms that were the backbone of Hong Kong's manufacturing industries had few government incentives or pressures to influence their activities and consequently they historically underinvested in technology and innovation. As a result they remained locked into low value-adding processes and products. Second, and facilitated by the latter problem, they have been allowed to disinvest in Hong Kong in order seek-out the almost unlimited possibilities for cheap, labour intensive production in China. They have thus been able to escape the economic pressure for upgrading that would otherwise have come from the colony's/SAR's tight labour market (Henderson 1994). Third, the relatively unfettered flow of domestic and foreign funds into property markets, that have been at the core of the territory's business cycle since the early 1970s – and thus its economic reversal in the late 1990s and early 2000s – have been a consequence not so much of economic ideology, but rather of the fact that Hong Kong Government has had an historic material interest in property market speculation, by virtue of its monopolization of land ownership and the significance of this to its revenue generation (see Chapter 3)

Economic bureaucracies

The final element in this particular jigsaw was the relative capacities of state economic bureaucracies in the region to regulate and direct investment flows, and more generally to orchestrate economic development. As will be clear from the thrust of the comments earlier, in the case of Thailand and Indonesia that capacity has never developed in an effective way, though the Malaysian record makes stronger claims to the model pioneered by its Northeast Asian neighbours. Furthermore, in an ambitious cross-national attempt to demonstrate the relationship between effective 'Weberian' state bureaucracies and economic growth, Evans and Rauch (1999) have shown that on a range of indices (meritocratic recruitment, promotion criteria, career stability, salaries, etc.) the more autonomous, technically proficient, coherent and authoritative economic bureaucracies of Korea, Taiwan and Singapore correlated positively with their record of economic development (as the related work by Henderson *et al.*, 2007, suggested it did with regard to poverty reduction). On the other hand, the less impressive performance of Malaysia and particularly Thailand, also correlated positively with their less effective economic bureaucracies as gauged against Evans and Rauch's 'Weberian' ideal. Although the Evans/Rauch work does not include Indonesia, it seems clear that there, as in Thailand, limited state capacities produced comparable failures, including the failure to deflect the counter-productive investment flows indicated earlier.

In Thailand, with a manufacturing contribution to GDP of about 31 per cent by 1993 (Jomo *et al.* 1997, Table 4.1: 56), some of the institutional trappings usually associated with a state developmental capacity did emerge as an adjunct to import substitution industrialization (ISI) from the 1960s onwards. The National Economic and Social Development Board (NESDB), for instance, was created to prepare five-year indicative economic plans and the Board of Investment (BOI) constituted an attempt by the state to oversee the course of economic development. However, policy formation was dominated by the Bank of Thailand and the Ministry of Finance and their obsessions with the financial sector ensured that industrial policy was very much the 'poor relation'. Furthermore, the ISI strategies that did emerge were cut-though with clientism and unlike companies in Korea and Taiwan, Thai companies benefiting from these strategies were not assessed on the basis of performance criteria. Additionally, the late development of Export Oriented Industrialization (EOI) strategies in Thailand – only from the mid-1980s (compared to the mid-1960s in Korea and Taiwan, and the early 1970s in Malaysia) – was intimately associated with the implementation of World Bank/IMF structural adjustment policies and hence with the neoliberal impulses underpinning them. Thus by 1990 the Thai Government was beginning to liberalize and eliminate controls on foreign exchange transactions and capital movements; two of the elements that had been important to the Northeast Asian developmental model.

In any case by the time of the Prem regime in the 1980s there had been an extraordinary proliferation of bodies involved, in some way, with economic policy formation. Thus in addition to the Finance Ministry, the Bank of Thailand, the NESDB and BOI, at least four others emerged.[8] To complicate matters further, the Chatichai and Anand regimes of the late 1980s and early 1990s effectively sidelined the formal agencies (except the Ministry and the Bank) with the appointment of personal economic advisors. The consequence was that the economic bureaucracy was fragmented, uncoordinated and had limited technical capabilities (Jomo *et al.* 1997: 75, Hewison 1997). Unsurprisingly, then, it was prone to vacillation in decision-making, subject to corruption and stymied by the need to constantly negotiate between competing political and business interests.

On top of all this, as the most authoritative study of Thailand's economic development up to that time notes (Muscat 1994: 261), successive Thai governments simply did not have the credibility or the authority to engage in the market leading activities typical of its Northeast Asian neighbours. Indeed, it appears that the bureaucrats themselves were sceptical of their abilities to perform such a role. The Thai state, in other words, seems neither to have been equipped with the institutional capabilities, nor the desire, to discipline business in the interests of deepening its development project. Consequently, while it did take a leading role in the development, from the 1980s onwards, of petro-chemical, steel and other industries associated with the 'Eastern Seaboard' programme in the Gulf of Thailand, in essence it was far more laissez faire – by default as much as by design – than its Northeast Asian counterparts. As a consequence it did not lever companies in the interests of technological upgrading, it did not in any significant way direct credit, it dismantled capital market controls, and fatally – as we saw in the previous section – it failed to deflect investment away from unproductive activities.

Among all the high performing East Asian economies, Indonesia has remained industrially the least advanced. While prior to the onset of the late 1990s crisis, there was certainly impressive growth in GDP, GDP per capita (with the former averaging nearly 7 per cent per annum in the 1989–93 period; Jomo *et al.* 1997, Table 6.2: 127), skill upgrading and the alleviation of poverty, etc., it remained the case that economic and social development has been something of a veneer. Indeed, of all of the Southeast Asian societies – together with The Philippines during the Marcos regime and Burma [Myanmar] throughout the period and through to the present day – Indonesia came the closest to approximating what Peter Evans (1995) calls a 'predatory state'.

The euphemistic 'guided economy' developed by the Sukarno regime subsequent to decolonization, riven as it was with rent-seeking by state officials (particularly in terms of their use of state-owned companies), generalized and ingrained political-economic corruption and macroeconomic chaos, in many ways set the foundations for the economic development that was to follow. The brutal birth of the Suharto regime in the mid-1960s (over half a million slaughtered by the military) and the creation of the military-state's own political party, Golkar, heralded a 'New Order' whose fundamental feature was that:

> the source of political power and political leadership (lay) within the state apparatus itself, and that political power and bureaucratic authority (were) appropriated and integrated by the officials of the state.
>
> (Robison 1993: 45)

Even though the course of economic development in Korea (1961–87) and Taiwan (1947–88) had been overseen by military regimes (with Taiwan, in fact, under martial law for most of that period), and the military in Thailand were an ever-present force in politics, in their cases the bureaucracy operated within a rational legal framework, and in the former two, with substantial autonomy from the political process. This was not the case, however, in Indonesia. There the economic bureaucracy became Suharto's personal preserve, with a proliferation of agencies such as the National Economic Planning Board, the Investment Co-ordinating Board, the State Logistics Board and the Technology Research and Development Board under his direct control (Robison 1993: 48, Robison 1997). While, in this context, economic bureaucrats played with initiatives typical among their Northeast Asian counterparts – state funded industrial projects, protection of upstream industries such as steel and petro-chemicals, etc., – they did so in the interests of appropriating state resources on behalf of particular members of the political and business elite (in the latter case, mainly Sino-Indonesian and *Pribumi* – 'native' – conglomerates and companies owned by members of the Suharto family). Thus in Indonesia, the politico-bureaucrats certainly had an interest in capital accumulation, but only as long as significant proportions of it accumulated into their own and their cronies' bank accounts.

The upshot of this was that industrial policy, such as it was, was invariably *ad hoc* and – by design or incompetence – was largely geared to short-term material gain, even where manufacturing projects such as automobiles or 'high-tech' initiatives (e.g. civil aircraft) were involved (Jomo *et al.* 1997: 131–32). As Hill (1996) notes, none of the policy instruments typical of the Northeast Asian economies (directed credit and selective protection conditional on meeting performance standards) were employed in Indonesia. Thus there, as in Thailand, no effective state capacity emerged that was capable of levering business in the interest of industrial deepening, technological upgrading, or indeed of guiding investment into productive activities and away from the easy (and lucrative) business of speculation.

By 1995, manufacturing industry in Malaysia was accounting for over 33 per cent of GDP and over 25 per cent of employment (Jomo *et al.* 1997, Table 5.1: 90). By that time the country had developed the 'deepest' industrial structure of any of the Southeast Asian societies except Singapore, but in the light of the discussions earlier and later and the experience of the Northeast Asian economies, that is not saying a great deal.

As with the other East Asian economies discussed here (except Hong Kong and Singapore), the Malaysian government, after 1970, built an export-oriented industrialization strategy alongside a pre-existing ISI strategy. In its case, however, the catalyst for EOI was inter-ethnic riots in 1969 and a subsequent desire to accelerate industrialization and redistribute wealth – as a pre-condition for ethnic harmony – at one and the same time. In furtherance of the aims of the resultant New Economic Policy (NEP), the Malay-dominated state turned not to the indigenous small and medium-sized manufacturing companies, for they were owned by ethnic Chinese, but to foreign capital (Jesudason 1989). Thus for example in the 1980s, when the Mahathir regime decided that a 'national car' (what became Proton) was required, it did not intervene to rationalize, technologize and upgrade the 21 auto assemblers (of imported kits) already in the country – for they were all Chinese-owned – but rather invited Mitsubishi into a joint-venture with the state-owned Heavy Industries Corporation of Malaysia (HICOM).

Along with the NEP came the institutional trappings of what, for a while, began to look like a 'developmental state'. In addition to the relevant Ministries (Trade and Industry – later, International Trade and Industry, consciously aping, but a pale reflection of, its Japanese counterpart – Finance, and Science, Technology and the Environment), there emerged the Malaysian Industrial Development Authority (MIDA), the Economic Planning Unit (EPU), various provincial development corporations, and state holding companies such as HICOM, PETRONAS (petrochemicals) and Sime-Darby (trading, rubber, etc.). The problem with all this, as Lubeck (1992) and Jomo *et al.* (1997, Chapter 5) have cogently argued, was twofold. First, unlike the Northeast Asian societies and Singapore, but rather like the other Southeast Asian cases, the economic bureaucracy in Malaysia was highly fragmented and at its core – the EPU – dominated, as part of the Prime Minister's office, by the whims of Mahathir and his cronies. The technocratic elite remained weak and any efforts to rationalize industrial policy were consistently undermined by the political elite's own interests, including their personal financial interests (Gomez and Jomo 1997). The consequence was a relative absence of linkages between the industries spawned by the ISI and EOI strategies and thus an inability of the economy to benefit from the synergies and spin-offs that could have been expected. Little serious technological upgrading has occurred in domestically-owned companies (a minuscule amount equivalent to about 0.4 per cent of GDP was spent on R&D in 1992) and evidence of adequate skill development – necessary for technological upgrading – is slim (Lall 1995, Jomo *et al.* 1997: 112–18; see also Chapter 6).

In the case of Malaysia, then, a 'semi-developmental', or what Evans (1995) calls an 'intermediate' state, did emerge subsequent to 1970. There, however, the economic bureaucracy ultimately was too weak and politically constrained to develop and implement the sort of policy regime that would have been necessary to deepen the industrialization project. In any case the overriding goal of industrial policy was not industrial deepening, but rather redistribution, and with it the expansion of opportunities for political rentierism. Thus whatever the promise of Malaysian attempts to emulate the East Asian development 'model' – and that promise was far greater than in Thailand and Indonesia – it seems clear that the state-institutional elements of the Malaysian version of the model have been largely 'still-born' (see Chapter 6).

The issue of the economic bureaucracy and industrial policy in Hong Kong provides an interesting contrast to both the Southeast and Northeast Asian cases. Ideologically-driven neoliberal commentary (infamously Friedman and Friedman 1982) notwithstanding, it is now clear that Hong Kong, under the British colonial regime, did evolve a variant of a semi-developmental or 'intermediate' state (Castells *et al.* 1990, Part I, Schiffer 1991, Henderson 1991; see also Chapter 3). In this case, however – as I have indicated earlier – its *dirigiste* elements were largely confined to land ownership, the provision of factory space, and the subsidization of the reproduction of labour power (particularly by creating, as a proportion of the population housed, the second largest public housing system in the capitalist world after Singapore). It did not seek to regulate capital flows, generate pro-active industrial policy, subject companies to performance standards, drive technological upgrading and the rest. In particular, in no sense did it seek to limit or deflect speculative investment. As a consequence, as well as for the other reasons indicated in earlier sections, speculation in real estate markets has now become the bedrock of the economy. Interestingly, however, the onset of financial crisis in 1997 propelled new initiatives by the Hong Kong SAR Government. In order to support stock market values and thus dampen pressure on the currency link to the US dollar, the Government's Monetary Authority acquired stakes in some of the SAR's major conglomerates. By 1998 it was reported to hold, for instance, around 10 per cent of the equity of the Hong Kong and Shanghai Banking Corporation, 11 per cent of the British-colonial conglomerate, Swire Pacific and 9 per cent of Li Ka-shing's flagship conglomerate, Cheung Kong (*Financial Times,* 1 September, 1998). While this was hardly nationalization 'through the back door' (and these stakes were subsequently relinquished), symbolically it represented a significant move away from the former colonial government's laissez faire commitments in this area of the economy.

In spite of the continuing significance of property markets to the 'health' or otherwise of the Hong Kong economy, the preponderance of investment in this sector has not been as damaging to the prospects of economic development and prosperity there as it was in the Southeast Asian cases. The reason for this is that for a considerable period – at least since the early 1980s – it had been inappropriate to consider Hong Kong as an economy distinct from that of China. Consequently although industrial deepening was always limited there and from the early 1990s the manufacturing industries were subject to massive disinvestment, the Hong Kong economy survived and prospered because of the service functions it performs for the Chinese economy (trading connections, managerial expertise, finance, professional skills, etc.). China, in other words, provides the manufacturing and heavy industry base which props–up the Hong Kong economy. Its economic viability, then, is now more dependent on China's continued transformation (and technological upgrading) as an industrial economy than it is on the whims of property speculators.[9]

If the encouragement, or failure, to deflect investment from flowing into unproductive activities such as real estate and stock market speculation, was a central component of the crisis in the Southeast Asian economies and Hong Kong, what of the region's other principal site of economic turmoil in the late 1990s: Korea? It is to the origins of crisis there that I now turn.

Deregulation, big business and the demise of Korea's developmental state

Subsequent to the post-war rise of Japan, Korea evolved perhaps the classic developmental state. Central to its developmental capacities were authoritarian regimes, with relatively autonomous economic bureaucracies, capable of mediating – especially financially – the relation between the domestic and international economies (Woo 1991). The state encouraged the expansion of huge conglomerates (*chaebol*), which were family-owned, managed in a semi-militaristic style and which aggressively competed with one another in a range of industries, and for ever greater market share. Additionally the state suppressed organized labour (until 1987), sought-out, adapted and disseminated foreign technologies, fed subsidized credit through state-owned banks in support of particular industrial initiatives, subjected those in receipt of credit to performance standards, engaged in capital controls, selectively protected the domestic market, etc. (amongst a considerable literature, see for example, Amsden 1989, Chang 1994, Kim, E. M. 1997 and Chapter 3). While this form of state-led development may have prospered in part because it was tolerated – indeed supported – by the US Government which was concerned to see South Korea built as a 'bulwark against bolshevism' (particularly 'bolshevism's' Chinese and North Korean forms), though seemingly only '. . . as long as it remained in the interstices of global capitalism' (Woo 1991: 202) – of which more later – it seems clear that South Korea evolved a form of capitalism that in the time-frame under consideration in this chapter (mid-1960s to 1997) was able to deliver one of the most spectacular development records the world has yet seen.

Unlike the cases of the Southeast Asian economies and Hong Kong, however, it appears that property market speculation did not figure prominently in the onset of crisis in Korea. I say 'appears' because the data that would give us some insight into the significance of property markets in the overall picture is unavailable, and none of the authorities on the Korean economy who have commented on the 1990s crisis raised this as a significant factor. However, it is clear that in terms of the inflow of foreign portfolio investment (FPI) Korea was not unlike the other crisis economies. For instance, while FDI flows into the economy increased from US$7.2 billion in 1990 to $19.5 billion in 1996, FPI in the same years increased from $9 billion to nearly $121 billion (Jin 1998 Table 4). Given the rapidity of urban development in Korea and the region more generally, during this period, it seems likely that a significant proportion of these funds did flow into property market speculation, as well as infrastructural development. Additionally, by the late 1980s, there were strong rumours in the country that the top 30 *chaebol* owned 65 per cent of urban land and had invested $16.5 billion in land speculation and luxury hotels (*Business Korea*, February 1991: 43).[10] Given such concentrated private ownership of land, Korea would have been peculiar economy indeed if profits, bank loans, portfolio investment, or some combination of the three, had not been used for speculative purposes, particularly in the light of the relaxation of state 'discipline' that emerged from the early 1990s (see later). Irrespective of the incidence of property market speculation, however, what is clearer is that speculation in housing markets was not as significant a component in the onset of crisis there as it was elsewhere. At least until the early 1990s the state sought to depress speculation and constrain housing prices (and thus, indirectly, subsidize wages) by placing price ceilings on smaller housing units and controlling the construction of larger units by restrictions on housing finance and planning permission and by the use of executive power (Kim, W. J. 1997: 147).

While the true story of the role of property markets and portfolio investment in Korea's economic demise during the late 1990s will have to await further research, it seems clear that the internal dynamics of the country's slide into turmoil were very different from its Southeast Asian counterparts. While in the latter the slide was intimately connected with their inability (or lack of interest) in developing effective developmental states, in the former it was closely related to the decline in the state's initially substantial capacities to mediate between the domestic economy – principally by way of controlling the activities of the *chaebol* – and the international economy.

Some of the work on East Asian transformation has suggested that authoritarian, non-democratic states have been a necessary precondition for successful 'late industrialization' in the region. The argument has been that such state forms were able to avoid the destabilization or deflection of economic policy that can sometimes result from the internalization into the political process of the contestation and conflict of interests typical of Western-style democracies. As a consequence they were able to override competing interests, disciplining both business and labour as necessary in the interests of national economic goals. Even where formal democracies emerged in East Asia – such as in Japan, Singapore and Malaysia – they were unlike their Western counterparts and in Johnson's (1982) phrase remained at least 'soft authoritarian'.

While estimates of the concentration of economic power in Korea (with the top 30 *chaebol* supposedly responsible for 80 per cent of GDP by the mid-1980s) were probably overdrawn, it seems likely that by the 1980s some *chaebol* were beginning to see their strategic interests as being better served by a selective relaxation of state regulation of their market activities. With the onset of formal democratization in the late 1980s, and particularly after the election of Kim Young Sam as President in 1992, such relaxation became a fact of economic policy.

With the end of the Cold War – which had helped induce US toleration of Korea's state-directed capitalism – and the arrival of Korea as a significant industrial power, the Korean Government began to come under increasing US and IMF pressure to deregulate its economy, and particularly the financial system. With the gradual spread of the neoliberal orthodoxy within Korean economic opinion and the growing influence of US-trained economists in the Ministry of Finance,[11] impulses towards deregulation, however, were not only external. Partly out of a desire to prepare for OECD membership – and thus a need to be seen to be a 'good citizen' of the world economy – the Kim Government began to perceive the supposed 'wisdom' of freer market arrangements.

A major casualty of the process was the Economic Planning Board (EPB), which had been Korea's equivalent, in terms of policy formation, of Japan's Ministry of International Trade and Industry. In 1994 the EPB was absorbed into the Ministry of Finance, effectively emasculating its ability to engage in long-term strategic planning. Additionally, while Korean governments had been masterly exponents of what I have called earlier, 'developmental corruption', the preferential treatment (support for strategic initiatives, subsidized credit, etc.) which this entailed had previously been directed to the *chaebol* in general. With the Kim Young Sam regime, however, preferential treatment began to be directed to particular *chaebol* as evidenced by the support given to Samsung to develop an automobile division (despite objections from the Ministry of Trade and Industry) and Hanbo, a steel industry (Jin 1998, Chang *et al.* 1998).

While the termination of industrial strategy, signalled by the treatment of the EPB, may well have contributed to what some (e.g. Pirie 2007) regard as the longer term neoliberalization of the Korean economy, the most important consequence of deregulation in the short to medium term was that state control over the *chaebol's* access to finance was abandoned. Like an alcoholic in a wine cellar, the *chaebol* rushed to drink of the funds the foreign (mainly Japanese) and domestic banks (principally new – since 1994 – and unsupervised merchant banks[12]) were more than willing to supply. While some of these funds were probably used for speculative activities, the bulk of them were almost certainly used to feed the determination of the heads of the *chaebol* (still at that point largely family-owned and controlled) to out-compete one another. Unlike the loans from state banks that had been a principal source of capital in earlier periods, these new loans were subject to short-term payback clauses. The consequence was debt-equity ratios that were unsustainably high, even by East Asian standards.[13] By the end of 1996 and in the case of some of the less prominent *chaebol,* these had reached 21:1 for Halla, 32:1 for Sammi, and a staggering 86:1 for Jinro (Jin 1998, Table 6). Once Hanbo (14th largest *chaebol)* had been declared bankrupt in January 1997, Sammi Steel (part of the 26th largest *chaebol*) in March and Jinro (19th largest) in April (Jin 1998) the Korean cat was well and truly out of the, by now, foreign dominated financial bag. Creditors panicked, a scramble to recover debts ensued, the value of the won collapsed, thus making debt repayments even more unlikely (due to the increasing costs of servicing loans denominated in foreign currencies). The IMF arrived and the Korean 'miracle' seemed, after all, to have been a mirage.

While the exogenous developments associated with the globalization of 'mad money' (Strange 1998, Glyn 2006, Henderson 2010) were as significant in the onset of the crisis in Korea as they were elsewhere in the region, the endogenous processes were different in Korea. Whereas the Southeast Asian economies slid into crisis in part because they had undeveloped or 'stillborn' developmental states, in Korea the problem was that its formerly highly effective developmental state, confronted as it was by pressure from the US and other neoliberal interests and from the concentrated economic power of the *chaebol*, was systematically dismantled during the 1990s. In none of the Asian crisis countries can the problems be traced to the over-regulation of their domestic economies. In all of the cases, but most spectacularly in Korea, a principal determinant – at the global economic moment it mattered most – was, on the contrary, *under*-regulation.

Sustaining effective *dirigisme*: Taiwan and Singapore

With the economic demise of Korea, Thailand, Malaysia and Indonesia, and recession in Hong Kong, the question remains as to why Taiwan and Singapore survived the turmoil of the late 1990s relatively unscathed (with the exception of currency devaluations – about 20 per cent in Taiwan – and falls in stock market values). While in both cases, substantial foreign reserves (relative to GDP, among the highest in the world) and a willingness to use them to manipulate exchange rates, were contributing factors, it is likely that the sustained capacities of the respective states to control their domestic economies and to mediate between these and the international economy, carry much of the explanatory weight. In both cases effective developmental states were constructed (in Taiwan from the early 1950s, Singapore from the mid-1960s) as central components of what Castells (1992) calls, the 'political economy of survival'. While their strategies of state-orchestrated economic development were inevitably different – given their different histories as colonies, as social formations, their different gearings to the world economy and geo-politics, etc. – they managed to navigate and deflect the external and internal pressures that compromised state economic governance in Korea. While this is not the place to investigate the detail of the continuing institutional vitality of the Taiwanese and Singaporean states, in line with the tenor of the argument developed earlier, a number of significant issues can be highlighted.

In the first place, the question arises that if property market speculation was a central component of the crisis in the Southeast Asian economies and Hong Kong, why was it not such a debilitating feature, at least through to the 1990s, of economic development in Taiwan and Singapore, in spite of the fact that both of them were (and are) thoroughly imbricated in Overseas Chinese business networks? For Taiwan part of the answer seems to lie in the fact that the Government was committed to channelling savings (as a proportion of GDP, an enormous 40 per cent by the late 1980s) and investment into productive activities. In order to achieve this, tight control of finance capital was essential.

After its expulsion from China in 1949, the Kuomintang (KMT) Government, by then established in Taiwan, developed a healthy suspicion of the activities and interests of financial institutions. Rightly or wrongly, Chiang and the KMT placed part of the blame for their defeat by Mao's Communists on the corruption and speculative activities of financial institutions which had undermined the economic base of their military effort and contributed to the loss of legitimacy of the Nationalist regime (Wade 1990, Seagrave 1985). Partly as a consequence of this experience and perception and partly because of the need to channel capital into productive activities, the dominant commercial and specialist banks (in the latter case for agriculture, industrial development, etc.) remained state-owned until the early 1990s and capital movements, through to and beyond the end of that decade, closely regulated.

As in Korea, but unlike the Southeast Asian countries, the Central Bank in Taiwan is legally committed to the promotion of economic development. As Lee (1990) argues, the Central Bank has usually interpreted this as its overriding commitment. Additionally, loans through the state banks always privileged 'tradeables' (principally manufactured commodities) over non-tradeables and until recently the Taiwan Government did not allow its citizens to hold foreign assets (Lin *et al.* 1996). In both cases these measures had the effect of supporting productive (and indeed export-oriented) activities and discouraged – in the context of a still under-developed stock market – the siphoning away of domestic funds for speculative investments overseas. While new privately owned commercial banks were allowed to develop from the late 1980s (17 were operating by 1993), unlike their equivalents in Korea (see earlier), they have been tightly regulated by the Central Bank (Yang and Shea 1996). Such regulations included reserve requirements (compulsory deposits held by the Central Bank) which by 1993 amounted to 24 per cent of deposits (Lin *et al.* 1996, Table 7.9: 221), a figure that is very high by international standards.

In spite of regulations such as these, significant speculation in real estate and stock markets did emerge in the 1980s. Although no data is available for real estate, the total trading value of stocks increased from NT$195 billion in 1985 to NT$25,408 billion in 1989. By 1993, however, it had declined to NT$9,057 billion (Yang and Shea 1996, Table 8.2: 232). The reason for the decline was that by 1990 the Central Bank had intervened to prick the bubble to prevent it from destabilizing the real (non-financial) economy. It did so, in part, by increasing the rediscount rate[14] and the reserve requirements. The effect was the dramatic contraction of the money supply and with it, the dampening of speculative activity (Yang and Shea 1996: 237).

The Taiwan Government, however, was not merely been concerned with controlling the financial sector domestically. On the contrary, while economic growth was encouraged to proceed by means of a full engagement with the world economy via trade, engagement via money-capital flows have continued to be controlled until very recently. While the Government did begin to dismantle controls on capital markets during the 1990s – in preparation for membership of the World Trade Organisation and partly as a consequence of US pressure – significant restrictions remained. For instance, through to at least the early 2000s there remained a US$5 million ceiling on the amount of money individuals could remit in and out of the country. Importantly, and as a lesson the Government seems to have learnt from the Southeast Asian crisis on the one hand, and the relative insulation of the Chinese economy from the regional turmoil of the time on the other, plans to further liberalize capital markets were subsequently shelved (*Financial Times,* 23 September 1998).

In terms of property and stock market speculation, Singapore has occupied an intermediary position between its Southeast Asian neighbours and Hong Kong on the one hand and the regulated markets of Korea (until the early 1990s) and Taiwan on the other. Although the country had experienced property and stock market bubbles – particularly in the early 1990s – with overexposure of domestic banks, the dangers inherent in this bout of speculation had been contained by 1996 as a result of tightened Government controls.[15] The Singapore Government, in spite of the image of the country as having an open economy, continued to exercise a strong influence over the arbitrage activities of domestic banks[16] and has been willing to manipulate exchange rates (using its substantial reserves) and generally and rapidly alter the rules of the investment game whenever it has deemed it necessary to 'cane the speculators' lest they destabilize the real economy (Woo and Hirayama 1996: 308, 324). Other parts of the Government's 'caning' project have involved some restrictions on capital flows (limits on foreign lending and borrowing by non-residents, for instance) and restrictive trading rules for the stock exchange. The latter have involved, for instance, the requirement that foreign stocks, other than Malaysian ones, be denominated in foreign currencies. As a consequence would-be local speculators have had to bear the exchange rate risk and this has depressed their activities. The implication of these regulations is that the Singapore Government has been more concerned to control the potentially disruptive effects of stock market speculation than it has to encourage stock market expansion for its own sake. One of the things that this has meant is that prior to the late 1990s crisis in other Southeast Asian economies, a much lower volume of trade was conducted on the Singapore than on the Kuala Lumpur stock exchange, in spite of the fact that the former is infinitely more important as an international financial centre (Jin 1996).

If stock market speculation was moderated in the ways indicated, so too was real estate speculation. While the latter has been much more significant in Singapore than in Taiwan (as any witness to Taipei's relatively drab urban-scape would attest), its destructive potential for the real economy and economic stability generally, has been contained. While strong urban planning controls, and their active application have helped moderate speculative activity in Singapore's built environment – in the way that they have not in Thailand, Malaysia, Indonesia or Hong Kong,[17] the state's decisive role in housing provision and finance has been a major contributing factor (Castells *et al.* 1990, Part II). State-enforced savings through the Central Provident Fund (by means of compulsory employer and employee contributions) have not only circumscribed funds that might otherwise have been available for speculative purposes, but have helped constitute the Fund as by far the dominant and preferential source of housing finance in the country. Contributions to the Fund can be used as a source of low interest loans to buy state-provided housing. As the state anyway, through the provision of public housing and housing for sale, is the provider of housing to over 80 per cent of the population (proportionately by far the highest level of state housing provision of any capitalist society), these initiatives have had the effect of substantially removing housing as an object of speculative investment.

In addition to the varying degrees of control over property and financial markets maintained by the Taiwanese and Singaporean Governments, they both continued through the period in question (though in different ways, and unlike Korea) to pursue long-term strategic economic planning. Where Thailand, Indonesia, Hong Kong and – to a lesser degree – Malaysia have in essence operated with the assumption that most, if not all, economic activities are equivalents when it comes to growth and development, Taiwan and Singapore have not. The Taiwanese Government pursued *dirigiste* industrial strategies which privileged manufacturing and related services over other sectors, and it attempted to move them into higher value-added, more technology intensive operations, with more success than probably anywhere else in the region with the exception of Japan. The Singapore Government similarly successfully levered foreign and domestic firms alike to invest in technological upgrading and higher value-added activities. This was done in the 1980s and 1990s partly through forcing-up labour costs (via increased Central Provident Fund levies on employers) and thus squeezing some of the labour intensive assembly industries out of the economy. Allied to this – indeed a precondition for its success–were significant and increasing investments in the skill base (particularly technical skills) of the economy. Paradoxically the fact that the Singapore economy is largely foreign-owned (around 70 per cent overall and 84 per cent of manufacturing industry by value in the early 1990s) has probably meant that there has been no need for the extraordinary levels of short-term portfolio investment – and its destabilizing potential – evident elsewhere in the region.

Whatever the ravages internationally and domestically deregulated finance capital wrought elsewhere in the region in the 1990s, in Taiwan and Singapore it was tamed. Amongst the instruments of its taming it is difficult to avoid the conclusion that the continuation of pro-active state policies and institutions, in both countries, remained decisive.

Conclusion

The discourse on the East Asian economic crisis conducted in this paper is intended to supplement, not supplant, those analyses that have emphasized the role of globalization – in the form of the deregulated activities of international finance capital – and the geo-political considerations of the US Government in its origins, progress and 'resolutions'. In my attempts at supplementation, however, I have insisted – against the tenor of some of the contributions to which I am otherwise highly sympathetic – that there were endogenous determinants of the crisis and that as these differed from one society to the next, they ensured different economic and political resolutions. While recognizing, as Cumings (1998) has argued, that all political formations in the region have been products of the historical rhythms of the world economic and geo-political system – infused as it is with US hegemony – on the one hand, and frequently-related internal social struggles on the other, the nature of state institutions, their actors and their actions, cannot simply be reduced to such world-historic processes. At any given historical moment the structures of the world system do set the political and economic parameters of the possible. But it is *only* the parameters that they set. Within those, states and their agencies and the political and bureaucratic actors they contain, continue to have real options. A theoretical implication of the East Asian turmoil of the late 1990s was certainly that different social formations have been bequeathed different political and economic parameters in which to operate. But another implication is that different states have used their ranges of political 'freedom' in their responses to similar economic contingencies, in dramatically different ways.

At a lower level of abstraction, I argued that in the cases of Thailand, Indonesia and Malaysia, the onset of crisis and its course were intimately associated with the absence, or limited nature, of the state's developmental capacities. As a consequence structurally weak economies – though with variations – emerged in each case and these were allowed to be distorted by speculative activities focused on stock, but particularly property markets. Amongst the principal actors in these developments large Overseas Chinese business corporations were prominent. The course of the crises in Southeast Asia suggested that unless they – and other domestic and foreign portfolio investors – were 'disciplined' by means of an effective developmentalist policy regime, their activities would be likely to disrupt the prospects for robust industrialization and development.

Though similar problems arose in Hong Kong (and for similar reasons), Hong Kong's long-standing absorption by the Chinese economy, together with the SAR Government's discovery, at the appropriate time, of the benefits of pro-active intervention (for instance in the stock market) meant that a severe recession, rather than full-blown crisis, was the order of the day. In the former economies the corruption of political elites (not relevant to Hong Kong) has taken an 'acquisitive' form and consequently has had negative consequences for possibilities of securing robust development (see Gomez and Jomo 1997, on Malaysia).

In the case of Korea, there emerged between 1961 and the early 1990s a classic developmental state. While corruption of political elites was evident there, it was not oriented towards rent seeking, but indeed towards the enhancement of productive investment. It was one of the best examples of 'developmental corruption'. Subsequent to 1992, however, the state's developmental capacities began to be dissipated. It abandoned long-term strategic planning and became increasing unable to mediate the relation (particularly the financial relation) between the domestic and international economies. The Wall Street-IMF-US Treasury view notwithstanding, the internal origins of the Korean crisis lay not in too much regulation, but ultimately, when confronted with deregulatory pressures and ideologies, in too little.

Taiwan and Singapore remained largely outside the web of crisis because they continued to have effective (though very different) developmental states. As a consequence they have been able to construct more robust economies than the others, partly by withdrawing property and stock markets as foci for speculative investment, partly by maintaining the institutional capacity and bureaucratic skill to – in the Singaporean phrase – 'cane the speculators', and partly by continuing to practice strategic economic planning. In the case of Taiwan, the retention of some controls over capital movements, into the 2000s, clearly helped to protect the economy from the worst effects of deregulated international finance capital, as did the restrictions on trading in foreign currencies imposed by the Malaysian government at the height of the crisis (Jomo 2001: Chapter1).

In the debates over the consequences of globalization for national economic governance, the analysis developed in this chapter points to the following general conclusions. Different states, for a variety of historical and social reasons, have developed different capacities to mediate between the national and the global and to lever both in terms of economic and social transformation. While these capacities change over time, and in general have probably diminished as a result of globalization, states who are determined to pursue *dirigiste* policies, and have the bureaucratic skill to do so, provide themselves with the economic and political space to make choices: to decide on the balance of economic activities within their borders, to decide to privilege some sectors as against others, to decide to transform corporate governance, to decide to redistribute, and so on. Though the East Asian crisis of the late 1990s was a crisis in the 'western' sense of that term, the current global financial crisis, for the moment, remains one whose immanent possibilities are best expressed through the Chinese version of the term. While we are very much in a period of significant danger, the opportunities to re-make (for instance) the architecture of international and national finance capital, are potentially substantial. In thinking through what that re-making might look like, an adequate understanding of both the exogenous and endogenous causes of the East Asian crises (shorn of their neoliberal overlays), and particularly of the significant variations in the latter, would go some way towards helping us get economic governance and regulatory policy 'right'.

5

GOVERNING GROWTH AND INEQUALITY

The previous chapter has underlined how significant variations in the institutions and practices of national economic governance were (and remain) for the possibilities of sustained economic transformation and robust development (or its absence) in East Asia. But the nature of economic governance there, as elsewhere, is arguably also closely tied to the prospects for building relatively egalitarian societies. This is an issue that, in general, is insufficiently understood, but it is one that we broach in this chapter.

A key element at the heart of contemporary (neoliberal) globalization has been the pressure to reform not only economic, but also welfare policy. This has been true not only in the developing world, parts of which continue to be subject to IMF and World Bank 'structural adjustment' programmes, but also in the developed world. In the latter, where the United States and Britain succumbed to these pressures in the 1980s, by the 2000s, even the social democratic heartlands of the European Union were under threat. In such exemplars of 'welfare capitalism'[1] as Germany, France and Sweden, for instance, neoliberal reformism has ravaged pension systems and other components of the social wage.

Where economic and welfare projects have been reconstructed along neoliberal lines, two outcomes (among many others), have been evident: significant increases in inequality (see, for instance, Pontusson 2005) and the weakening or abandonment of strategic economic planning (for the latter – in spite of the current global financial crisis – remains the institutional *bete noir* of neoliberal economic theory). An important question that arises here, is whether these consequences are related to one another not merely by virtue of their origins – neoliberal reformism – but whether they are themselves causally connected; namely, whether the weakening of state planning capacities, in the context of neoliberal globalization, in itself adversely impacts on the incidence of inequality and poverty. While there is a growing body of work that addresses the relation between globalization, welfare policy and inequality (see, for instance, Deacon 1997, Gough 2001), there is hardly anything that broaches what may be the more fundamental question: the relation of *economic* policy – and thus economic governance – to inequality.

In assessing the relationships between globalization and economic governance, the East Asian crisis of the late 1990s has taken on totemic significance. In the previous chapter I argued that while 'mad money' (Strange 1998) undoubtedly provided the global context for the onset of the crisis, in its national representations the crisis was facilitated either by the historic absence of strategic economic planning capacities – as in Thailand or Indonesia – or by the erosion of previously robust ones, as in South Korea. Given that in many cases the crisis was accompanied by steep rises in inequality and poverty, the presence or absence of such capacities was no idle matter. On the contrary, the East Asian crisis, those that came in its wake (such as Argentina's in 2001) and the current global recession, have underlined not merely the question of the appropriate form (or forms) of economic governance in an age of globalization, but also the issue of the relation of economic governance to poverty and inequality.

It is against the backdrop of globalization's consequences for inequality and poverty[2] that the remainder of this chapter proceeds. It is especially concerned with the crucial 'intervening variable' in the globalization/inequality-poverty matrix: the role of national economic governance. As we shall see, however, the role of economic governance in this matrix is not clear-cut. Thus while it yields a story line of general import, it is by no means a simple one. Rather, economic governance and its relation to inequality has been formed and transformed by the 'messy' historical specificities of the countries concerned. While we shall return to this point later, the chapter proceeds by sketching two essential building blocks in the argument: the relation of economic growth to inequality and of economic governance to the growth record. It then turns to an examination of the globalization-governance-inequality/poverty matrix in two of the East Asian countries most affected by the economic crisis of the late 1990s: South Korea and Malaysia. Assessing their contrasting experiences (both historically and in the aftermath of the crisis), the chapter ultimately concludes that *especially* in an age of neoliberal globalization, the maintenance of state capacities for strategic economic planning seems to be essential if economic growth and transformation is to be achieved and sustained with reasonable levels of social equity.

Growth and inequality

At first sight many people tend to assume that there must be an inverse relation between economic growth and inequality. Unfortunately that is not at all clear. Indeed, assessments of the relationship between growth and inequality have led something of a tortured existence, in at least two senses. Historically, the various forms of socialism (from state-socialism to European-style social democracy) have tended to prioritize the need for building materially egalitarian societies without linking them directly to concerns with economic growth.[3] Much neoliberal theorizing, on the other hand, has tended to assume that growth and inequality are inversely and inextricably linked, such that the problems of material inequality can be solved largely as a consequence of the benefits of growth 'trickling down' the income and social hierarchy. As regards the empirical record – at least for the developing world – the situation is ambiguous. For instance, most recent discussion in the standard economics literature has been concerned not with the impact of growth on inequality, but with the reverse: how inequality might affect growth (Kanbur 2000) and indeed, with how high levels of inequality might be harmful to growth (Persson and Tabellini 1994, Clark 1995).

With regard to the more specific relationship between growth and poverty, there has been an assumption that pro-poor growth,[4] which by definition would reduce absolute poverty, also tends to moderate the maldistribution of income. While this may well be the case, there are many situations in which growth benefits the 'non-poor' as well as – inevitably – the wealthy (lifting many of the former into a new middle class, as in China and other parts of East Asia, for instance) and thus improves income distribution overall, but tends to leave levels of absolute poverty more or less the same. Work by Ahuja *et al.* (1997), for instance, shows that in Thailand the poor have hardly benefited from an otherwise generally good growth performance. Notwithstanding these reservations, however, the work by Dollar and Kraay (2001) suggests that, on average, income poverty reduces as levels of GDP per capita (the usual proxy for economic growth) increase.[5]

Irrespective of the position taken in the debates sketched earlier, all of them (except those over socialism and inequality) suffer from two major theoretical silences: (a) the absence of institutional mechanisms though which growth is achieved, and (b) how those mechanisms, together with growth, subsequently influence inequality. It is to those mechanisms that I now turn.

Governing growth

While concerns with the relation of economic policy to growth go back at least to the dawn of classical political economy in the eighteen century, concerns with the nature of state institutions and their relation to economic growth are of more recent vintage. While inclinations of these were evident in Austrian political economy of the late nineteenth century (Hodgson 2001), it was Weber who became the first to systematically elaborate the institutional bases of (what we now refer to as) effective economic governance.

For the best part of a century, then, it has largely been work in the Weberian tradition (albeit given particular specificity by Polanyi 1957) that has argued that effective public institutions are a cornerstone of economic growth and development. In spite of such a long period of theoretical gestation, however, it was only recently that such arguments began to be operationalized for the empirical analysis of the growth record. In a widely cited paper, Evans and Rauch (1999; see also Rauch and Evans 2000) demonstrated that state bureaucracies, measured according to their 'Weberianness' (a scale based on meritocratic recruitment to the civil service, provision of long term and rewarding civil service careers, etc.) have significant implications for economic growth. On the basis of their analysis of 35 developing and middle-income countries they show that when controlling for initial levels of economic growth and the skill base, variations in the 'Weberianness' of state bureaucracies captured, for instance, 'a key institutional element of the "high performing" East Asian economies while pointing to an institutional deficit that may help explain low rates of growth in Africa' (Evans and Rauch 1999: 757).

Governing inequality

If there is a strong relationship between bureaucratically competent economic governance and the growth record, as the Evans-Rauch work attests, it is reasonable to hypothesize that there should be a similar relation between such state capabilities and the record on inequality and poverty. Recent econometric analysis of the relation of a state's 'Weberianness' to poverty reduction – for a sample of 29 developing and middle income countries – does indeed support such a hypothesis (Henderson et al. 2007).[6] The problem with this and the Evans-Rauch work which preceded it, however, is that – inevitably – it works at a level of empirical aggregation that makes it impossible to understand the significance of the historical contexts (nationally and internationally) in which these relations are forged, and the institutional detail involved in the policy processes (including the politics and political economy of policy formation and implementation). Related work, however, which studied these issues ethnographically in a small sample of countries, allows us to begin to grasp the dynamics in question (for a summary see Henderson and Hulme 2002; see also Phillips et al. 2006).

While the econometric work referred to earlier supports the contention that there is a relation between a state's competence for economic governance and its ability to reduce poverty, it provides no sense of the extent to which pro-active economic policies were involved in the more successful poverty-reducing countries, nor whether effective economic governance was at least, in part, associated with the state's ability to manage the interface between its domestic economy and the international economy (a combination that I refer to as 'strategic economic planning'). Furthermore, this work is unable to enlighten us as to whether explicit anti-poverty policies (and, at least implicit, redistributional policies) were part of the story of poverty reduction in the more successful cases. Both of these, however, are very important issues (not least because they go to the heart of neoliberal propositions) and in order to engage with them, we need to introduce explicitly such 'global' and policy dimensions into our considerations; we need to focus, in other words, on how inequality is 'governed'. This we proceed to do by paying specific attention to the cases of South Korea and Malaysia.

From the mid-1970s South Korea (hereafter, Korea) was perceived as not merely an exemplar of rapid industrialization and economic growth, but also as a society where substantial reductions in inequality and poverty seemed to have been largely a reflex of economic growth; seemingly providing, in other words, empirical support for the 'trickle-down' hypothesis of increasing human welfare beloved of neoliberal theorists.[7] Although the reasons for Korea's economic development were contested across the ideological and paradigmatic divides, on the basis of the realist tests of empirical adequacy and plausibility (Sayer 1984), it seems clear that the country hosted what was perhaps the classic developmental state, at least until 1993. As I have argued in Chapter 4, continuing democratization associated with Kim Young Sam's term of office as President, and the beginnings of neoliberal reform consistent with OECD membership, resulted in attempts to dismantle Korea's version of *dirigisme*. In particular the principal agent for strategic planning, the Economic Planning Board (EPB), was absorbed into the Ministry of Finance. As a consequence, the Ministry not only enhanced its role in economic policy-making more generally, but also became the main institutional conduit for the dissemination of neoliberal ideas within Government circles. The abandonment of a strategic planning capacity that these developments represented, contributed to the deregulation of domestic financial institutions and thus led directly to the economic crisis of the late 1990s and to the growth of inequality and poverty that arrived in its wake.

Unlike the Korean case, Malaysia has been one of the very few instances in the history of capitalism where anti-poverty and redistributional policies have been instituted as a central moment of a national development project (see Chapter 6). Although not as impressive as Korea's, from the mid-1970s Malaysia achieved a very credible growth record. Seemingly as a result of its welfare policy initiatives, it had also made in-roads into poverty and inequality that were far better than any of its Southeast Asian neighbours, with the exception of Singapore. These successes had been achieved – unlike its counterparts in East Asia – while having a racially diverse population (with the attendant tensions and conflicts often associated with such societies).[8] While the Malaysian state had evolved, since the late 1960s, with the trappings of the developmental model (in its case, the Economic Planning Unit – EPU – being the rough equivalent of Korea's EPB), it had never been as effective in guiding and encouraging economic development as had its counterparts in Korea, Taiwan or – indeed – Singapore. In spite of this, Malaysia's limited strategic planning capacity was not dismantled in the 1990s, as Korea's was, and thus while its economy was badly affected by the crisis towards the end of that decade, the Government's new planning agency – the National Economic Action Council (NEAC) – managed to contain the situation by recourse to currency controls and other policy initiatives that ran against the grain of neoliberal prescriptions (Jomo 2001: Chapter1, Henderson *et al.* 2002b). Partly as a consequence, and unlike Korea, Malaysia had no need of IMF assistance and the crisis had limited consequences for the incidence of inequality and poverty.

With Korea and Malaysia we seemingly have two disparate, but still related, cases of how states that had traditionally attempted to orchestrate economic transformation (with differing degrees of success) had responded to the increasing globalization of their economies and, particularly, to the challenges posed by the liberalization of international finance capital. While their approaches to inequality and poverty were seemingly quite different, in what follows we look briefly at their recent development projects. We do so in order to uncover their experiential realities but also to identify some of the lessons they might have for the encouragement of growth with relative equity.

Governing growth and inequality

Recent work on Korea (such as Henderson *et al.* 2002c) has confirmed the broad outlines of the accepted account of that country's dramatic record on reductions in poverty and seemingly inequality also (at least until the late 1990s); namely, that these improvements in human welfare were largely a consequence of improvements in economic growth without significant recourse to explicit anti-poverty or redistributional policies. However, what many commentators often fail to recognize is that both the growth record and the reductions in inequality were underpinned by extensive land reform (that is, redistribution to the peasantry) which began under the Japanese occupation after 1910 and was completed by the Korean government in the 1950s. Supplementing the material and social effects of land reform, however, were a series of policies – from the late 1960s – which though designed to regulate the power of the *chaebol* in certain domestic markets, had the effect of subsidizing the wage for, at least, urban workers. These included price controls over key foodstuffs (such as rice, vegetables and meat) and price ceilings on smaller housing units together with planning and financial controls over the construction of larger units (Kim W.J. 1997: 147).[9]

Notwithstanding these policy initiatives and given that we know that the relation of economic growth to inequality is, in general, ambiguous (discussed earlier), if economic growth was the principal factor in the reductions in inequality and poverty in Korea, that still begs the question as to what it was about the *nature* of economic growth there, that made it capable of delivering these improvements in human welfare. Arguably the key issue here is not that of growth per se, but of the economic structure that underpins the growth. We know from countries in the developed world, for instance (Britain being a good example), that where growth is delivered largely through financial and related services and through low value-adding services such as retailing or tourism, it tends to be associated with significant levels of income and social inequality (Sassen 1991). Where growth is largely associated with high value-added manufacturing and related services, however, the prospects for material and social equity tend to be better, as such activities are usually associated with an increased demand for people with higher manual and technical skills and thus hold the promise of a higher wage economy with more generalized prosperity.

On the basis of this line of argument, the question in the developing world is not merely one of economic growth – though that in itself is very important[10]–but whether a given country will be able to evolve an approximation to the latter economic structure by a combination of 'market signals' (to domestic and foreign companies) and 'market facilitating' policies (instituted by the state), as typically recommended in neoliberal policy advice. As argued in earlier chapters and detailed at length in a plethora of publications stretching back nearly 20 years (for instance, Woo 1991, Chang 1994, Kim E.M. 1997), we know from the implications of the Korean development model (among others), that this is unlikely. Rather it seems that more pro-active state policies, supported by authoritative and bureaucratically competent governance agencies (or, in short, a capacity for strategic planning and implementation) is better able to deliver the types of economic structure that, historically, have been more closely related to generalized prosperity.

In Korea, that economic structure was anchored in heavy industries such as steel and shipbuilding as well as manufacturing industries such as automobiles, consumer electronics, semiconductors and, more recently, telecommunications.[11] That many of these industries were induced (and subsequently moved into higher value-added production) by state agencies working in particularly close relationships with the large, private (and family owned) conglomerates – the *chaebol* – is now a matter of historical record. As a result partly of the demands for skilled manual and technical labour that these industries generated, as well as the militancy of the trade unions that began to organize their workforces, by the early 1980s significant upward pressure on wages began to be evident (Deyo 1989). Together with the expansion of labour markets in these industries consistent with the increasing international competitiveness of the principal *chaebol*, a dynamic towards a relatively high wage economy was set in train, and with it, the possibilities for generalized prosperity.

These developments are reflected in the data for poverty and inequality. In the mid-1960s, for instance, 60–70 per cent of the Korean population was estimated to be still living in poverty, the vast majority of whom continued to be peasants and agricultural workers. By the mid-1990s, however, absolute poverty had declined to just over 3 per cent of the population (undoubtedly consistent with urbanization and proletarianization), giving Korea one of the best poverty records among OECD member countries. In terms of inequality more generally, gini coefficient data suggests that by 1996 it had fallen to about 0.31 which was, again, a record that was very impressive by any standards (Park 2001; see Henderson *et al.* 2002c: 1–6).

While these spectacular achievements seem to have been largely a product of the nature of the economic structure that had evolved as a consequence of Korea's state orchestrated form of capitalism ('plan rationalism'), rather than of economic growth in a simple sense or of anti-poverty policy, we need to mark that the Korean state was not immune to welfare considerations. In addition to the welfare implications of price controls and housing policies indicated earlier, from the mid-1970s there had been a concern within the EPB about the need for unemployment insurance. It was not until the early 1990s, however, that the EPB – against opposition from some government and business interests – managed to get unemployment provision included in the 7th Five-Year Economic Plan (Henderson *et al.* 2002c).[12]

Such expressions of welfare policy were short lived, however, subsequent to the absorption of the EPB into the Ministry of Finance in 1993. They were eliminated as the latter's fiscal conservatism became the dominant ethos of Korea's economic governance system, which began to shift from a planning to a more directly market–and, indeed, a finance – driven one (Pirie 2007). Consistent with these developments, and as indicated earlier, the regulatory regime that had underpinned the country's economic stability was weakened. As explored in Chapter 4, this development became especially problematic with the increase in the numbers of private banks during the 1990s, for it was their unregulated borrowing and corporate lending activities that were the single most important trigger for the country's economic crisis which began in 1997 (Chang 1998).

Among other things, the crisis of the late 1990s had profoundly negative consequences for poverty and inequality. In the case of the latter, gini data suggest that by early 1999, inequality had risen to 0.34; an increase of around 9 per cent in less than three years. With regard to poverty, government data suggests that by early 1999, 8.5 per cent of the population had become poor. These data, however, were based on earnings only, whereas other data, based on household expenditures, suggest that by early 1998 poverty levels had already risen to encompass 23.5 per cent of the population (PSPD/UNDP 2000; see also Henderson *et al.* 2002c: 3–4). Either way, however, it seems clear that the Korean economic crisis produced a significant decline in the county's social welfare. As we see later, this was in stark contrast to the situation in Malaysia during similar economic turmoil.

As indicated earlier, Malaysia has been perhaps the only developing country (other than state-socialist ones) to have explicitly pursued anti-poverty and redistributional policies as a central component of its development project. Driven by concerns with racial conflict, the New Economic Policy (NEP) of the 1970s and 1980s was designed to irradicate the link between race and class by shifting resources to the bumiputera[13] (Malays and other indigenous peoples) majority, and to irradicate poverty irrespective of race. The policy tools deployed to these ends included employment quotas in the private sector, affirmative action (formal and informal) in the public sector, material support for rural development (and hence for the overwhelmingly bumiputera peasantry) and a major expansion of state equity participation in the economy through holding companies involved in manufacturing, petroleum, plantation agriculture, trading, etc. Underpinning and securing such initiatives were programmes to attract foreign investment in manufacturing and related services, especially in electronics, automobiles and similar industries.

On the face of it, such initiatives have made significant inroads into poverty, though this has been less true for inequality. For instance, while over 49 per cent of the Malaysian population were poor in 1970, immediately prior to the NEP, by 2000 the poor represented no more than 6 per cent of the population. Even rural poverty – always the more intractable in Malaysia (as elsewhere) – had declined from nearly 59 per cent to around 13 per cent over the same period (Henderson *et al.* 2002b, Tables 1 and 2: 2). Credible reductions in inequality, however, have been less evident. Gini data, for instance, suggests that between 1970 and 1997, the index dropped from 0.50 to 0.46; a reduction of only 8 per cent (Roslan 2001; Henderson *et al.* 2002b, Table 3: 3). While more recent gini data for Malaysia is unavailable, it is notable that in contrast to the Korean experience, the economic crisis in Malaysia seems to have had only marginal consequences for the incidence of poverty. Between 1997 and 1999 – the period when the crisis was at its zenith – both rural and urban poverty in Malaysia increased by only 1.4 per cent (calculated from Henderson *et al.* 2002b, Table 2: 2).[14] In terms of the consequences the crisis had for poverty, these data, then, seem point to the relative 'superiority' of Malaysia's economic governance system compared with the system that had been created in Korea subsequent to the early 1990s.

Although significant improvements in some aspects of inequality in Malaysia have been made over the past three decades, from the point of view of our current concerns, two questions remain: can these improvements be attributed largely to the government's anti-poverty and redistribution initiatives; and what was the role of economic governance in achieving these ends?

The Malaysian experience of economic governance over the past 30 years underlines the fact that while, in principle, there seems to be a correspondence between economically pro-active states and growth with relative equity, as argued in Chapter 4, there are significant differences between such states in terms of the coherence, authoritativeness and competence of their planning agencies (see also Evans and Rauch 1999) which have implications for inequality and poverty. Thus in Malaysia it seems clear that the well-documented corruption within the political elite coupled with the gradual decline in the quality of the civil service has resulted in a less impressive record of reducing inequality than would otherwise have been the case. For instance, while the aforementioned state holding companies could have been significant tools for the redistribution of wealth, in practice the bulk of their material benefits have flowed to particular individuals and groups close the Prime Minister (particularly for over 20 years until 2003, Mahathir Mohamad), and the leadership of the ruling party, UMNO (Gomez and Jomo 1997: Chapters 3–5) thus restricting the impact they would otherwise have had on inequality. Additionally, while from the 1970s to the 1990s, well over 20 per cent of the annual development budget (itself around 20 per cent to the total state budget) was allocated to poverty reduction, year on year between 19 and 32 per cent of the development budget – including the funds earmarked for poverty reduction – remained unspent, thus raising questions about the civil service's ability to engage in effective project implementation (Henderson *et al.* 2002b: 20–28).

If these problems raise questions about the extent to which reductions in poverty and inequality can be attributed to anti-poverty and related policies per se, then to what extent can they be attributed to the nature of economic policy – and thus strategic economic planning – in Malaysia?

While the system of economic governance in Malaysia has achieved some spectacular 'own goals'[15] and has continually failed to address significant weaknesses in innovation, the skill-base, etc. (Rasiah 2001), it has still been largely responsible for crafting an economic structure that would have been inconceivable had the Malaysian government, since 1970, adopted an uncritical relationship to neoliberal ideas about trade, investment, etc. It is this economic structure, with its manufacturing industries on Peninsula Malaysia's west coast (now responsible for about

35 per cent of GDP) that has allowed poor peasants to transform themselves into a relatively well-paid urban working class.[16] It is in this sense, then, that strategic economic planning in Malaysia (in spite of its institutional weaknesses relative to Taiwan, Singapore and Korea prior to the early 1990s; see Chapter 4) has had a positive impact on poverty and inequality there. Anti-poverty and redistributional policies – as enshrined in the NEP and NDP – have been, perhaps, less significant. The real achievement of these social policies seems to have been the creation of a Bumiputera middle class and thus the delivery of social stability via the avoidance of racial conflict.

Conclusion

I cautioned in the first section of this chapter that the way a national system of economic governance emerges and develops over time, whether it manages to create and sustain an institutional apparatus capable of the effective management of the domestic economy and – crucially in an age of globalization – of the interface between the domestic and international economies, depends on a whole series of historical contingencies (including the particular politics and political economies of development) specific to the countries in question. Given this reality, it is not surprising that particular national development projects will have their own gearings to poverty, inequality and the means by which they can be reduced. Having said this, the foregoing brief examination of the somewhat similar, but mainly contrasting, Korean and Malaysian experiences does allow a number of general conclusions.

The Korean and Malaysian cases both suggest that while robust and sustained economic growth is a *sine qua non* for significant reductions in inequality and poverty, in itself it is insufficient to the task. This does not mean, however, that explicit anti-poverty and redistributional policies are necessarily essential to the process (though they undoubtedly help) as the Korean case demonstrates by means of their absence and the Malaysian case, by means of their ineffectiveness.[17] What seems to be more important is that the economy evolves with a structure that supports industries capable, over time, of delivering higher value-added activities that can underpin relatively high wages (and that these can be sustained through subsequent movements into innovation-led growth and development). Almost without exception since the beginnings of the first industrial revolution through to the present day, the achievement of national economic structures of these sorts has been associated with various forms of state intervention, as the work of Chang (2002) on practically all the now developed economies (when they were themselves developing) and Amsden (2001) on the 'late industrializers', attests.

From the analysis sketched here it seems that those forms of national economic governance that continue to prioritize institutional capacities for strategic economic planning (in other words, forms of plan rationalism), are vital to the types of economic structure, and thus the forms of economic growth, that are most conducive to reducing inequality and poverty and can sustain that downward trajectory during the inevitable periods of recession and even crisis. This conclusion, of course, runs counter to much neoliberal theorizing and the policy prescriptions that tend to flow from it. As neoliberal globalization, and particularly its 'financialized' variant, has brought with it the threat of increased economic turbulence at national, regional and now (since 2008) global levels, it is a conclusion that demands serious attention from national and international agencies and from the development community at large.

6

LIMITS TO INDUSTRIALIZATION

(with Richard Phillips)

Policy initiatives, whatever the intentions behind them, often have unintended con-sequences. Chalmers Johnson (2003), in his penetrating analysis of the impacts of US foreign policy, has termed these, 'blowback'. In the previous chapter I discussed how the Malaysian style of strategic economic planning was, during the crucial crisis period of the late 1990s, more robust than that of Korea. Unfortunately the social and redistributional programme associated with Malaysian economic plan-ning seems to have generated its own blowback. While the programme's contribu-tion to social stability has been decisive for Malaysian transformation and develop-ment, in the longer term, it seems to have contributed to a 'stalling' of the country's industrialization process. In the contemporary era, when Chinese competition in manufactured commodities is increasing, this is a dangerous situation for a political economy to be in. In this chapter, we use the Malaysian experience to analyse how certain social policy agendas – no matter how well intentioned – can sometimes begin to constrain, or indeed set limits, to continued industrialization.

Social policy and economic transformation

In the study of economic transformation, issues of social policy tend to enter the analysis by attention to 'human capital' and the means by which it might be 'improved'. The focus, therefore, tends to be on educational provision and the strengthening of the skill-base of labour markets. In accounts of the East Asian economic 'miracle', for instance, much was made of the link between the abil-ity of those countries to deliver a relatively well-educated and increasingly skilled workforce (at low cost) and their rapid economic growth (see, for instance, World Bank 1993).

In its concern with social policy, this chapter takes a different tack. Its focus is anti-poverty and redistributional policy on the one hand and migration policy on the other. Notwithstanding the undoubted contributions of such initiatives to social welfare, we are not concerned with these, but rather with their implications for industrialization.

The history of Malaysian industrialization, and its present condition, provides us with particularly interesting materials with which to 'think laterally' about the relation of social policy to economic development.[1] Since the early 1970s, Malaysia has achieved a highly credible industrialization record. Indeed, it has become the first 'Muslim majority' country to industrialize.[2] Importantly, and relatively unusually, it has managed this feat on the basis of a multi-racial society, with all the additional social bases for division and conflict (additional, that is, to class and gender) that this implies. As argued in the previous chapter, while inequality remains problematic, Malaysia's economic development has been accompanied by dramatic poverty reduction and, unlike in many of its East Asian neighbours, this has been sustained during periods of economic crisis.

Whatever the successes of Malaysia's industrialization project, and the benefits derived from it (and they have been considerable), it now appears that the project has begun to stall. The problem does not seem to be cyclical and short-term in nature, but structural. In examining Malaysia's most important manufacturing industry (in terms of GDP contribution, employment, export performance, etc.), electronics,[3] the question remains as to why, after nearly 40 years of electronics manufacturing in Malaysia, this should have been the case? While this chapter does not claim to provide a complete answer to this question (in addition to it, see Phillips and Henderson 2009) it does attend to the role that anti-poverty and, more recently, immigration policy might have had in producing the situation.

It is important to understand the reasons for this 'stalling' of the Malaysian industrialization project not merely because of the damage it is likely to inflict on the Malaysian economy and the social fall-out that may be associated with it, but because the prospects of Malaysian policy-makers (and others) thinking and planning their way out of the problem will depend on how they interpret its causes. Additionally, we need to recognize that Malaysian experiences of industrialization may have implications for other countries attempting to achieve economic growth with social equity, while being confronted – as a result of Chinese (and to a lesser extent, Indian) development – with a 'race to the bottom' (see Kaplinsky 2005). Among such countries, South Africa and Brazil (both, like Malaysia, multi-racial societies) immediately come to mind.

Our substantive discussions begin by marking the promise and achievements of Malaysian industrialization, but acknowledging that there is an underlying reality that raises serious questions about the future viability of the country's industrialization project. In the subsequent section, we turn to a discussion of the social policy contexts within which Malaysian industrialization emerged and evolved. We suggest that while crucial to social stability, these contexts have had the unintended consequence of perpetuating the structural weaknesses of the country's industrial base. Only through the intervention of regional government agencies – of which those in Penang are the principal examples – has this structural weakness been partially moderated. Additionally, we suggest that recent immigration into the country, largely of lower-skilled workers from elsewhere in Southeast Asia, has had the effect of releasing companies from the tight labour markets and thus wage pressures they would otherwise have been under, and that in other countries (Taiwan and Singapore, for instance), helped propel industrial upgrading. In the next section we demonstrate the continuing technological weaknesses, particularly in the electronics industry, and subsequently sketch the nature of China's competitive threat. In conclusion, we summarize the reasons for the stalling of Malaysia's industrialization project and outline the general implications of our analysis.

Industrialization: hope and reality

While much of this chapter is critical of what has become of Malaysia's industrialization project, we need to be clear from the outset that there is much to applaud in the country's record of industrial development. Putting its decisive contribution to growth, poverty-reduction and well-being to one side for the moment, and looking at the internal evolution of Malaysia's manufacturing industries, there is evidence (though fragmented) to support claims that technology and capabilities transfers have occurred between the TNC subsidiaries that dominate manufacturing, and locally-owned firms. For instance, Malaysian Industrial Development Authority (MIDA) officials and some analysts make much of the rising technological capabilities of locally-owned electronics companies that have emerged and have been absorbed into the production networks of TNCs such as Intel and Maxor[4] as they do (though less frequently) of those that have been emerged to supply the car producer, Proton.

Such performance did not go unnoticed in international development circles. Indeed, in 2000, then UN Secretary General, Kofi Annan, singled out Malaysia as a leading exemplar for other developing countries attempting to grow through foreign direct investment (Yanus 2000). Such praise, if anything, increased the interest in understanding Malaysia's supposed ability to foster linkages between indigenous small and medium-sized enterprises (SMEs) and TNCs (e.g. UNCTAD 2001, 2002; Rasiah 1999a, Best and Rasiah 2003). While there has indeed been much to praise in Malaysia's record of industrialization, the lessons to be learned from its FDI-led strategy are not as straight-forward as many observers would have us believe. As we suggest later, Malaysia's successes in building global-local industrial linkages have been overstated; over generalizing the role of TNCs and ignoring severe limitations in Malaysia's ability to deviate from a low-cost, labour-intensive form of integration into the global production networks (GPNs) of TNCs.[5]

The problem – for the future of the Malaysian economy and some developing countries currently trying to industrialize on the basis of FDI-led, export-oriented strategies – is that some of the most important lessons to be learnt from Malaysian industrialization, may be associated with other matters. Firm-level industrial successes in Malaysia, while evident, have been limited. They do little to offset concerns about the underlying competitiveness of domestic producers and the extent to which industrial upgrading has been able to move the country away from its original mode of integration into global manufacturing. Malaysian electronics – the sectoral focus of this chapter – as with its ASEAN equivalents, is still widely recognized to be not only foreign-dominated, but – unlike Singapore – with local SME suppliers disproportionately engaged in 'lower tier' functions (JICA 2001, Ernst 2003).

Evidence of this can be seen in employment data. For instance, even in Malaysia's most advanced manufacturing region – in and around Penang – over 74 per cent of all manufacturing employment was still based on production work in 1990,[6] after nearly 20 years of electronics manufacturing in the region.[7] By 1998, the situation had improved only marginally, with just over 67 per cent of manufacturing employment still in production work (Ong 2000). As of December 2003, 17 per cent of all production workers in Penang's electrical and electronics sector were officially classified as 'unskilled', with about 80 per cent of them classified as 'skilled' or 'semi-skilled'. Even so, PDC analysts (who know more about Penang's electronics industry than anyone else) estimate that over half of all those employed (of whatever skills category) in the region's electronics industry, may still be performing low-value assembly functions.[8] Such findings are endorsed, for Malaysia as a whole, by the relatively modest changes that took place through to the mid-1990s in the skills composition of workers employed by US-owned TNC subsidiaries. In 1977, for instance, 74 per cent of those employed by US TNCs comprised unskilled production workers. By 1994, the unskilled still comprised 72 per cent of all those employed by such subsidiaries (Slaughter 2002).

From the aforementioned data, it seems that the successes of Malaysian electronics production may have been over-emphasized at the expense of under-estimating and – as we argue later – misrepresenting the dynamics that have limited Malaysia's ability to deviate significantly from its original, low-cost, labour-intensive form of integration into GPNs. There are two problems here. First, much of the debate about Malaysia's ability to upgrade by 'levering' FDI has paid insufficient attention to broader changes affecting the organization of the global electronics industry (for an exception, see Phillips and Henderson 2009). Second, the effects of government policy on Malaysia's indigenous electronics base is often only selectively examined and, even then, limited to a narrow reading of 'industrial policy'. It is this second deficiency that the current chapter addresses.

Policy contexts of the evolution of the electronics industry

The evolution of the Malaysian electronics industry is well-trodden ground in the specialist literature (e.g. Jomo 1990, Rasiah 1995, Ismail 1995, Jomo *et al.* 1999) and needs no recuperation here. Important for our purposes, however, is the fact that the industry developed as part of a particular model of 'pro-poor' growth based upon rapid industrialization through foreign investment, coupled with a highly politicized 'affirmative action' programme to achieve greater equity in the distribution of employment and wealth. Contextualizing the industry's evolution in this way is important for understanding why support by the Malaysian Federal government for electronics was both piecemeal and re-active. We argue that while there clearly have been exogenous reasons for the 'stalled' upgrading of Malaysia's manufacturing industries, and of electronics in particular (see, for instance, Phillips and Henderson 2009), there have also been important endogenous reasons for this. We suggest later that the latter have been associated with the unintended consequences, for the country's industrial-corporate structure and its technological base, of two social policy agendas: anti-poverty and redistribution from the early 1970s and immigration from the late 1980s. Only in the case of Penang state, and for particular political-institutional reasons, have these consequences been (partially) circumvented.

Policy origins of structural weakness

The colonial division of labour developed by the British in the Malayan Peninsula and western Borneo during the nineteenth century was the origin of the multi-racial society evident in contemporary Malaysia. By the late 1960s persistent poverty, coupled with the superimposition of racial and class divisions, provided the context for anti-Chinese riots. In their wake came economic and social policy initiatives (the 'New Economic Policy' – NEP – and its successors) that have sustained, over nearly 40 years, an effort to achieve economic growth and, at the same time, a more equitable distribution of wealth. As such, Malaysia has been one of the very few capitalist societies (perhaps the only one) to institute anti-poverty and redistribution ('affirmative action' in the interests of the Bumiputera majority) programmes as central components of its development project.

Success for the country's anti-poverty and affirmative action initiatives, however, was predicated on its ability to achieve rapid economic growth. Unlike South Korea, Taiwan and Hong Kong (but like Singapore) successive Malaysian governments chose to mobilize foreign, rather than domestic, capital. As Jesudason (1989) has argued, this choice was probably seen as a way of limiting further capital accumulation among wealthier Malaysian Chinese, as it was they that would have been the primary beneficiaries of the state's mobilization of domestic capital for industrialization purposes. In a racialized state, dominated by the Bumiputera political elite, this would have been an unacceptable outcome. Thus the use of foreign capital represented a way of both avoiding politically-sensitive ties between the state and local Chinese capital, as well as a means of 'crowding out' the latter's influence on the Malaysian economy (Lim and Pang 1991). As we discuss later, this combination of foreign-driven industrialization with the 'crowding out' of Malaysian Chinese industrial interests has had negative consequences for the evolution of Malaysia's industrial structure and, ultimately, for the country's ability to sustain its industrialization project in the face of increasing international competition.

While the social-structural change initiated by the NEP and subsequent programmes was central to social order in Malaysia, inadvertently, they generated problems for the economy. In particular, they helped to discourage those groups

– especially Malaysian Chinese entrepreneurs – that were most likely to develop the SMEs capable of linking with the TNCs and thus essential to the maximization of the benefits of FDI. Added to this was the fact that by expanding the opportunities for generating wealth through rentier activities – via participation in a growing stock market and in the state-owned holding companies (HICOM, Petronas, etc.)[9], the government (again, inadvertently, no doubt) detracted the attention of Malaysians – of whatever race – from manufacturing.

Paradoxically, given the government's interest in economic growth with equality, rentierism associated with the state-holding companies, has had the particular effect of depressing direct Bumiputera involvement in manufacturing industries. While the government has been well aware of this problem since at least the late 1980s (Salih 1988, Salih and Yusof 1989; see also Lubeck 1992), the problem has remained. The Japan International Cooperation Agency, for instance, reports that of Malaysia's locally-owned manufacturing SMEs in 2000, only 20 per cent of them were owned by Bumiputera and of these, the majority were small, rather than medium-sized companies (JICA 2001: 2–7). It needs to be borne in mind that while rentier activities are perhaps the easiest way to capital accumulation (short of inheriting assets), manufacturing must be amongst the hardest. It is manufacturing and related services, however, that are central to the prospects for building high value-added economies capable of delivering generalized prosperity with low levels of inequality.

Enter Federal industrial policy

Stimulated by fiscal and other incentives from the Federal government and the provision of export processing zones, foreign investment – mainly in electronics – began to flow into Malaysia from the early 1970s. What the Federal government did not do, however, was to tailor domestic corporate and institutional circumstances to the changing needs of the TNCs so as to try to anchor them in the country on the bases of higher value-added, and thus higher wage operations. In as far as this was done, it was left largely to state governments, but with very mixed results, as we shall see later.[10]

Strategic industrial policies, from the Federal government, only emerged in the 1980s and, with the exception of encouraging SME entrepreneurship (only among the Bumiputera, however), they did not target electronics. With hindsight, the Federal government's relative lack of interest in the electronics industry was surprising given that by then it had become the country's most important manufacturing industry; it was already clear that technologically it was falling behind those of some of its regional neighbours (Salih and Young 1987); and that it was becoming increasingly dependent on the more capital intensive, higher skill operations, performed by foreign companies in their plants in Hong Kong and Singapore, rather than in Malaysia (Henderson 1989: Chapter 4).

Though surprising, the Federal government's lack of interest in the electronics industry was, perhaps, not unexpected. The government was certainly concerned with growth, but it was also concerned with redistribution, which it mainly interpreted as the transfer of assets to the Bumiputera (and, in practice, only to small numbers amongst them; see Gomez and Jomo 1997). Consequently, given that it had eschewed the joint-venture route to developing the electronics industry in the country's first phase of industrialization, by the mid-1980s this was not now an industry amenable to Bumiputera equity participation. Following the experiences of Japan and South Korea, the government targeted heavy industries such as steel, petro-chemicals and automobiles, all of which were ripe with joint venture opportunities and thus with significant possibilities for Bumiputera capital accumulation. Orchestrating the emergence of these industries thus provided a convenient solution to the political need to balance growth with redistribution (and avoid creating further opportunities for capital accumulation by Malaysian Chinese), while creating opportunities to expand Bumiputera rentierism, via participation in HICOM and similar state holding companies (see Gomez and Jomo 1997).

With the Federal government's attention focussed on heavy industrialization and other projects that could enhance the opportunities for further wealth expansion by the growing Bumiputera middle class, it was left to state governments to do what they could to anchor electronics FDI in the country and encourage linkages with local companies.

Enter Regional industrial policy

FDI in electronics has generally flowed into three distinct regions in Peninsula Malaysia: Penang and more recently, the adjacent state of Kedah; the Klang Valley in Selangor, adjacent to the Federal capital, Kuala Lumpur; and along the southern edge of the Melaka Straights extending into the state of Johor, adjacent to Singapore. Generally speaking, Penang and, to some extent, Kedah, represent the most coherent concentrations, dominated by the foreign-owned manufacture of electronic components (semiconductors and hard disc drives), together with some locally-owned SMEs engaged in manufacturing support functions. In Penang, investment has tended to come from the US and Europe. In contrast, Selangor has attracted investment from Japanese and Taiwanese firms who produce a broad range of consumer electronics including household appliances. The Melaka and Johor concentrations developed as a result of Singapore-based firms (foreign and Singaporean) relocating their labour intensive assembly operations as Singaporean labour costs increased in the 1980s (Parsonage 1997). These firms have specialized in computer peripherals and consumer electronics assembly. While absorbed into the production networks of the Singapore-based firms and subsidiaries, Johor, in particular, has attracted 'autonomous' investment particularly from US contract manufacturers seeking to tap into the region's high volume assembly capacities.[11]

While Federal incentives and labour market reforms (helping to maintain relatively low labour costs) were critical for attracting foreign investment, it was state institutions at the regional level that were instrumental in operationally influencing where this investment located and in promoting linkages with local firms (where and in as far as they existed). Consequently, and arguably, it has been the institutional capacities developed by the regional states – rather than the Federal state – that have been decisive for even the limited industrial upgrading that has occurred in the Malaysian electronics industry.

Although this division of labour between Federal and regional state agencies is not normally problematic for industrialization and industrial upgrading, in the context of Malaysia, it has been. There, the relative lack of Federal Government support for regionally-based industrial development agencies has resulted in their unevenness, both in incidence and performance. In fact, only in Penang has there emerged a significant institutional capacity to deal with the electronics sector (Rasiah 1999a), though even there the capacity has remained limited. In Selangor, – the second largest region for electronics manufacturing in the country – electronics has always been a minor concern among a diverse range of unrelated industries with which the local economic development agency engages. The question arises as to why this state of affairs has arisen; why, in other words, that of all the regional states where electronics is an important part of the local economy, only Penang has developed an institutional capacity capable of encouraging upgrading in the industry?

Malaysia's best examples of industrial upgrading, both in foreign-owned TNC subsidiaries and in locally-owned firms absorbed into their production networks, occur in the Penang electronics industry. Indeed, most of the information on the Malaysian electronics industry and its successes derive from Penang.[12] This is because it is only in Penang that a political and institutional infrastructure has emerged that has a coherent industrial focus, combined with high levels of administrative expertise, encouraged by state politicians oriented towards industrial development (see Haggard *et al.* 1998, Rasiah 1999a, 2002a). At the core of this infrastructure is the Penang Development Corporation (PDC).

Founded in 1969, the PDC has become a unique agency in the development of Malaysian electronics. Since then it has provided Penang with a critical institutional asset: a pro-active and adept administrative intermediary through which to co-ordinate relationships between the TNCs and local firms and between the industry and the Federal government. Over time the PDC has emerged as the leading centre for research and expertise on the electronics industry anywhere within the government bureaucracy (Federal or state), and is now a key source of information about the electronics industry for Federal decision-makers. By contrast, the Selangor Economic Development Corporation (SEDC) has focussed its efforts on the development of land and infrastructural services (housing, retail complexes, transport networks, for instance) for the hinterland of the nation's capital. Unlike Penang, Selangor has failed to develop the institutional capacity for pro-active engagement with the region's significant electronics industry. Engaging with the question of 'why Penang, but not Selangor', raises the question of ethnic politics and returns us to the Federal government's policy preferences.

A product of the spatial division of labour associated with British colonial control, Penang's principal city, Georgetown, became (like Singapore), a focus for Chinese migration. By the beginning of the post-colonial period in the late 1950s,

Georgetown – and Penang more generally – had a predominantly Chinese population. The problems of economic decline (associated with the collapse of Georgetown's entrepot functions) were compounded by the fact that, as the principal
location for political mobilization among the Malaysian Chinese, Penang was not a
state favoured by a Bumiputera-dominated Federal government. The consequence
was that the Penang government had to look to the state's internal resources to
help drive economic development. The institutional key to this was the PDC.
With the institution of the Federal government's New Economic Policy in 1971,
Penang, with Malaysia's principal concentration of skilled technical and engineering personnel, was uniquely placed to take advantage of FDI flows in electronics.
The state became the obvious place in Malaysia for TNCs – whose most capital-
intensive operations were in Singapore – to locate their secondary operations (see
Haggard *et al.* 1998).

In contrast, politicians and business interests in Selangor have never seen a need
to engage with the state's electronics industry in order to encourage its upgrading.
The reasons for this seem to be two-fold. First, ethnically dominated by Malays,
Selangor politics was always more closely aligned than Penang's to Federal politics
in general, and to that of the ruling party, UMNO[13] in particular. Consequently,
and by virtue of the fact that the state constituted the immediate hinterland of the
Federal capital, Kuala Lumpur, there was no particular need for business and political interests there to forge their own economic destiny. It seems likely that with the
explosion of Kuala Lumpur as a real estate and services market – and its absorption,
in these senses, of the Klang valley and other parts of Selangor – there was no material reason why the Selangor Economic Development Corporation needed to work
with the electronics firms to upgrade their operations, deepen their linkages with
local SMEs, and thus improve their contribution to generalized prosperity. Indeed,
the SEDC's primary focus on land development – and thus real estate – provided
a far better prospect than the electronics industry for rentier accumulation (and,
indeed, for accumulation by corruption). In principle, such economic activities are
also a faster route to accumulation by Bumiputera and this, after all, was what the
Federal government was principally interested in, even though it did little for the
productive basis of the economy or for income inequality.

Federal policy change and regional initiatives

The economic recession that affected Malaysia and other Southeast Asian countries in the mid-1980s (doubling unemployment to 7.4 per cent by 1986)[14]
and Prime Minister Mahatir's imminent re-election campaign, seem to have
provided the contexts for a re-think of Federal government strategy towards
industrialization. The result was the country's first Industrial Master Plan (IMP1)
which ran from 1986 to 1995. IMP1 was the Federal government's first concerted
attempt to promote the upgrading of technological capabilities and skills coupled with the creation of greater linkages between the TNCs and locally-owned
SMEs.

Over the previous 10–15 years, manufacturing FDI, particularly in electronics, had developed few linkages, of technological significance, to indigenous manufacturing companies. TNCs invested in Malaysia knowing that the vast majority of the components and sub-assemblies required for their export activities would have to be imported (discussed further later). Even though manufacturing SMEs were hardly evident at that time and the government had failed to lever the TNCs in terms of joint-venture ownership arrangements, there were no incentives – that might otherwise have emanated from the nature of corporate governance – to link with locally-owned companies. As Table 6.1 shows, foreign ownership of the 'Malaysian' electronics industry has remained, since the industry's inception, very high. Consequently, unlike industrialization experiences elsewhere in East Asia, FDI-led industrialization in Malaysia has not stimulated significant, nationally-owned, export industries. Given that local input has remained towards the lower end of the production chain, there has been no 'product life-cycle effects' associated with the production strategies of the TNCs themselves, that might otherwise have provided incentives for local companies to upgrade to meet their requirements for higher value-added supplies, or opportunities for the latter to enter the export markets vacated by the former (cf. Jomo *et al.* 1997, Felker 2003).

In this context IMP1 introduced new training and skills development initiatives. A Human Resource Development Fund (HRDF) was created and, from 1993, improvement in the skills base of workforces was now a regulatory requirement for all firms with 50 or more employees. With a private-public contribution to the Fund amounting to one per cent of each firm's annual payroll, the government attempted to induce larger (effectively foreign) firms to begin investing in the skill-upgrading of the Malaysian workforce. A firm's contributions to the Fund could be reclaimed by sending workers to approved training courses, or deducted where in-house training programmes were provided. Any surpluses in the Fund were intended to contribute to the training of workers employed by locally-owned SMEs.

In the mid-1990s the second Industrial Master Plan (IMP2) was launched. With this Plan – more than 20 years after the start of electronics production in the country – the Government finally provided a framework for long-term

TABLE 6.1 Foreign ownership of fixed assets in electric/electronics industries, 1968–1998

Year	Foreign Ownership (%)
1968	70
1975	84
1980	80
1985	73
1990	89
1993	91
1998	83

Source: Rasiah (2002b)

industrial upgrading. As part of the country's 'Vision 2020' (the date by which it was hoped Malaysia would have joined the ranks of the advanced industrial nations) and indebted to Porter's (1990) notions of developing national competitive advantage, IMP2 adopted a strategy to move industries along the value chain to higher value-added activities such as research and development (R&D). In a conscious attempt to compete with Singapore, IMP2 (coupled with the government's 'Multimedia Super Corridor' project initiated in 1996 and located in the Klang Valley adjacent to Kuala Lumpur), represented an attempt to attract investment in more value-generating and durable projects such as regional headquarters of TNCs.

Following the East Asian economic crisis of the late 1990s, the Government pursued several time-limited measures to maintain Malaysia's attractiveness to foreign investors in export sectors. Many of these took the form of market liberalization. For instance, it relaxed export conditions that had limited foreign firms in export-oriented industries from servicing the domestic market. It also increased the tax incentives and exemptions available to export sectors and the (limited) local sourcing conditionalities that had existed were allowed to lapse in conformity with ASEAN and WTO trade agreements. These flirtations with pro-active industrial policy resulted in the creation by Intel and Motorola (among others) of their own supplier development programmes. While each TNC could have developed 'in-house' programmes these could also be delivered in an aggregated fashion in regions like Penang where coherent sets of manufacturing activities had already been created by TNC co-location practices.

In principle, these new regulations did help to foster greater linkages between multinationals and local suppliers. In practice, however, it was only in Penang that the local institutional capacity necessary to the maximization of the possibilities for, and benefits of, these linkages, successfully emerged. Indeed, as with so much else in the Malaysian record of trying to convert electronics FDI into a tool for genuine development, the state of Penang was ahead of the game.

By the late 1980s, facilitated by the PDC, TNCs in the region had created a unique skills development programme. From 1989, the Penang Skills Development Centre (PSDC), with the active participation of TNC executives on its Board, began to provide specialist training courses. With the PSDC as a model, similar skills development centres, subsequent to the aforementioned Federal Government initiatives , were later created by other Malaysian states, but none of them have been as successful as the PSDC, nor harnessed as much commitment from the multinational firms[15] (cf. Best and Rasiah 2003).

Alongside its attempts to improve the skill base of the labour force, the government also attempted to promote linkages between the TNCs and local SMEs. To complement the tax incentives to encourage TNCs to engage in R&D, etc. an Industrial Linkage Programme (ILP) was instituted in the early 1990s. Whatever government hopes for the Programme originally might have been, today the ILP is little more than a database of local suppliers that MIDA provides for the TNCs. Where their subsidiaries source from locally-owned firms on this list, they are entitled to further tax allowances. Unfortunately, the ILP seems never to have been used by any electronics TNC to access local suppliers.[16] The ineffectiveness of the ILP underlines the limits of fiscal strategies (to connect TNCs with local suppliers) where the technological and skill base of SMEs is underdeveloped.

In the 1990s Malaysia was a recipient of a second wave of US and Japanese investment, together with increased flows from Taiwan and South Korea. To the former staples of the Malaysian electronics industry (semiconductors and consumer electronics), this new investment added computer peripherals and hard disk drives (HDD) in particular. Again Penang was the preferred site and received major investments by the likes of Maxtor, Conner, Hitachi Metals, Control Data and Applied Magnetics. Between 1990 and 1996, for instance, employment by HDD firms in Penang increased from 2,600 to nearly 32,000. By 1996, the HDD segment provided 27 per cent of all employment in Penang's electronics cluster (Haggard et al. 1998). Many of Malaysia's 'show-case' local firms (all of them in Penang) emerged from this wave of FDI. Trans Capital Holdings, for instance, evolved at this time from initial ties to Connor into a relatively diversified contract manufacturer. Eng Teknologi and UNICO were early spin-offs (by local managers) from Intel's operations in Penang. Incorporated in 1992, the former developed into an upper tier OEM[17] supplier from initial ties to Maxtor (Rasiah 1999b). Symptomatic of the problems addressed here, however, very few other Malaysian-owned electronics firms have achieved this status.[18] While we pick up the significance of this point later, we first need to examine the economic consequences of the second social policy issue with which we are concerned: immigration.

Enter migration policy

Compared with other East Asian countries, Malaysia has fared relatively poorly in terms of its investment in R&D and in the production of scientific, engineering and technical personnel (Table 6.2). Consequently, many commentators have

TABLE 6.2 Technology indicators for selected East and Southeast Asian countries

Country	R&D (% of GDP)	High-tech exports (% of manufactured exports), 2001	Scientists and Engineers per million capita	Tertiary Science and Engineering Students (% of population), 1998
Hong Kong	0.45 (2000)	19.5	n/a	0.49
Korea	2.68 (2000)	29.1	2,319 (2000)	1.65
Taiwan	2.3 (2000)	35.0 (1998)	2,980 (1998)	1.06
Japan	2.98 (2000)	26.0	5,095 (2000)	0.64
Singapore	1.88 (2000)	59.7	4,140 (2000)	0.47
Thailand	0.1 (1997)	31.1	142 (1997)	0.19
Indonesia	0.1 (1994)	13.4	206 (1998)	0.23
Malaysia	0.5 (2000)	56.9	159 (998)	0.13
Philippines	0.2 (1999)	70.2	179 (1996)	0.55

Source: Ritchie (2005: 753)

emphasized Malaysia's need to import more of its advanced technicians and researchers (cf. Ernst 2003).

Unfortunately, the supposed skills shortages do not seem to be reflected in the employment needs of the companies themselves. A shortage of technical and engineering personnel would only be evident if the Malaysian electronics industry were, indeed, upgrading decisively to more capital intensive and higher value-added operations. In contrast to beliefs that linkages to TNCs encourage techno-logical upgrading by local firms, recent findings by Clarke *et al.* (2002) suggest this has not been true of Malaysian electronics. As we have argued earlier, it is more likely that electronics TNCs have continued to treat Malaysia as a relatively low-cost assembly platform; a common strategy, particularly for East Asian TNCs in Southeast Asia (Yamashita 1991, UNDP 1994, Taylor 1995).

Noor *et al.* (2002) suggest that Malaysia's problem stems from the fact that too large a technology gap (between TNCs and local firms) now exists for spillovers to occur. Questions about the willingness of multinationals to transfer skills and tech-nology remain important, but alongside these are concerns about Malaysia's own abilities to manage its manufacturing labour markets. We suggest that the govern-ment's inability to 'tighten' the labour market in lower-skilled occupations is also important to an understanding of the current situation in Malaysian electronics.

We know from the contrasting experiences of Hong Kong and Taiwan in the 1980s that where governments allow lower-skilled labour markets to be system-atically replenished through migration (as did the colonial government of Hong Kong), they tend to depress the likelihood that firms will invest in higher-value operations that require less lower skilled labour (Henderson 1994). Unfortunately for Malaysia, it has followed the Hong Kong 'model' in this sense, rather than the Taiwanese one. Rather than experiencing a decisive increase in the demand for technical and engineering personnel, the Malaysian electronics industry has become increasing dependent on the import of lower-skilled migrant workers.

Growth in the import of lower-skilled labour (largely from Indonesia, but with smaller numbers from other Southeast and South Asian countries) coincided with the liberalization of the economy and the boom in foreign investment in the late 1980s and early 1990s. In absolute terms, the use of migrant labour in the electri-cal and electronics industries mushroomed from 1,024 in 1990 to 46,470 in 1996 (10.7 per cent of all employment in the sector). While the crisis years of 1997–99 saw decreases, by 2000 the proportion was back to 10 per cent (Table 6.3) and has continued on an upward trend ever since.[19] As a consequence, electronics is now running the construction industry (typically, in many countries, a large user of migrant labour) close as an importer of migrant workers.

Migrant labour is a key dynamic affecting one of the potential gains from FDI: skills transfers associated with capital deepening. While government guidelines place limits on the extent to which firms can import low-skilled labour (one-third of the domestic labour employed), in practice the government allows as much as half of a firm's workforce to be low-skilled foreign migrants. When subcontracting arrangements are taken into account, finished or semi-finished products exported

TABLE 6.3 Proportions of semi and unskilled migrant workers in Malaysian manufacturing, 1981–2000

Year	Total Manufacturing (%)			Electrical & Electronics (%)		
	Total	Local	Migrant	Total	Local	Migrant
1981	100	99.0	1.0	100	99.7	0.3
1982	100	98.8	1.2	100	99.7	0.3
1983	100	98.7	1.3	100	99.7	0.3
1984	100	98.4	1.6	100	99.7	0.3
1985	100	98.4	1.6	100	99.6	0.4
1986	100	98.5	1.5	100	99.7	0.3
1987	100	98.4	1.6	100	99.7	0.3
1988	100	98.3	1.7	100	99.7	0.3
1989	100	98.3	1.7	100	99.7	0.3
1990	100	98.0	2.0	100	99.5	0.5
1991	100	98.3	1.7	100	99.4	0.6
1992	100	96.8	3.2	100	99.1	0.9
1993	100	93.8	6.2	100	96.7	3.3
1994	100	91.2	8.8	100	94.5	5.5
1995	100	89.8	10.2	100	93.0	7.0
1996	100	85.9	14.1	100	89.3	10.7
1997	100	86.1	13.9	100	90.6	9.4
1998	100	86.4	13.6	100	91.3	8.7
1999	100	86.8	13.2	100	91.9	8.1
2000	100	86.1	13.9	100	90.0	10.0

Source: Department of Statistics, Government of Malaysia, Malaysia Manufacturing Census

by TNCs must have utilized thousands of imported workers staggered across different labour-intensive sites in the production network.

While the import of lower-skilled foreign workers seems to have contributed to the depression of wages (Wangle 2001),[20] it may have had a more deleterious 'lock-in' effect. The increased import of lower-skilled labour throughout the 1990s may have insulated the electronics industry from the competitive effects of lower labour costs in neighbouring countries. In other circumstances – those of tight low-skilled labour markets – such low wage competition could have contributed to increased investment in more capital intensive and higher valued-added processes and products (as it did in Singapore, for instance). In Malaysia, however, the availability of foreign migrants, willing to accept lower wages (see Ishida and Hassan 2000) seems to have helped many foreign firms to maintain their traditional utilization of Malaysia as a regional hub for low-cost, labour-intensive assembly of imported intermediate goods.

Stalling industrial upgrading

The stalling of Malaysia's industrialization project stems directly from the problems of industrial upgrading. In the electronics industry, the prospects for upgrading had many favourable conditions. In terms of time and access to relevant knowledge, for instance, Malaysia has had nearly four decades to 'learn' from foreign multinationals and develop its indigenous manufacturing capabilities. For most of that period, global competition was far less intense than it would be now for a developing country seeking to industrialize through electronics production. Additionally, and in spite of our earlier criticisms, compared with the large majority of developing countries, Malaysia has had a well-established system of economic planning with a range of financial incentives and – if we take into account local state initiatives – proactive industrial policies. Yet Malaysian industrialization exhibits many signs of a process that has begun to stall with local electronics firms unable to successfully deviate from their original mode of integration into the GPNs of foreign multinationals.

Some, such as Best (1997), have argued that the competitive advantage of Malaysian electronics has shifted from its original model as a low-wage, labour-intensive manufacturing platform to a provider of low-cost, high-volume products based on increasingly automated manufacturing activities and specialist capabilities in assembly, testing, and packaging. While Best admits that this transition is not yet sufficient to compete with nations of superior production and innovation capabilities (such as Taiwan and Singapore), he still over-estimates the extent to which the electronics industry has shifted away from low-wage, labour intensive functions. With large segments of Malaysian electronics continuing to be oriented to the production of commoditized goods, its export performance is now under threat from China's increasing competitiveness in electronic and other manufactured products (cf. Lall and Albaladejo 2004, Yusuf and Nabeshima 2009).

Other reports and commentaries arguably provide a more realistic assessment of upgrading in the country's electronics industry. Commissioned by the Penang Development Corporation in 2001, and probably the most authoritative report on Malaysia's electronics SMEs to date, notes that there is:

> A sense of crisis regarding a possible decline of local industrial activities . . . (and) that the development of the capability of local companies to supply parts to MNCs is an urgent necessity.
>
> (JIAC 2001: 1–1)

So pessimistic is this report about the state of Malaysia's electronics SMEs that it is worth quoting two of its observations.

> . . . there is a general shortage of such SI (supporting industries) as parts and processing service industries (precision machining, precision stamping, precision plastic processing, heat treatment, electrical and electronic parts and plating), materials industries (resin . . . metal . . . and chemicals) and other industries (industrial waste treatment, jigs, press dies, plastic dies and automation machinery) to support the operation of MNCs.
>
> (JIAC 2001: S-2)

> the ratio of SMIs (small and medium industries) which have reached the level (excellent) required by MNCs is quite low, ie. 24% in terms of processing, 14% in terms of production control and 15% in terms of management control out of the 103 SMIs diagnosed . . .
>
> (JIAC 2001: S-3)

Another of the report's observations hints at the root of the problem.

> . . . the level of awareness of problems on the part of SI is rather low when it comes to the necessary improvement of quality control and floor control, both of which are key ingredients of production. The situation is judged to be the result of the fact that *SMIs are not fully aware of the importance of production engineering because of their status as subcontractors of MNCs and the fact that their production activities follow the instructions given by MNCs.*
>
> (JIAC 2001: S-3, emphasis added)

Here the report's authors seem to be suggesting that the SMEs have remained content with their original roles in the GPNs of the various TNCs, and have failed to lever their involvement in the GPNs to upgrade their processes and products. Whatever assistance has been available from the federal or regional governments, it seems, has been ineffective.

As Ernst's (2003) assessment of the industry suggests, Malaysia has never developed a deep, multi-tiered industrial supply structure in electronics. Rather, with the exception of the few mentioned earlier, the contribution of indigenous firms to export performance continues to be dominated by SMEs disproportionately engaged in low-value 'lower tier' assembly activities. The relative lack of local suppliers in higher-tier supply positions implies a shallow level of industrial specialisation and thus a 'thin' range of domestic supply capabilities. While there has been no research on the structural asymmetry in local supply activities (detailed supply-chain mappings have only been conducted for the Malaysian automobile sector), circumstantial data is available to support our contention.

It seems that Malaysia has been historically more dependent upon the import of intermediate components in electronics than other East Asian NICs. For instance, Takeuchi (1997, referenced in Ernst 2003) found that in the late 1980s, 43 per cent of Malaysia's final product exports were based upon intermediate imports, compared with 37 per cent of Korea's. Such figures have worsened since then. For instance, in 2003, RM108.7 billion (US$28.5 billion), or 73.1 per cent of all electronic imports, stemmed from intermediate components used in the production of finished and semi-finished electronics exports.[21] In that same year, the import of intermediate components represented over 54 per cent of the total value (RM199.5 billion – US$52.5 billion) of electronics exports. Thus the value of locally produced content was 46 per cent of electronics exports and from all we know about the asymmetrical structure of the Malaysian electronics industry, the majority of this must have been produced by TNCs rather than by locally-owned firms.[22]

Other data points to the relative weakness of Malaysia's local supply base. For instance, total factor productivity (TFP) – a proxy for the extent to which knowledge and technology transfer has occurred between foreign multinationals and local suppliers – dramatically declined in the 1990s, from an average of just over 14 per cent in the first half of that decade, to just 2 per cent by 1996 (Ernst 2003) and is currently in decline once again (Yusuf and Nabeshima 2009). This decline in TFP underlines the extent to which local firms have failed to benefit from spill-over effects, technology transfers and other linkages to the foreign TNCs.

Malaysian electronics in the 'race to the bottom'

This limited upgrading in the Malaysian electronics industry means that it is now exposed to the competitive pressure of China's export 'machine'. While recent high-profile plant closures, and a re-location of their operations to China,[23] have spurred Malaysian government officials to fear for the future of the country's electronics industry, the surprise is that it has taken so long for these concerns to be acknowledged. After all, China's rise as an electronics exporter emerged long before its accession to the WTO in 2001. For instance, by 1990, China had exceeded Malaysia in terms of all FDI inflows, capturing 9 per cent of the world total, as against Malaysia's 7 per cent. By 2002, China's share of FDI inflows had increased to 33 per cent while Malaysia's share had dropped to a mere 2 per cent.[24]

By the mid- to late 1990s, China had effectively equalled Malaysia in its export performance in electronics. Between 1995 and 1999, for instance, Malaysia supplied 6.4 per cent, and China 6 per cent, of world exports in electronic products (Sturgeon and Lester 2002). Over this period and, indeed, since the mid-1980s, China had been involved in much the same mode of GPN integration in the global electronics industry as had Malaysia; namely, it had been focussed on labour-intensive assembly activities that transformed imported intermediate goods into finished or semi-finished products. The crucial difference was that China had rapidly, and more effectively than Malaysia, upgraded its indigenous production capacities and, in so doing, decreased its need for imported intermediate components. Additionally, it had far outstripped Malaysia in terms of its scientific and research base (Shafaeddin 2004).

Lall and Albaladejo (2004) have argued that any East Asian country with industries based on medium and lower level technologies are at risk from China's industrialization and export drive. Malaysian industries, as they suggest and as we have indicated earlier, fall into this category. In the concluding section we summarize the reasons why this has happened and indicate the general implications of our analysis.

Conclusion: The limits to Malaysian industrialization and what it might mean

Although the Malaysian industrialization project has not yet reached its limits, or 'stalled', from the perspective of the country's electronics industry and in the light of China's increasing competitive advantage, its prospects seem, at best, uncertain. How might we summarize the reasons for this and what lessons might be drawn from the experience?

The first and most general point to be made, is also the obvious one: it is one thing for a manufacturing industry to emerge, but quite another for it to move, over time, into higher value-adding operations that are a *sine qua non* for high-wage economies capable of delivering generalized prosperity. Achieving this, in developing economies, often involves working against the grain of their supposed 'comparative advantage' to encourage process and product upgrading, and thus engagements with the world economy that rely less on lower skilled, lower value, assembly activities. The history of 'late industrialization' in East Asia and elsewhere shows that rarely can this be left to individual companies responding to 'market signals'; manufacturing needs to be treated as a strategic industry and thus one that is supported by state planning.

Where the bulk of the given industry is foreign-owned – as with the Malaysian electronics industry – this support, in practice, involves encouragement for the growth and upgrading of locally-owned SMEs. It is of decisive importance that these SMEs emerge from the lower tier supply functions that they originally provided for the TNCs and alter the nature (in terms of knowledge and technological basis) of their integration into the global production networks of the TNCs concerned. It is only in these ways that the benefits of GNP-local firm linkages can be maximized for the domestic economy as a whole.

In as far as the problems for the upgrading of the Malaysian electronics industry have been domestically derived, there seem to have been three related issues. The first was the fact that the industry emerged from the context of a politically-charged, racially divided society, where – rightly – the government instituted an anti-poverty and re-distributional programme as a route to social harmony and as a central moment of its development project. The problem with this was that as the programme involved 'affirmative action' on behalf of the Bumiputera, it had the consequence of depressing the prospect that Chinese (or Indian)-Malaysians – the group in Malaysian society that originally (1970s) were best placed to become manufacturing entrepreneurs – would invest their resources and talents in that economic activity. Furthermore, the government support that was given to entrepreneurship from the 1980s onwards was not only heavily weighted towards encouraging entrepreneurship among the Bumiputera, but had no brief for encouraging manufacturing entrepreneurship in particular.

The second and related issue, was that the government sought to improve prosperity among the Bumiputera and, indeed, all sections of Malaysian society by any economic means available. This meant that opportunities for speculation and rentierism, far from being discouraged – as they had been in South Korea and Taiwan, for instance (in the interests of encouraging greater investment flows into productive activities) – were encouraged in spectacular fashion. The consequence, in addition to persistently high levels of inequality, rampant corruption and a key trigger for the economic crisis of the late 1990s (see, Chapter 4, Henderson *et al.*

2002b, Gomez and Jomo 1997), has been that Malaysians, of whatever race, have tended to avoid manufacturing entrepreneurship.[25]

Within this latter context (opportunities for rentierism) the Federal government has encouraged and supported the automobile and heavy industries but, until late in the day, left the electronics industry largely to its own devises. Only in Penang, via the state government's PDC and related agencies, has the electronics industry been given systematic strategic attention. Unfortunately these efforts, on their own, have been unable to lift Malaysian electronics SMEs into the upgraded, higher tier supply operations that are essential to the industry's long-term survival.

The third issue that has constrained the prospects for electronics upgrading has been the government's migration policy. Just as in Hong Kong a generation earlier, the government's refusal to engineer a tight labour market for lower-skilled occupations has meant that electronics firms – TNCs and SMEs alike – have been able to remain competitive without having to invest in more knowledge-intensive, higher value-added operations. With China's (together with India, the world's ultimate low cost producer) assault on world electronics markets, this strategy (low wage, low to medium technology production) now seems to be unsustainable.

For over 20 years, Malaysian analysts of the country's industrial scene (for instance, Salih and Yusof 1989) have been pointing to the folly of the government's lack of attention to manufacturing SMEs. Seemingly for ideological reasons, these warnings were not heeded. With the Chinese dragon looming large on the manufacturing horizon, the window of opportunity within which the electronics industry could have been upgraded is now rapidly closing. It may not be too long, therefore, before the Malaysian industrial project lurches from 'stalling' to 'stalled'; before, in other words, its limits have been reached.

7

CHINA AND GLOBAL TRANSFORMATION

At various points throughout the preceding chapters the transformation of the Chinese political economy has inevitably entered the frame. On those occasions, however, only limited attention has been paid to China's internal development since the late 1970s and even less to its external consequences. In this chapter I begin to look more closely at what appear to be some of the implications of the contemporary re-emergence of China as a global economic and political actor. In the following (and final) chapter, I extend the analysis broached here to a consideration of what the rise of China might mean for the nature of globalization. In both chapters my predominant focus is on the consequences, for the rest of the developing world, of China as the world's most significant 'rising power'.

China and the crisis of the developing world

Recuperating the notion of crisis first utilized in Chapter 2 (crisis as a dialectic of danger and opportunity), in this chapter I turn to the impacts of China's contemporary engagement with the developing world by examining the empirics and logic of that engagement along a number of 'vectors': processes that carry and project China's transformative dynamics. Among the vectors that reasonably could warrant attention here, given space constraints, I can deal only with three of them and in a schematic way at that. Consequently this chapter does not tackle such vital questions as the environmental impacts of China's global expansion or how the Chinese government, with its US$2 trillion plus foreign exchange reserves, is responding to a disfunctional international financial architecture. Similarly, it does not deal directly with some of the more general questions of global governance or with the geo-political implications of China's re-emergence on the world stage. It does, however, attend to some of the other 'big questions': namely, the consequences for the developing world of China's trade dynamics, its aid and human rights policies and its search for energy security. Even in themselves these three vectors, taken both separately and collectively, are clearly ones on which much of the future of the developing world will depend. With regard to energy security, in particular, they are also vectors around which geo-political tensions are already reverberating.

Trade

Imports: The sheer scale of the dramatic and sustained growth of the Chinese economy has massively expanded China's dependence on the import of primary commodities from elsewhere in the developing world. Thus with the continuing reduction in agricultural land (consequent on urbanization) and the flow of peasants into the cities (as result of the rising demand for industrial workers on the one hand and rural poverty on the other), agricultural productivity in China has stagnated. As a result, the country has become increasingly dependent on the import of food and other agricultural commodities. Thus by 2004, China's trade deficit in foodstuffs amounted to US$3.7 billion (Kaplinsky 2005: 206). While much of this – in grains, for instance – was composed of imports from the developed world (and the USA in particular), some of the shortfall has been sourced from the developing world. Well-known examples include the import of soya and oil seeds from Brazil and Argentina. Thus, for instance, China's share of Brazil's total oil seed exports rose from 20 per cent in 2001 to 30 per cent in 2004 (Gottschalk and Prates 2005).

Similarly, China's increasing demand for metals to feed its industrial revolution has impacted on developing world exports. Thus increasing proportions of Zambia's copper exports are heading for China, as are the Congo's exports of cobalt and copper, Zimbabwe's exports of cobalt and Ghana's exports of aluminium (bauxite). China's share in Chile and Peru's exports of copper, for instance, increased respectively, from 9 and 8 per cent of the total in 2001 to 17 and 19 per cent by 2004 (Gottschalk and Prates 2005). Although most of these metal exports continue to be in the form of ores rather than the higher value-added processed metals, it is still the case that the rising prices that they have helped induce are, in principle, beneficial to the economic welfare of the countries concerned. The fact that many of these benefits may not be reaching the workers in these industries, nor the bulk of the populations of the countries concerned, is not China's responsibility, but is rather a product of the inequalities of wealth and power evident in those countries themselves.

There is, however, at least one primary commodity where China's import demand is having a detrimental effect. With its burgeoning furniture and pulp industries, China is now one of the world's largest importers of timber. Unfortunately, in the process, it has become the world's largest importer of illegally-logged timber, particularly from the rain forests of Burma, Malaysia, Thailand, Indonesia and Papua New Guinea (Rapa 2007). As a consequence, some of China's demand for timber is having adverse environmental implications and at the same time is having few positive welfare implications for the countries concerned (in terms of poverty reduction, for instance).

With regard to China's rising demand for manufactured commodities the picture, for the moment, is more clearly positive than mixed. Given the nature of China's industrial economy – with its predominant emphasis on textiles and garments, electronics and engineered metal products (e.g. automobiles) – the principal regional source of manufactured imports from the developing world are the industrializing (and recently industrialized) countries elsewhere in East Asia. Thus, with regard to textiles – though definitely not garments (see later) – there is evidence to suggest that China has been increasing its imports from other parts of East Asia and from South Asia (e.g. Lau 2007). With regard to electronic products, most of China's component imports have come from South Korea, Taiwan, Singapore, Malaysia and Thailand (and, of course, from Japan, which by definition does not figure in the current analysis). So far, this dynamic has had a positive impact in terms of employment, wages and other economic benefits for the countries concerned. What is unclear, however, is how long such import demands will continue. With the reconfiguration of electronics production networks in East Asia, consequent on rising skills, but lower production costs in China, investment strategies of TNCs and rising costs elsewhere in the region, it seems likely that some component production (at least for those that embody medium level technologies, such as hard drives and some other computer peripherals) is likely to shift to China itself. Evidence of this is beginning to emerge, for instance, from Malaysia and Thailand (see Chapter 6, Phillips and Henderson 2009, Yusuf 2008, Yusuf and Nabeshima 2009).

Exports: If the implications for the developing world of China's demand for imports is mixed (with both dangers and opportunities involved), the consequences of the fact that it is a manufacturing and exporting powerhouse seem more clear-cut.

China's capacity in labour intensive manufactured exports seems to be helping to drive a 'race to the bottom' in parts of the developing world. With regard to textiles, a recent World Bank study (Winters and Yusuf 2007: 89–92) reports that while exports to China have thus far benefited East Asian producers, by 2020 the situation is likely to have reversed with Indonesia and Vietnam, for instance, suffering contractions in their respective industries of around 9 per cent. The study's projections suggest that garments industries will be hit more heavily with declines of around 19 per cent in Vietnam and North Africa (principally Egypt), for instance. Other research reports the consequences of China's exports to the US, EU, etc., for garments industries elsewhere in the developing world. Subsequent to end of Multi Fibre Agreement, Lesoto's garments industry has all but been wiped out, while South Africa's supply of garments to its domestic market has declined from 80 to about 25 per cent (Kaplinsky and Morris 2008). Furthermore, recent estimates suggest that between 2003–5, 130,000 workers were laid-off in Sri Lanka's garments industry as a direct result of Chinese competition in third markets (Perera 2006).

With further regard to Chinese competition in exports to third markets (e.g. USA) – including higher technology products such as electronics and auto components – much recent research on Latin America has been equivocal about the extent to which China poses a threat to their indigenous or foreign owned manufacturing industries, in spite of evidence in the media that suggests that Mexican-based producers, for instance, have been badly damaged with growing unemployment in the maquiladoras bordering the USA. The work of Jenkins and his colleagues (2008), however, is more consistent with media concerns. He shows that with regard to Latin American manufactured exports to the USA, Chinese competition is likely to have more serious consequences than has been recognized in the scholarly literature. With regard to East Asian manufacturing industries, work by Lall and Albaladejo (2004) suggests that low and medium technology industries there are seriously at risk from Chinese competition. This includes not only recently industrialized countries such as Malaysia (Chapter 6, Yusuf 2008), but also more mature industrial economies such as South Korea.

Aid and human rights

China's foreign aid derives largely from four central government and a variety of provincial government agencies. The former consist of the Ministry of Commerce, the China Export-Import Bank (Exim), the China Development Bank and a variety of less significant actors (which can be grouped as the fourth agent), such as the Ministries of Health, Education, etc. Of these the Ministry of Commerce (which contains the Department of Foreign Aid) and the Export-Import Bank are currently the most important, though the Development Bank is reputed to have substantial reserves. In 2005, Exim alone had a larger investment portfolio in Africa – US$15 billion – than any of its equivalents from the US, Japan or Britain (Alden 2007: 24). The latter have also become significant actors in their own right, with the governments of Anhui and Sichuan, for instance – via their state-owned construction firms – having direct links with particular provincial governments in Angola, and Sichuan currently co-operating with the government of Ogun State, Nigeria, to build a US$50 million pharmaceutical plant (Alden 2007: 29).

With this multiplicity of funding sources and the diverse (indeed, given Provincial involvement, competing) interests associated with them, it is probably a misreading of the situation to assume that there is a unified 'strategy' when it comes to China's aid programme. That question notwithstanding, there seem to be at least two issues worthy of comment here: the consequences of China's aid regime and the potential human rights issues as Chinese firms begin to expand their investment in other parts of the developing world.

Given its historic (official) commitment to non-interference in the internal affairs of other countries (Taylor 2006), it is, perhaps, unsurprising that China's overseas aid programme is effectively circumventing the political conditionalities now associated with 'Western' aid, whether the latter comes from international or national agencies. Judged against the dubious lending standards of the World Bank or – particularly – USAID in earlier periods, for instance, China's current aid programme (which, among others, includes grants and loans to countries with dubious human rights records such as Burma, Turkmenistan, Uzbekistan and Sudan) seems relatively unproblematic. If there is a problem, however, it is that international lending standards (at least formally, if not informally), have moved on. Thus while Chinese loans and other forms of assistance provide a politically easy route to development finance for cash-strapped regimes, they release those regimes (some of them highly corrupt and, indeed, predatory on their populations) from the pressures they might otherwise be under to drive through political reform. Unlike their international counterparts, it is a matter of course, for instance, for Chinese aid agencies to refuse to engage with NGOs concerned with the human rights and governance implications of their policies and – to take one Chinese example – the China Export-Import Bank consistently fails to conduct environmental and social impact analyses (now routine for international aid agencies) prior to investing in given projects (Alden 2007: Ch. 1). One example of recent Chinese loan activity will suffice to underline the general problem.

China, as with USAID, and many other national aid programmes, lends money predominantly in accord with its commercial and strategic interests. For instance, given its involvement in Angola's oil industry (referred to later), it is not a surprise that the Angolan regime has been a recipient of China's largesse. Angola, however, is a country where around 25 per cent of state revenues 'disappear' year on year and one that has a President who is believed to be implicated in these 'disappearances'. In 2005, China's Exim Bank delivered US$2 billion in aid to the Angolan regime. Whereas much of this has been invested in much-needed transport and infrastructure, the government partners in receipt of aid were not the relevant ministries, as is usually the case, but the President's office, raising questions as to what proportion of the loan in fact ended-up in productive investment.

While China's foreign aid programme seems to herald both dangers and opportunities for recipient countries, a recent series of agreements with the Congo may be destined to put Chinese aid to the developing world on a different plane. In September 2007, the China Exim Bank agreed to provide US$8.5 billion to support infrastructure development in the Congo, a country that is home to 10 per cent of the world's copper reserves and over 30 per cent of the world's cobalt. In early 2008, China provided a further US$5 billion in development loans to the Congo. These latter funds are destined to support the provision of hospitals, schools and two universities. Additionally, Socomin, the Chinese-Congolese joint venture company that will mine the metals, will be required to commit 0.5 per cent of all investment on training the workforce and on technology transfer, while 3 per cent will be spent on social provision for the local community. Furthermore, Socomin is specifically required to subcontract 12 per cent of its work to Congolese companies and limit its Chinese workforce (an increasing bone of contention in Africa; see later) to 20 per cent of the total (Komesaroff 2008).

While China is set to make between US$14 and 40 billion (the estimates vary) from its copper and cobalt mines, confirming that this is far from an arrangement driven by altruism, these agreements between the Chinese partners and the Congo government are unprecedented in the history of foreign aid to the developing world. Already, the Congo government has begun to renegotiate its agreements with European and US mining companies, using the Chinese arrangement as a benchmark. Consequently this development seems potentially to be highly positive for the Congo. Should it become a model for aid and investment activity elsewhere in Africa, it could help to revolutionize the principles on which international aid, in general, is provided.

Set alongside such positive developments, there is beginning to be concern about the types of labour processes and working conditions that are likely to result from Chinese FDI or, indeed, Chinese outsourcing in the developing world. It is in some African countries that these problems are likely to be experienced initially as Chinese firms are now the leading foreign players in the development of transport infrastructure there and are increasingly prominent in telecommunications, mining, logging and, of course, energy extraction. Alden (2007: 14), for instance, reports that more than 800 Chinese companies are now operating in 49 African countries with 480 of these involved in joint ventures with African firms. While these investments are undoubtedly positive in terms of economic development, their implications for social development are less clear. Notwithstanding the fact that many of these companies generally prefer to bring (indentured) Chinese workers with them – thus leaving local Africans unemployed – it is likely that working for such companies leaves much to be desired. While the working conditions in the sub-contracted plants of the US and European companies that drive, for instance, many of the garments and footwear production networks in the developing world remain highly problematic (among a vast academic and popular literature underlining the problems, see McVeigh 2007), this should not absolve the activities of Chinese firms. While there is little evidence available from the developing world on which to base robust conclusions about working conditions in Chinese-invested operations, the treatment of rural migrants in Chinese industrial cities such as Dongguan and Guangzhou (who suffer working and living conditions that would have been familiar to Engels in 1840s Manchester)[1] and across the country's urban-industrial landscape, does not augur well for the treatment of workers in, say, Pakistan or Nigeria, Indonesia or South Africa, where China's 'cultural ethnocentrism' is likely to further influence management attitudes to their workforces.

Energy security

Among the vectors discussed in this chapter, it is China's search for energy security that is probably attracting the most attention; if not from researchers, then certainly from those concerned with international security policy. Among the countries where China already has exploration and/or supply contacts are, for oil, Kazakhstan, Iran, Saudi Arabia, Qatar, Sudan, Nigeria, Angola, Venezuela; and for gas, Turkmenistan, Burma, Bolivia and Algeria (Boekestein and Henderson 2005). While, in principle, Chinese demand is likely to bring economic benefits – and thus considerable opportunities – to such resource rich countries, in practice that is only true where the revenues are redistributed and/or invested in productive projects (only in Venezuela are revenues currently redistributed). Beyond the question of the economic – and broader welfare – benefits that may be derived from China's search for secure supplies of oil and gas, at least two other issues arise that are politicising developments along this vector.

The first of these concerns China's bilateral relations with some very dubious regimes. In 2003, for instance, 41 per cent of Sudan's exports and 23 per cent of Angola's went to China (Jenkins and Edwards 2006, Table 1: 25). In both cases, these exports were almost totally made up of oil shipments. Like the Sudan, Angola is also an example of a country with an authoritarian, corrupt, predatory regime. Unfortunately the majority of oil rich countries have regimes that are variations on this theme, so China cannot be faulted with allowing its (state owned) oil companies to do business with them, just as there has been no attempt, by US and European governments, for instance, to constrain the activities of many of 'their' oil companies in countries where the respect for human rights verges on the non-existent.

In spite of the ether of hypocrisy surrounding pronouncements by politicians and the media in the US and EU on China's role in some oil rich countries, the charge that does seem to stick against the Chinese government, is the nature of its relations with Sudan. Given the Sudanese government's complicity in the genocide taking place in the Dafur region and its export dependence on China, as indicated earlier, China, in principle, must have significant leverage over the regime in Khartoum, particularly given the inability of the regime to sell its oil (at least legally) to other major consumers.[2] That this leverage has just begun to be exercised seems to be indicative of two things.[3] While the lack of respect for human rights in China is now a matter of (a very long) record, given the fact that since 1949 this has rarely involved the suppression of its own minorities (though there remain deeply problematic issues with regard to Tibet and with the Uighurs in Xinjiang), a reluctance to lever the Sudan regime is unlikely to be a product of the fact that the Chinese government is oblivious to human rights issues. For the moment, it is more likely to be a consequence of China's traditional bilateral relations with African countries, which going back to the 1950s have emphasized (at least officially) non-interference in the internal operations of other states (Taylor 2006). Second, the relative absence of a popular concern in China with the human rights implications of China's external operations (the significant exception to this general rule is Hong Kong) is, once again, a reflection of a tightly controlled media (with an absence of a tradition of investigative journalism)[4] and the underdevelopment of an autonomous civil society.

The second question concerns the interface between China's search for oil and gas security and the geo-political ramifications of this. Among an array of issues that could be picked-up here, only two will be touched upon: SCO and the 'string of pearls'.

Founded in 2001, on the basis of a Chinese initiative, the Shanghai Co-operation Organization (SCO) now includes – in addition to China – Russia, Kazakhstan, Tajikistan, Uzbekistan and Kyrgyzstan as full members, while India, Pakistan, Iran and Mongolia have observer status (Lanteigne 2005: Chapter 4). Pakistan and Iran are currently seeking to become full members. While Chinese motives in SCO are many and diverse, it is likely that the principal reason for the Chinese initiative was its concern to wean the central Asian states from their economic and political reliance on Russia. Beyond that, the development of stable political relations with the potentially major oil and gas suppliers in the region has been high on the list (Boekestein and Henderson 2005). Although the physical logistics of supply from the various former Soviet republics are potentially problematic (though, for instance, China is currently constructing a pipeline to supply gas from a non-SCO member, Turkmenistan), inter-governmental relations via SCO should help to secure supplies should problems arise in the 'bottlenecks' of China's oil supply lines from the Persian Gulf: the Straits of Hormuz and Melaka. More recently, SCO members have begun to conduct joint military exercises and this has prompted speculation that SCO could develop into a military alliance similar to NATO (Alexandroni 2007).

Consistent with my earlier point about physical 'bottlenecks' turning into geopolitical ones, China seems to be engaged on a number of initiatives in the Indian Ocean which at least, in part, could constitute the early stages of a strategy to protect its oil supply lines from the Middle East and Africa. At Hambantota in Sri Lanka, for instance, Chinese companies are building a new port that could serve as a refuelling and docking facility for the Chinese navy as it extends its presence (currently confined to helping police pirate activities off the Horn of Africa) across the Indian Ocean. Additionally, and perhaps more importantly, in Pakistan's ethnically turbulent Balochistan province, the Chinese-built port at Gwadar became fully operational in 2009, turning an isolated sandy peninsula on the Arabian Sea into what could become the country's principal commercial port. Run by the Singapore Government's Port Authority (a favoured partner in the management of China's own ports), Gwadar has opened up new sea-borne trade routes to Afghanistan and Turkmenistan, along with China's Central Asian partners in the Shanghai Co-operation Organization and its own, land-locked, north-western provinces.

With an estimated total investment of around US$1.2 billion (including oil refineries) from China's Exim Bank, the Chinese government's interests seem more than commercial. After all, Gwadar comes complete with a new naval facility that both the Pentagon and India's Ministry of Defence assume will emerge as a base for Chinese as well as Pakistani warships.

A Chinese naval presence in the Indian Ocean is nothing new. In the early fifteenth century, when China was at the zenith of it economic, political and cultural power, warships under the command of the legendary admiral, Zheng He, reached India, Arabia and East Africa establishing trade routes for Chinese silk and African ivory. Six centuries later, the main commodity shipped across the Indian Ocean, and of interest to China, is oil. At the core of both the Gwadar and Hambantota developments lies China's search for energy security. Fuelling its double-digit economic growth, China's demand for oil doubled between 1995 and 2005. By 2020, some projections suggest this demand will rise to 10 million barrels a day, or the equivalent of about 70 per cent of Saudi Arabia's oil output, an increase of two-thirds over 2007. While some of this demand will come from pipelines through Kazakhstan and Turkmenistan, more than 85 per cent will need to cross the Indian Ocean (Zajek 2008).

Like all powers, and particularly aspiring great powers, China needs to protect its energy supply lines. But the Indian Ocean presents special problems. Oil tankers loaded with Iranian oil in the Persian Gulf have to transit the Strait of Hormuz. Once across the Indian Ocean they, together with those from Saudi Arabia, Sudan and Angola (China's other principal suppliers) must negotiate the Straights of Melaka; sandwiched between Indonesia, Malaysia and Singapore and often reckoned to be the most actively pirated waterway in the world.

But piracy is unlikely to be China's real concern. Both the Straits of Hormuz and Melaka are bottlenecks that could be easily blocked by a future military rival. Chinese energy and military planners have to assume scenarios where within the next decade or so America might become a less benevolent observer of China's growing power than it currently is. With the US fifth Fleet patrolling the Indian Ocean, and an airbase on the British island territory of Diego Garcia sitting in the middle, China's fears about blocked oil supply lines could easily become reality should tensions over Taiwan, for instance, escalate into a Sino–US confrontation.

To pre-empt such a threat, the Indian Ocean is emerging as a focus for Chinese logistical and naval expansion. In addition to Pakistan and Sri Lanka, China is developing another container port with possible naval access in Chittagong, Bangladesh and a fourth port alongside the Burmese naval base at Kyaukphyu. On the Burmese island of Ramree, they are also developing oil and gas terminals.

A clear logic seems to lie behind all this activity. Gwadar is only 72 kilometres from Iran, and discussions are underway for a pipeline to link the port to Iran's oil fields. Having processed the oil in the Chinese built refineries, it would then be tankered to Burma. From there another two pipelines would take over, from Ramree to Kunming in China's Yunnan Province: one for gas from Burma, the other for oil from Gwadar, Saudi Arabia and Africa.

Other projects are being developed to circumvent what Chinese President, Hu Jintao, has termed the country's 'Malacca dilemma' (Lanteigne 2008, Kaplan 2009).[5] An Iranian funded pipeline to be built across northern Malaysia has been mooted since 2007, while there is an ambitious aim is for a 'Panama style' canal across the thin Kra isthmus of southern Thailand. If either of these were to come to fruition, they would dramatically shift the geo-politics of China's energy security.

Unsurprisingly these developments and their possible implications are beginning to alarm both the US and Indian governments. The Pentagon, obsessed by the prospect of China's naval expansion, refers to the new ports as China's 'string of pearls'. Even a casual monitoring of Pentagon-related and neo-conservative websites reveals how quickly China's Indian Ocean expansion has moved up America's security agenda in recent years. The emerging rivalry with India is, potentially, just as acute. As long ago as 1993 Zhao Nanqi, then head of the general logistics department of the People's Liberation Army (which controls China's navy), remarked that: 'we can no longer accept the Indian Ocean as an ocean only for the Indians' (quoted in Kaplan 2009). The Indian government seems to have taken note of possible Chinese intentions and has begun to modernize its navy. It plans to add three nuclear submarines and three aircraft carriers to its fleet by 2015. China, similarly, has built a submarine base on the island of Hainan, in the South China Sea, and it has recently announced plans to build four new aircraft carriers, naval vessels essential to the protection of oil tankers. If, into this mix, we add the possibility of a Japanese naval presence (subsequent to a possible change in the country's constitution)[6], the result of the China's legitimate search for energy security seems to be the likelihood of an increasingly militarized Indian Ocean.

Conclusion

I have briefly identified a series of 'crisis' dynamics that are arising along three vectors associated with the re-emergence of China as a global power. Consistent with the Chinese 'reading' of crisis employed here, it seems that 'rising China' and its international expansion, are likely to carry both dangers and opportunities for economic, social and political development in other parts of the developing world and, indeed, in some developed countries also. This is confirmed by other work, for instance on the role of China in the WTO and other institutions of global governance (e.g. Gu *et al.* 2008, Bergsten 2008) and by Kaplinsky's (2005) analysis of the implications of China's export competitiveness for industrialization in Sub-Saharan Africa. A key methodological (also political and policy) point arising from this chapter, however, is that rather than 'read-off' the likely consequences of China's external impact on the basis of our assumptions, hunches or prejudices, we need to be guided, on a case by case basis, by the empirical realities as they emerge. These realities are diverse and this needs to be appreciated. Only subsequently will we be able to develop the sort of aggregated picture that will be necessary to confirm whether or not the China-driven trajectories of transformation currently in-train, point to a better future for the developing world than that which the last 60 years (and more) of global transformation has delivered them.

The work in this chapter, in one sense has been similar to other work on the external implications of China's rise: it has treated China's interface with the rest of the world in a conceptually unmediated fashion. What has been largely missing here, as elsewhere, has been reflection on the possible consequences of China's growing economic and political power for the nature of globalization.[7] Yet in its own right, this is a potentially significant issue. It is so, because China's increasing global engagement across the economic and political spectra is changing the rules of the game. As a consequence, when China engages with any particular country or world-region (sub-Saharan Africa, Latin America, etc.), its companies, work forces, migrants, diplomatic personnel and (perhaps ultimately) its military, carry with them characteristics that are not only specifically Chinese (in terms of culture, values, priorities, etc.), but attributes that arise from the shifting power relations, organizational forms and associated expectations at the global level.

In an attempt to stimulate debate around these questions, the concluding chapter focuses on what the rise and international expansion of China may mean for the nature of the global economic-political order.

8
TOWARDS A GLOBAL-ASIAN ERA?

At the end of the twenty first century's first decade we stand, once again, at a hinge of history; one of those moments in social evolution where the superimposition of multiple contradictions from the past, is generating extraordinary economic and political turbulence and uncertainty. That these are reverberating on the human condition, from the individual psyche at one polarity to the geo-political relations of nation states at the other, is no surprise (cf. Appelbaum and Henderson 1995). The rise of China, and soon perhaps of India also, is beginning to compound existing contradictions and this is likely to further complicate the problems of our contemporary epoch.

Hinges, by their nature, are turning points. They allow doors to swing open to reveal new vistas, new possibilities, but they also allow them to swing back, at least partially closing down those possibilities. Until the trajectories for the future have been revealed and stabilized, the world is inevitably cast into crisis. As has been argued in earlier chapters, however, the crisis of the human condition we now confront should not be understood in the largely negative sense, evident in European languages. Rather, the dialectical process now afoot should be seen in a more positive light: one certainly fraught with danger (perhaps particularly environmental and political), but at the same time, one that exhibits major opportunities for continued economic development, human progress and prosperity.

In Chapter 2, I mobilized this notion of crisis to reflect on the current condition and future possibilities for the East Asian region in general. In Chapter 7, I utilized it to discuss some aspects of China's current engagement with the developing world. In this concluding chapter, it is mobilized as an heuristic devise once again, in order to grasp the implications of the rise of China for the nature of globalization.

In exploring this question of the future of globalization and thus the global political-economic order, I do not wish to imply that the nature of our global future – in so far as it may be a product of Chinese and, more generally, Asian developmental trajectories – has been immanent within the course of East Asian development for the last half-century or so. This has clearly not been the case. The only Asian country during that period that could have projected itself in such a way as to make a political difference globally (it certainly made an economic difference) was Japan. Successive Japanese governments since the 1960s, however, chose not to try to forge a world in Japan's image largely because of the terrible catastrophe that resulted in 1945 from their earlier attempt to forge East Asia in that image. Consequently, if we are on the cusp of a new form of globalization, it will be a form whose origins have arisen, first, from the re-emergence of China as a global power and, second, from a number of Asian powers that are emerging in its wake: India certainly, but further down the line perhaps a number of East Asian countries that might currently be conceived as the 'rising middle': for instance, Vietnam and Indonesia. It may even be a form of globalization that re-engages Japan as a key driving force.

The possible global implications of a 'rising India' and certainly of a 'rising middle' would require us to go far beyond the bounds of currently reasonable speculation. Consequently, the commentary presented in this chapter limits its speculative remit to the nature of globalization that seems currently to be implied by 'rising China'. Given that as social scientists we can never predict the future, then the best we can do is to try to identify the trajectories of the possible. As a consequence, the discussion and argument advanced here is couched in terms of a 'working hypothesis'. Specifically, I suggest that we may be on the verge of a new form of globalization: a 'Global-Asian Era' (GAE). If we are, then what might be the nature of a possible GAE and what might make it distinct from what has gone before?

Future globalizations

That the structures and contours of contemporary globalization are in flux is a proposition that would be accepted by nearly all analysts of the global political economy.[1] The issue, then, is not whether change is occurring, but rather the direction (or directions) of change and the nature of its possible outcomes. Consistent with the discourse of transformation that has informed my argument in this book, it is possible to envisage changes in the global economic-political order that could lead to a number of outcomes. Whatever they might be, it now seems unlikely that one of them will be the affirmation of the unipolar, US dominated order that I will refer to later as 'neoliberal globalization'. The Russian Government's reassertion in the Caucasus, in August 2008, of its geopolitical interests vis-á-vis the US and NATO, has surely symbolized the end of that particular possibility (Milne 2008). If it does, the outcome of the change process is unlikely to be a bipolar world, either, be it geo-politically and certainly not economically. There has been 'too much history' since the historical rupture of 1989–91 (the implosion of European state socialism) – not least with the rise of China – to allow for that.

If a bipolar world is not a serious prospect, then a multipolar one may be.[2] This is a prospect that has received significant scientific attention (see, for instance,

Ikenberry 2005, Buzan 2008). While the geographic specification of multipolarity tends to vary, depending on the analyst in question, even a 'minimalist' version of the concept would seem to imply at least three world-regional political-economic orders centred on the US, Russia and China and perhaps a fourth (subsequent to the ratification, in 2009, of the Lisbon Treaty and the beginnings of coherent mechanisms to advance foreign policy), the European Union.

Among these visions of our global future, this chapter suggests that the prospects of a Global-Asian Era (GAE) may be worth taking seriously. While there is beginning to be a literature that points to a possibility such as this (e.g. Frank 1998, Mahbubani 2008), including from affiliates of the US Central Intelligence Agency (NIC 2004), this chapter is less categorical than certainly the former tend to be. It presents the GAE merely as a possible global future, but a possibility worthy of consideration and debate.

The GAE hypothesis sketched here recognizes that while China may be its initial driving force, we need to acknowledge that there are many factors that could delay or even derail the emergence of a GAE, or at least prevent it from becoming the relatively stable formation that the notion of an 'era' implies. The differing histories, natures and interests of the Asian political economies themselves – and hence their geo-political relations – are cases in point, as are the deep, mutual suspicions associated with Sino-US relations. The fact that the Chinese economy may be 40 per cent smaller in GDP terms than was thought as recently as 2007,[3] in itself may mean that a GAE's gestation period may be longer than otherwise might have been the case. If we append to such uncertainties the growing evidence that the Chinese economy itself may be heading for a massive overaccululation crisis[4] (i.e. a crisis in the 'western' sense of the term) with the prospect of serious knock-on effects for social and political stability (Hung 2008, 2009), then, clearly, it may be some time before we are in a position to judge the validity of the GAE hypothesis. In the meantime, however, we can begin to evaluate its plausibility.

Globalization today

In order to assess the nature and dynamics of a potential GAE, we need first to characterize the current phase of globalization; a phase that has been both a cornerstone of China's economic success and one from which any future GAE is likely to emerge.

The current form of globalization is conventionally charted from the early 1970s, though as the work of Hirst and Thompson (1999) and Held et al. (1999), among others, can be taken to imply, this 'starting date' has been more a product of business school and media 'hype' than it has of historical reality. Rather, the contemporary form of globalization can be seen as being characterized by a deepening and geographic dispersal of a number of dynamics that emerged at various times in the post World War II period. Four of these seem to have been particularly important.

- The electronics and ICT revolutions that followed the invention of the modern computer and the emergence of semiconductor technology in the late 1940s have subsequently transformed economic transactions, politics, work and everyday life through the global expansion of cyber networks (a dynamic captured best in Castells' trilogy: Castells 2000a, 2000b, 2003).
- The grafting of a conservative ideological project onto neoclassical economic theory, that began with the Mont Pelerin Society in the late 1940s, led to the rise and expansion of neoliberalism as a relatively coherent set of economic, political and social practices and as the principal ideological 'glue' of contemporary globalization (Harvey 2005, Henderson 2010).
- From the early 1980s, as an adjunct of the neoliberal project, there has emerged a new regime of accumulation – 'financialization' – associated with the progressive subjection of all other forms of capital to the particular interests and rhythms of finance capital (Boyer 2000, Glyn 2006).
- Consistent with the rise of neoliberalism and particularly since the historical rupture in Eastern Europe of 1989–91, the United States has emerged not only as the dominant military power, but as a global power whose foreign policy has been progressively militarized (Harvey 2003, Johnson 2004).

As for much of the period since the end of the World War I, the United States has been confirmed as the dominant political economy during the current – what we can now term 'neoliberal' – form of globalization (roughly mid-1970s onwards). While this dominance has always been contested – by other states, ideologies and by social movements – it has been successfully reproduced over time not merely because of the US's military power, but because the US has been the principal source, and the principal commercial and political exploiter, of many of the innovations associated with the first three of these dynamics. Underlying this dominance, however, are deep structural weaknesses in the US economy (Brenner 2003, 2005), such that the consequences of these dynamics is that the world economy and its geo-politics have become increasingly unstable. The global financial crisis of 2008, with its origins on Wall Street, has underlined and deepened these problems.

Transformational dynamics

In attempting to grasp the transformation of the prevailing form of globalization towards a possible GAE, we need to identify what it might have been that has delivered China to its current global position. While this is not the place to recuperate the relevant arguments in any detail (though see, in particular, Arrighi 2007), it is important to note that whatever the underlying determinants, China's rise from the mid-1980s would have been inconceivable without at least two historical processes having become entrenched in the immediately preceding period. The first of these was the 1949 revolution and the subsequent social project associated with Maoism. While acknowledging the disasters of the Great Leap Forward and the Cultural Revolution, it is easy to forget that without the Maoist version of state socialism, China would not have emerged by the 1980s with a largely literate and healthy population and one whose considerable population size was under control. The stark contrast with its closest comparator, India, in the same time frame as well as today, underlines the substantially positive developmental legacies of the Maoist social project.[5]

The second historical process central to China's rise – and the one to which I alluded in the previous section – was the significance of neoliberal globalization. The beginning of China's economic reform process coincided with the 'first wave' international extension of the neoliberal economic project. This was not simply a matter of China benefiting from increased FDI flows, for that had been true for other parts of East Asia since the mid-1960s and, in any case, most of the initial flows into China came from 'Overseas Chinese' territories such as Hong Kong and Taiwan (Henderson 1991: 175). Probably of more importance was the progressive freeing of trade in manufactured commodities (under the auspicies of the GATT and, subsequently, the WTO) – from which China was uniquely placed to benefit – coupled with the abandonment, by the 1980s, of state concerns in the neoliberal heartlands (particularly Britain and the USA) to maintain vibrant, internationally competitive manufacturing industries of their own. More recently, with the financialization of the world economy – and the reduction in national controls associated with that process – state-owned Chinese 'sovereign equity' funds have been allowed to make inroads into some of the core companies of global finance capital.[6]

Notwithstanding the neoliberal resonances in China's own development project (explored, for instance, in Harvey 2005: Chapter 5, Liew 2006), there are strong reasons to believe that any transition from the current form of globalization to a Global-Asian Era is likely to be highly contentious. Among the reasons for this are the following.

China is a dramatically different socio-political formation from the USA and other countries that dominate contemporary globalization

With few signs, as yet, that the Communist Party's hold on power is weakening, China remains a neo-Stalinist state. As a consequence, the Party formally absorbs the state apparatuses, the state is fundamentally authoritarian and repressive, and though change is afoot, China lacks a vibrant civil society that could act to moderate its authoritarianism (Nolan 2004a, Pei 2006). Although Britain, the United States and other major global players were nowhere near as democratic as early, or as deeply, as their national mythologies suggest (Chang 2002: Chapter 3), and from the Peterloo massacre of 1819[7] through the 'labour wars' of the late nineteenth and early twentieth centuries, to the McCarthyite 'witch hunts' of the 1950s, their governments could certainly be repressive, the repression there was never as systematic or as prolonged as it has been in China.[8] In a nutshell, as Hutton (2007) has argued, China does not subscribe to 'enlightenment' values. While, again, the extent to which Britain and the United States have themselves subscribed to enlightenment values has been uneven and patchy, depending on political expediency and prevailing perceptions of the 'national interest',[9] the key difference relative to historic (since the revolution of 1911) and contemporary China, is again the dramatic differences in the development of their respective civil societies and thus in their relative capacities for the mobilization of political opposition in support of enlightenment values.

To the peoples of the currently dominant countries (and the 'Occident' more generally), China represents the 'Great Other'[10]

In 1511 when the first modern maritime colonial power, Portugal, made contact with Chinese merchant ships (in Melaka, now part of Malaysia), China was at the zenith of its power as the regional hegemon in East Asia. While it was to slide gradually into economic and geo-political decline over the following four centuries or so, China began to be perceived by Europeans and, subsequently, Americans and other peoples of European origin, as the 'Great Other' (Jullien 1999, Zhao 2007). While part of this perception was undoubtedly positive, in terms of an appreciation among the middle and upper classes of the aesthetic representations of Chinese culture and of the early Chinese advances in science and technology, elements of it were profoundly negative. China came to be perceived as the polar opposite of European cultures. The size, wealth and cultural sophistication of China, coupled with the fact that it had been controlled by a unified state since the third century BC, began to transmute, by the late nineteenth century, into a sense of China as a potential 'civilisational' threat. With the triumph of the People's Liberation Army (PLA) in the civil war of the 1930s and 40s and the founding of the 'Communist' state in 1949, China began to be perceived – particularly in the USA – as not merely the cultural Great Other, but ideologically, as profoundly alien, a perception that was probably compounded when US troops were confronted by the PLA during the Korean War (cf. Cumings 1997: Chapter 5). US and European racism, of course, were a central component of this perception.

While Japan, at least since the mid-nineteenth century, was also viewed culturally in European societies and the United States in similar ways to China, with the exception of the 1930s through to 1945, it was never perceived as an ideological and military threat. On the contrary, with the exception of that period, from the Meiji Restoration (1867) through to the present, the Japanese state has specifically linked its political fortunes (arguably in a subservient form) to those of the prevailing dominant power: Britain through to World War I and the US subsequently (Murphy 2006).

With the size of the temporary and permanent migrations from China that have been associated with recent globalization and the 'ideological/spiritual pollution' that has been a result of the absorption of China into the global economy and, particularly, its cyber networks and cultural forms, it is possible that the negative perceptions in the Occident of China and in China of the Occident (on the latter see Dikötter 1992), are being moderated. Whether that moderation has penetrated the power centres of the global political economy, including those of China itself, not to mention the vast majority of their respective populations, however, must remain a question for history.

The geo-political context within which China is the principal 'rising power' is arguably more fragile than at any time since World War II

If the leading analyst of the relation of war to the economic decline of the 'great powers', Paul Kennedy (1989) and the world's greatest living historian, Eric Hobsbawm (1994) are in pessimistic agreement that we live in perilous times, then we all need to take note. In both their cases, as in the work of many 'global historians', there is a sense that the contemporary period is remarkably reminiscent, in terms of economic instability and inter-state rivalry, of the decade or two preceding the World War I. As I have indicated earlier`, there is a sense that the US economy, in its structural fabric, is beginning to come apart. We must add to this the facts that finance capital, with all its inherent instabilities, has been 'unleashed' internationally (Glyn 2006) – contributing to potentially serious recessions in the US, Britain and elsewhere – the US and some of its allies are militarily over-stretched, Russia and Japan may be on the verge of re-militarization,[11] poverty in the developing world (with the significant exception of China), if anything, continues to increase (Davis 2006) and global warming threatens to deliver devastating climatic shifts. Into this maelstrom, China is now stepping. It thus seems axiomatic that China has re-entered the global political economy at a moment when geo-political relations are more fragile than at any time since World War II, and thus probably in recorded history.

Globalization tomorrow?

We are now in a position to sketch some of the key elements that could influence the nature of a future Global-Asian Era. As with the current form of globalization, the nature of a GAE will probably be associated with the 'peculiarities' of China's political economy and social formation; its history and its current condition. Arising from these, two elements could be decisive.

The sources of China's competitive dynamic

There are at least two factors that are important here: that China has a 'giant' economy and that its economy is constituted as an unusual form of capitalism.

The 'big country' effect

While its various indices of economic growth are not dissimilar to those of Japan, South Korea or Taiwan in earlier periods (Winters and Yusuf 2007, Figure 1.1, p.9), with a population of over 1.3 billion, a low-wage labour force matched historically in size only by contemporary India, and with increasing skill and innovative potential in abundance, the difference between China and the other East Asian late industrializers (or, indeed, any other country that has industrialized) is the sheer scale at which these economic and social dynamics are being brought into play. The following data will serve to underline this comment.

In terms of shares in the growth of world exports, for instance, whereas China was second to the USA between 1995 and 2004, with 8.9 per cent relative to the latter's 10.7 per cent of the total, its share in the growth of world exports between 2005 and 2020 is projected to be 15.4 per cent compared with the USA's 9.9 per cent (and Japan's 6.3 per cent and Germany's 3.8 per cent) of the total (Winters and Yusuf 2007, Table 1.3: 15). With regard to the structure of exports, China is now the world's largest producer of electronic and ICT products (Winters and Yusuf 2007: 42) and in terms of higher skill and technology intensive products, China's performance is beginning to approximate that of South Korea (extrapolated from Winter and Yusuf 2007, Figure 2.1: 40). This capacity to move into higher valued-added, more technology intensive products – at a far earlier stage in the industrialization process than other late industrializers – is underpinned by a dramatic expansion in the graduate labour force, with over 600,000 people in engineering now graduating annually (McGregor 2006). Add to this a competitive position in innovative technologies that one would not expect to find in a developing country at this stage in its development – such as nanotechnology, where around 1200 scientists at the Chinese Academy of Sciences alone, are acting as principal researchers (Appelbaum *et al.* 2006; see also Appelbaum and Parker 2007) – and we can see the reasons for the World Bank's conclusion in its report on China and India that 'even though China is not the dominant force in the world economy, the shock it is administering to the world is unprecedented' (Winters and Yusuf 2007: 11).

Form of capitalism

Far from being a monadic economic system, capitalism is extraordinarily diverse in its organizational composition, state-business relations, managerial priorities, etc. (from a vast literature see, for instance, Lazonick 1991, Henderson 1998: Chapter 1, Whitley 1999, Coates 2000, Hall and Soskice 2001, Lane and Myant 2006). One of the implications of this reality, as Chang (2007a) has stressed for the developing world, is that far from there being one 'royal road' to development, as neoliberalism in its various guises would have us believe, there are a multiplicity of potentially successful routes to high performing economies capable of delivering generalized prosperity. China's form of capitalism may well be one of these. If it is, and if China becomes a dominant economy, then it will be a very odd form of capitalism to have constituted the core of a new phase of globalization.

While Chinese capitalism is a complex, hybrid, phenomenon (see, for instance, Nolan 2004b, Nee and Opper 2007; see also Chapter 2), sharing some similarities with the 'state orchestrated' capitalisms of Japan, Taiwan and, particularly, South

Korea, it is unique in two ways. First, it is the only significant globalizing form of capitalism to have at its core a neo-Stalinist state that continues to pay lip service to, if not respect, some of the principles of socialism.

Second, it is the only political economy where state-owned companies are at the cutting edge of globalization. As a consequence, it is reasonable to assume that the managerial priorities, time horizons for returns on investment of such enterprises are not only very different from US, European, Japanese or South Korean firms, as Nolan's (2001, 2004b: Chapter 2) work implies, but that their primary concerns are not merely about profits (though they are about that), but with China's national development strategy. If the considerations behind particular investments in particular places are not just commercial, but are driven by the Chinese state's strategic interests, then almost by definition, the logic of globalization during a GAE, and its consequences for countries absorbed into it, could be dramatically different from earlier phases of globalization.

China's unusual nationalism

China is the first potentially dominant economic-political power, other than the US, to have been subject to colonization and, relatedly and importantly, the first to be populated by non-white peoples. The legacies of colonialism, and perhaps issues of race, are consequently likely to influence China's bilateral and multilateral relations, certainly with the US, the European powers and Japan and – in different ways – those with the developing world. Central to the issue (and unlike most other major country and great power nationalisms) seems to be a sense of historical grievance associated with a perceived 'one hundred years of humiliation'. From 1842 (the end of the first 'Opium War' with Britain) to 1949 (the socialist revolution), China was subject to imperialist incursions by the USA, Britain, France, Germany, Italy and other European powers and, particularly, by Japan ('particularly', because it involved military invasion and extreme brutality) which seem to have left deep scars on the national psyche (Chang 2001, Gries 2005).

With the decline of Maoism as the ideological 'glue' of Chinese society, the key legitimations for the continued rule by the Communist Party have become its ability to deliver sustained economic growth, coupled, as the occasion arises, with its determination to right the perceived historic wrongs perpetrated against China by foreign powers. In that the latter seems to be increasingly associated with a concern to re-assert its supposed 'rightful' place in the global economic and political order, Chang's (2001: 175) assessment that one of Deng Xiaoping's key contributions to China's development was to transform Maoism into a developmental nationalist ideology, seems valid.

Chinese nationalism has often been seen as a 'top-down' affair; essentially as a propaganda strategy designed to legitimate Party rule in the face of the deepening contradictions and rising conflicts associated with capitalism and increasing corruption (see Shirk 2007: 6–9). Events of the last decade or so, however, such as the US bombing of the Chinese embassy in Belgrade in 1999, the mobilizations against

Japan's refusal to apologize for its suppression of China in the 1930s and 1940s, and the 'anti-western' response to international protests (focussed on the Olympic torch) about the 2008 crackdown in Tibet, arguably point to the emergence of a grassroots, 'popular nationalism' (Gries 2005: Chapter 7, Anderlini 2008). Domestic responses to the success of Chinese athletes in the 2008 Olympic Games, where the celebration of individual endeavour seems to have been subordinated to the greater glory of the state, may be further evidence of the rise of popular nationalism.

Whatever the sources of China's 'new' nationalism, however, it seems to be infused with a deep sense of victimization and if Chang (2001) and Gries (2005) are correct, this has contributed to a mass psychology of insecurity.[12] Given that China has territorial ambitions in East Asia (Taiwan most obviously, but also with regard to control over the potentially oil and gas rich Paracel and Spratley islands in the South China Sea; islands also claimed by Vietnam, Malaysia and The Philippines) and its self-perception seems to be as much a product of 'cultural ethnocentrism' (Taylor 2006 and more directly – mobilising discourses of race and racism – Dikötter 1992, Jacques 2009) as that of the US and its allies, it seems likely that a GAE could be marked by less than pragmatic responses, both on China's part and on the parts of its potential adversaries, to some of the geo-political tensions that will inevitably arise.

Conclusion

As a consequence of the aforementioned dynamics, China's global economic and political footprints are likely to be markedly different from those associated with previous global powers. With the emergence of a GAE, therefore, we could expect an economic and political world order markedly different from that established under US/British/European dominance. For instance, with a GAE we might expect less emphasis on the ideal of democratic governance systems, or on human rights and humanitarian issues (perhaps even rhetorically). Also – and this could be positive for the developing world – the 'demonstration effect' of China's development may encourage others to further question neoliberal policy agendas. Consequently, and consistent with the Chinese 'reading' of crisis employed here, it seems clear that should a GAE emerge, it is likely to carry both dangers and opportunities for economic, social and political transformation in developing (and undoubtedly, developed) countries.

Whatever view is taken of the possible global implications of the rise of China, it seems clear that we are on the verge of a new episode in global history; one that will see, as Frank (1998) and others suggest, the return of China to an historically central role in the global political economy. While there will be many positive attributes associated with such a trajectory, both for the Chinese people and for our collective global future, there are clearly a number of very serious inherent dangers. Unfortunately, among these, may be the possibility of a Sino-US war.

Paul Kennedy, in concluding his magisterial 500 year survey of the *Rise and Fall of the Great Powers*, emphasizes that:

the fact remains that all of the major shifts in the world's *military-power* balances have followed alterations in the *productive* balances; and further, that the rising and falling of the various empires and states in the international system has been confirmed by the outcomes of the major Great Power wars, where victory has gone to the side with the greatest material resources.

(Kennedy 1989: 567; original emphasis).

The implications of Kennedy's conclusion for US-China relations seem all too obvious. The United States is in economic decline relative to China, not least in the manufacturing and other productive components of its real economy. If we add to this the fact that there appears to be a structural logic at the heart of US foreign policy which has resulted in its progressive militarization; (a political-economic dynamic that, among other things, has been driven by the fact that since 1941, the US has been almost perpetually at war somewhere on the planet),[13] then irrespective of the Chinese government's official desire for 'harmonious development', it seems inevitable that there will be tensions and possibly future confrontations between the two powers. If these are to be prevented from spilling over into military conflict, they will have to be mediated by third parties; and ones with the global power and legitimacy for their mediation to be effective. As the United Nations has historically proven itself incapable of effective mediation when the stand-off is between permanent members of the Security Council, there seems to be only one agency which, in principle, could perform this role: the European Union. While the EU remains a fractious institution (not least because of the unwillingness of successive British governments to engage with its political project), the fact that it is now in a formal position to forge its own foreign policy (which will need to be distinct from both the USA and China), may well be vital not only for China, the USA and the EU itself, but for the future of global humanity.

NOTES

1 Making sense of East Asian transformation

1 The principal texts in each case being: Karl Marx, *Capital*; Max Weber, *Economy and Society*; John Maynard Keynes, *The General Theory of Employment, Interest and Money*; Josef Schumpeter, *Business Cycles*; and Karl Polanyi, *The Great Transformation*.
2 Collectively referred to in the following chapters as 'newly industrialized countries', NICs, or sometimes 'first generation NICs'.
3 For an argument about Britain's need for 're-industrialization' and what East Asian experiences may have to say to this, see Henderson (1993).
4 See bar chart at: http://www.nationmaster.com/graph/eco_gro_nat_inc_percap-gross-national-income-per-capita#source (accessed 17 March 2010).
5 Brunei is a non-industrial, 'rentier' micro state (with a population of around 400,000 in 2008), whose GNI is almost entirely composed of royalties from oil production. Consequently, it does not figure in the discussions developed in this book.
6 The gini coefficient measures income inequality on the basis of 0 (total equality) to 1 (total inequality). Consequently, the higher the coefficient, the more unequal is the society in question. The OECD is the source for the data presented here: http://stats.oecd.org/index.aspx?QueryId = 11112&QueryType = View (accessed, 17 March 2010).
7 By 'scalar' I have in mind both institutional (macro, meso, micro) and spatial (global/international, world-regional, national, sub-national/regional, local) levels of analysis.

2 Danger and opportunity in the transformation process

1 I am grateful to Suet Ying Ho for alerting me to this conception of crisis in the Chinese language.
2 I am thinking, for instance, of the re-emergence of oppositional movements – in some cases including armed struggle – in The Philippines, Indonesia and Thailand. In China, the Government admitted in 2005 over 87,000 'social incidents' (mainly attacks on police by peasants illegally dispossessed of their collective land use rights and strikes by urban migrants who work in the country's manufacturing and construction industries).
3 With Malaysia and Thailand, for instance, badly exposed in developed country markets to competition from Chinese manufactured exports (Yusuf and Nabeshima 2009).

4 Between China and Taiwan most obviously, but with the ever present possibilities for Sino-Japanese conflict.
5 For accounts of the significance of East Asian development models for transformation elsewhere, see the essays collected in Henderson (1998) and the work of Chang (2003, 2007 a).
6 Frank's (1982) explicitly negative assessment of East Asian development is a particular example of the flawed reasoning involved here.
7 By 'structural adjustment' the IMF and the World Bank refer to the belief that the reform of economic and political institutions, together with the liberalization of macro-economic policy, are the preconditions for market-driven economic growth (the only form of growth they conceive as possible). Such reforms and policy changes – together with their insistence on 'good governance' – have increasingly become preconditions for IMF and World Bank loans. In many developing countries through to the present and in Eastern Europe in the 1990s and early 2000s, these involved, *inter alia*, the abandonment of market protection and import-substituting industrialization (ISI) strategies, whole-sale privatization of state assets and dramatic reductions in government expenditures on welfare, etc., with their inevitable human consequences. For an analysis of the 'iconic' Central-Eastern European case, Hungary, see Phillips *et al.* (2006).
8 Beginning, as far as I am aware, with Chalmers Johnson's (1977) book chapter on Japan's Ministry of International Trade and Industry.
9 Advice that in the current (2009) economic climate, many governments (including Brit-ain's, given that country's finance dominated and dangerously asymmetrical economic structure) would be wise to heed.
10 The literature on the forms – or varieties – of capitalism is replete with typologies. For other suggestions see, for instance, Whitley (1999), Coates (2000), Dore (2000) and Hall and Soskice (2001).
11 For a thorough analysis of the data on the consequences of China's export competition for some Southeast Asian countries, see Yusuf and Nabeshima (2009). For a counter view, see Ravenhill (2006).
12 Because, of the exception of a number of German-owned firms (Volkswagen, Siemens, Bosch, etc.) and Philips (The Netherlands), Nokia (Finland), Ford, GM, Motorola (US), EU and US firms have either vacated high-volume manufacturing, have limited inter-national competitiveness in them (as with Fiat of Italy or Peugeot-Citroen of France), have never engaged in high-volume manufacturing (e.g. Mercedes Benz or Miele of Germany), or have sold their assets to non US or EU firms (e.g. Jaguar of Britain, via Ford, to Tata of India; and Volvo Cars of Sweden, again via Ford, to Geely of China).
13 For the classic analysis of Japan's 'flexible rigidities', see Dore (1986).
14 Calculated from Statistics Bureau data, Ministry of Internal Affairs and Communications, Government of Japan. Available from: http://www.stat.go.jp/english/data/handbook/c11cont.htm (accessed 22 February 2010).
15 Calculated from the US Census Bureau's Foreign Trade Statistics. On Japan: http://www.census.gov/foreign-trade/balance/c5880.html On China: http://www.census.gov/foreign-trade/balance/c5700.html (both accessed 22 February 2010).
16 As a result of the global production networks in which Chinese companies are entan-gled. For instance, it has been estimated by University of California at Irvine researchers that of the $300 sale price for an Apple I-Pod assembled in, and exported from China, only $4 is retained in the Chinese economy. (*China Daily*, 6 April 2010).
17 See aforementioned discussion in section on 'economic fusion'.
18 Original equipment manufacturing (OEM) involves the manufacturing by one company of products designed by another and marketed under the latter's brand name. This is the basis for much electronics manufacturing (e.g. computers, mobile phones, etc.) in East Asia where the brand name companies are headquartered in the USA, the EU or Japan.
19 http://en.poly.com.cn/newEbiz1/EbizPortalFG/portal/html/index.html (accessed 8 April 2010).

20 Fieldwork in Guangzhou, April 2006. I am grateful to Wing Shing Tang of the Hong Kong Baptist University for further information. Of subsidiary interest, it might be noted that lying behind the 'urban village' phenomenon is a uniquely Chinese process of class formation. Historically and in all other industrializing countries, peasants were and are normally turned into industrial workers. For some peasants in China, however, it appears that the class formation process has turned them directly into rentiers!

21 Official estimate provided during a lecture at Sun Yat Sen University, Guangzhou, by a senior member of the Guangdong Academy of Social Sciences, April 2006.

22 In some cities, even the local police seem to be systematically implicated in crime. For instance, during field visits in 2005 and 2006 to Dongguan in Guangdong Province, we were warned, on both occasions, by our local organizer not to leave our hotel after dark as there was a possibility of being mugged by the police.

23 Though empirically dated, the debate between Goldstone and Huang in *Foreign Policy* provides useful references points for this scenario (Goldstone 1995, Huang 1995).

24 Lying implicitly behind many of the political analyses of China's 'trapped transition' (Pei 2006) to capitalism is the belief that the 'western'-style liberal-democratic state is the 'best shell' for a dynamic capitalism capable of delivering generalized prosperity. While this is not the place to engage in this particular debate, it seems clear that if we contrast the economic, social and political histories of China and India since the early 1950s, for instance, and compare their respective contributions to social development, then the liberal-democratic state may not be as crucial as many make it out to be. On this, see the debate, in *Prospect*, between Will Hutton and Meghnad Desai (Hutton and Desai 2007).

3 States and transformation

1 Via such things as exceptional taxes on bank profits, restricting employee bonuses, breaking retail banks from investment banks, as occurred in a number of countries in the wake of the 2008 crisis.

2 For the USA, Britain and other western European countries, the books by Coates (2000) and Pontusson (2005) take us some way down that road.

3 Chalmers Johnson, commenting on Milton Friedman's claim (in a US television programme) that 'the image of the Japanese having had an industrial policy which explains their success, is a myth' notes that 'Friedman does not read Japanese and has made no study of the Japanese economy. He does not have to because he is speaking as one of the world's most eminent economic theorists' (Johnson 1988:80).

4 There are two peculiarities with Porter's (1990) discussion of East Asia, which may indicate deeper problems with his account than their mere passing significance would suggest. First, his account of South Korea makes no reference to Alice Amsden's (1989) seminal work on the role of the state in that country's industrialization. Though his own book was probably finished before Amsden's was published, this is no resolution of the problem, as at the time when their research was being conducted and manuscripts written, they were colleagues together at Harvard Business School! Second, while Singapore was originally part of Porter's research programme, no more than a few brief comments on that country appear on his book. Given that Porter's thesis is rooted in an argument about intense competition among domestic firms, and that about 70 per cent of Singaporean economy, by the mid-1980s, was foreign-owned (Mirza 1986), therein may lie an explanation for this omission.

5 For important accounts of the origins of the contemporary financial crisis see, Elliott and Atkinson (2008) and Stiglitz (2010).

6 Until relatively recently, no more than 20–25 per cent of investment finance for the major Japanese business corporations was raised via capital markets.

7 By the mid-1980s this was the highest proportion of non-taxation revenues raised by any government anywhere in the capitalist world.

8 Singapore has the largest public housing system in proportional terms. Hong Kong has the world's second largest public (and subsidized ownership) housing system, though in terms of numbers housed, it is larger than that of Singapore.

9 With regard to income inequality, the principal exceptions in the region have been The Philippines and Burma throughout the period in question, Hong Kong since the 1980s and now China more generally. On Chinese inequality, see Chen (2007).

10 I am grateful to my colleague, Junko Yamashita, for pointing me to this data and helping me to interpret its significance.

11 Some of the reduction may have resulted from legislation that reduced the working week from six to five days. Though the legislation emerged in the late 1970s, it was the early 1990s before it began to have much of an effect on the length of the working week. Even so, given employer and cultural pressure on workers to commit to long working days and weeks, the impact of this legislation on average work years may have been limited. Similarly, while statutory paid vacations in Japan approximate those in other advanced industrial countries (in the Japanese case between 25 and 35 days, depending on seniority with one's employer), the same pressures on workers mean that relatively few Japanese take their full holiday entitlement. I am grateful to my colleague, Junko Yamashita, for these observations.

12 Calculated from the average hours worked per year in The Netherlands, Norway, Germany, France, Luxemburg, Sweden, Belgium, Denmark, Ireland, Austria, Spain, Switzerland, the United Kingdom, Finland, Iceland and Italy.

13 GDP data based on 2009 exchange rates. See CIA (2010).

14 It is possible that the 'socialist' form of state planning in Taiwan may have derived in part from the fact that in the early years of Kuomintang's rule in China itself (through to the late 1920s), leading elements in the Party were enamoured of developments in the Soviet Union. For instance, Sun Yat Sen, the figure head and driving force behind the republican revolution of 1911, conducted a long correspondence with Lenin and from 1918 until his own death in 1925, had Soviet advisors (Seagrave 1985).

4 Economic crises and governance failures

1 Needless to say, the warnings from the East Asian collapse were not interpreted as such by neoliberal (orthodox) economists and governments around the world, and were thus not heeded.

2 For a detailed account of some of the social consequences of the crisis, see the International Labour Office report (ILO 1998).

3 Examples included the closure of Siemens' and Fujitsu's semiconductor plants in the Northeast of England (*The Observer*, 2 August 1998).

4 Though the state could be involved particularly where public housing was a significant component of the housing stock.

5 Though, as we have been told regularly by orthodox economic opinion since the onset of the current crisis, no one predicted the possibility of collapse. In response, we might suggest that this view depends on whose work one reads, or more pertinently, does not read.

6 In Berger's hands culturalist explanations surfaced as a form of inverted racism. Witness the following comment: '. . . it is inherently implausible to believe that Singapore would be what it is today if it were populated, not by a majority of ethnic Chinese, but by Brazilians or Bengalis – or, for that matter, by a majority of ethnic Malays.' (Berger 1986: 166).

7 As it has been in the US and remains a potent influence in Italy, Greece, Bulgaria and perhaps other EU economies. In terms of sheer scale, however, political-economic corruption in East Asia (particularly at local and provincial levels), seems to have reached its zenith in China.

8 The Council of Economic Ministers, the National Economic Policy Steering Committee, the Joint Public-Private Sector Consultative Committee and the Eastern Seaboard Development Committee (Muscat 1994).

9 The vitality of the property market in Hong Kong is now intrinsically associated with the viability of the SAR's financial sector. Should there be a significant relocation of financial services to Shanghai (by no means inconceivable given inter-urban competition for investment in China and Shanghai's considerable political clout with the central government and within the Party), then the property market and the Hong Kong economy in general, would be in very serious trouble.

10 I am grateful to Dr Jong-Chul Jeon, formerly of Manchester Business School, for the additional information he provided on this matter.

11 Personal communication from a former employee of the Korean Ministry of Finance.

12 Jin (1998) shows that by the third quarter of 1997, 19 of the 24 merchant banks established after 1994 had non-performing loans that exceeded the value of their own capital.

13 Though 1:1 debt-equity ratios would normally be regarded as unacceptably high by Anglo-American standards (except, of course, in the run-up to the current crisis), Japanese, Korean, Taiwanese and probably other East Asian companies – importantly backed by secure, long-term credit – had thrived on debt-equity ratios of 3:1 or even 5:1.

14 In effect, the interest rate at which the Central Bank supplies funds to the commercial banks.

15 Personal communication from Professor Pang Eng Fong, now of Singapore Management University.

16 Arbitrage refers to price differences between currency and stock markets in two economies. It constitutes a form of speculation in which banks normally engage. Occasionally, like any form of gambling, arbitrage activities can generate serious problems, as it did in the case of Barings Bank, which collapsed in 1993.

17 Lax planning regulations in Thailand, Malaysia, Indonesia and Hong Kong – or often the non-application, as a result of corruption in the former three cases, of those that exist – has boosted the accumulation potential of investments in the urban fabric. It has done so by allowing higher building densities and lower safety and environmental standards than would be tolerated by US or Western European planning authorities, or by those in Japan. I am grateful to Harry Dimitriou, Bartlett Professor of Planning Studies, University College London, for this observation.

5 Governing growth and inequality

1 As I indicated in Chapter 2, there is no consensus on the terminology used to depict national forms of capitalism. For the purposes of the current chapter, I adopt Dore's (2000) categorizations.

2 While poverty is a particular form of inequality and particular forms of poverty (relative or absolute) can increase or decrease relative to changes in inequality, for the purposes of the current discussion (which tries to establish a theoretical proposition for the relation of economic governance to inequality, generally conceived), the significance of these distinctions does not require explicit attention. Although there are various ways of conceptualizing poverty (for a discussion see Henderson *et al.* 2007), it is used here in the sense of material deprivation.

3 Note that economic growth clearly was prioritized under various types of socialist regime (witness the staggering growth record of the USSR between the late 1920s and late 1960s, for instance). The point being made here is that, generally speaking, it was assumed that inequality could be dealt with by means of a policy agenda that was disconnected from concerns with economic growth.

4 A term developed in the mid-1990s as it became clear that economic growth on its own was insufficient for poverty reduction.

5 Dollar and Kraay's analysis has been used extensively by the World Bank and similar agencies. However, it has been subject to increasing critical attention, some of it methodological, some of it questioning the utility of drawing policy conclusions from country averages. See, for instance, White (2002).

6 Though arguing from different bases, some of the work collected in Houtzager and Moore (2003) comes to similar conclusions.

7 The empirical basis for the arguments about South Korea and Malaysia, developed in this chapter, can be found in Henderson *et al.* (2002b, 2002c).

8 Though Singapore is usually assumed to have a multi-racial society, in practice it has been dominated by peoples of Chinese origin (as of 2008, about 77 per cent of the population).

9 Hong Kong and Singapore were the classic examples, however, of how to use such policies – particularly with regard to housing – as development tools (see Castells *et al.* 1990).

10 Let us be clear that economic growth, however generated, is crucially important to the global poor. While global capitalism inevitably involves exploitation and some forms of the growth it generates bring with them harsher forms of exploitation than do others, tens of millions of people in Sub-Saharan Africa and elsewhere, know from their daily lives that there is one thing worse than the exploitation of global capitalism: being detached from it and thus subject to no exploitation at all!

11 Additionally it involved 'lighter' forms of industrialization associated, for instance, with footwear manufacture for international brand name companies. For some years in the 1980s and early 1990s, Korea was the principal producer of sports shoes marketed under the Nike and Reebok brands amongst others.

12 Korea, as with Taiwan, used a planning mechanism – the strategic five year plan – that was more typical of state-socialist societies, than it was of capitalist ones.

13 Meaning, literally, 'sons of the soil'.

14 From 11.8 to 13.2 per cent and from 2.4 to 3.8 percent respectively (Henderson *et al.* 2002b, Table 2: 2)

15 Largely wasted investments in steel and automobiles and other 'flagship' projects, for instance. Arguably these funds would have been better used in stimulating rural industrialization (perhaps along Chinese lines) and the development and upgrading of small and medium sized firms capable of linking more effectively with the foreign-owned manufacturing companies (see Chapter 6).

16 The peasantry in general have benefited from the growth of manufacturing industry, though many of the jobs have gone to women.

17 Mark, however, that redistributional policies are essential for dealing with spatially uneven development. For a general argument on this, see Scott (2002).

6 Limits to industrialization

1 We refer to this as 'think[ing] laterally' because the vast majority of work on social policy and development is concerned with *social* development (with the exceptions of work on education, etc., as noted earlier) in a way that tends to ignore the contributions of social policy to economic development. For a major exception, see Castells' work on Hong Kong and Singapore (Castells *et al.* 1990).

2 We are grateful to Paul Lubeck of the University of California at Santa Cruz for this observation.

3 Electronic and electrical products have consistently comprised well over half of Malaysia's gross exports, increasing from nearly 57 per cent in 1988 to 71 per cent by 1999 (Ismail 2001). They also account for 29 per cent of the country's workforce and over 30 per cent of its total value-added (JICA 2001: 2–7).

4 Fieldwork interviews, July/August 2002 and June 2004. MIDA is the Malaysian Government agency responsible, among other things, for attracting and organizing foreign manufacturing investment.

5 For an account of the general theoretical issues involved in the integration of local companies into global production networks and the consequences of this for economic development, see Henderson *et al.* (2002a). On the problem of the shifting architectures

and governance systems of global production networks and the consequences of this for recent Malaysian industrialization, see Phillips and Henderson (2009).

6   Unpublished Penang Development Corporation (PDC) data. Production workers are distinguished from engineering, technical and other managerial and supervisory workers in this data.

7   In this chapter we use the term 'region' as in traditional geographic parlance; as a sub-national space.

8   Fieldwork interviews, June 2004.

9   HICOM, the Heavy Industry Commission of Malaysia, is involved in automobiles, steel and other heavy industries, Petronas in petroleum products and petro-chemicals.

10   Malaysia has a federal political system consisting of 13 state governments in addition to the Federal Government in Kuala Lumpur.

11   Contract electronics manufacturing (CEM) refers to a particular type of outsourcing model based on manufacturing service firms with particular capabilities to manage the global supply chain functions on behalf of 'brand name' electronics multinationals. This model has particular implications for understanding upgrading in developing countries, particularly given their particularly high use of temporary and flexible labour (see Lüthje 2002, Sturgeon and Lester 2002 and Phillips and Henderson 2009).

12   Interviews carried out in June 2004, with a number of Federal and regional agencies, attested to the association, in the minds of policy makers, between Penang and Malaysian electronics in general.

13   United Malay National Organisation.

14   Department of Statistics, Government of Malaysia.

15   Interviews with MIDA officials, August 2002 and PDC officials, June 2004

16   Interview with MIDA officials, June 2004.

17   See note 18 chapter 2.

18   Other higher-tier, locally-owned companies do exist in Malaysian electronics, almost exclusively in Penang. These are: BCM, Globetronics, UNICO and LKT, but very few others. Their degree of success, however, is questionable, given that one of the largest, UNICO, became insolvent in 2003 due to Intel's decisions to source motherboards from China.

19   Unpublished statistics, Ministry of Trade and Industry.

20   This has been confirmed in a recent study conducted on behalf of the National Economic Action Council (NEAC) by Ratings Agency Malaysia (RAM). Interview with RAM consultant, June 2004.

21   MIDA data provided to an industry seminar in Penang, 15 June 2004. The public presentation of these data suggests that the 'gap' between firms in lower and higher tier levels of participation in GPNs is widely recognized in federal government agencies.

22   For instance, in 1994 only 9 per cent of the total value of US electronics exports was accounted for by locally-owned suppliers (Driffield and Noor 1999).

23   See endnote 18.

24   UNCTAD data available at: www.unctad.org. (accessed 21 January 2006)

25   While there are now calls from leading politicians to abandon the 'affirmative action' programme, the government is seeking to encourage further Bumiputera participation in real estate speculation (*The Economist* 2006)

7 China and global transformation

1   Fieldwork notes, April 2005 and April 2006. For rich ethnographic detail on the problems confronted by female migrant workers, see Pun (2005).

2   Chinese oil companies are not the only ones dealing with Sudan. The state owned Malaysian company, Petronas, for instance, operates in the country.

3   That the Chinese Government agreed in 2007 to send military personnel to Dafur, as part of a UN force, was widely assumed, in the US and European media, to have been

a decision driven by their desire to avoid a boycott of the 2008 Olympic Games in Beijing.

4 This is not unique to China, but is a general problem with the media throughout East Asia. The principal exception is The Philippines.

5 Malacca is the anglised name of the Malaysian city (which gives its name to the Ocean straight) known in Bahasa Malay as Melaka.

6 In May 2007, the Japanese Government approved a referendum on whether the Constitution should be rewritten to remove the clause that currently limits military expenditure and participation to defensive purposes only (Onishi 2007). Though participation in the various multilateral forces that are a significant feature of contemporary global politics has been the immediate context for this development, the principal reason seems undoubtedly to have been security concerns occasioned by the rise of China.

7 Though for a partial exception see Pieterse (2008).

8 Towards a global-Asian era?

1 As this chapter focuses predominantly on some of the economic and political aspects of globalization and the structures of power associated with them, I use the terms 'globalization' and 'global economic-political order' interchangeably.

2 Richard Hass (2008) has even predicted a world order characterized by 'non-polarity'.

3 Calculations in 2007 by the Asian Development Bank, subsequently given the World Bank's seal of approval (Keidel 2007). The ADB calculations also reveal that the extent of grinding poverty in China (those existing on less than US$1 a day) is, at 300 million people, three times higher than was thought.

4 And one in which real estate speculation could be central to the internal dynamics of the crisis, as it was in some of the East Asian economies in the late 1990s (see Chapter 4).

5 For the record of China's superior performance in health, vis -á- vis India and most other developing countries see Reddy (2007). Since the marketization of China's health care system, this performance has declined, but remains significantly better than that of India.

6 Taking equity stakes, for instance, in Barclays Bank (UK) and Merrill Lynch (US). Such developments complement the Chinese Government's long rumoured equity stake in the Hong Kong and Shanghai Banking Corporation (HSBC).

7 Caused by a military attack on an unarmed crowd attending a pro-democracy rally in Manchester.

8 Political authoritarianism and repression in China pre-dates the revolution of 1949, having been a feature of 'modern' China since the republican revolution of 1911 (repression in Imperial China is not relevant to this discussion). Taiwan is the only Chinese society ever to have evolved a democratic polity based on liberal-representative principles.

9 In over a century replete with instances where enlightenment values have been sidelined, witness, for instance, the US overthrow of the nascent nationalist government in The Philippines in 1898 (Miller 1984), the bombing and gassing of civilians by the British in Mesopotamia (now Iraq) in the 1920s (Glancey 2003), or the overthrow of democratically elected governments in Iran in 1953 – by the British and Americans (Halliday 1979) – Guatemala in 1954 or Chile in 1973, both with the active assistance of the US government (Globalsecurity NDa, NDb).

10 I use the term 'Occident' in preference to the ideologically-loaded, Cold War term, 'The West', with its geographical and cultural confusions (are Japan and South Korea, for instance, part of 'The West'?).

11 See Chapter 7, endnote 6.

12 With a nationalism rooted in an historic sense of victimization, Chinese nationalism seems more akin to Polish nationalism and those of small European countries such as Estonia, Latvia or Croatia (or, indeed, German nationalism between the two world wars)

than it does to the nationalisms – founded on imperial confidence – of former great powers such as Britain and France or, indeed, of the USA today.

13 Certainly if we take into account the extensive presence of US military bases on foreign soil and the activities of 'special forces' in helping to overthrow governments, assassinate politically inconvenient leaders and pursue the 'War on Terror'. Among a substantial literature that, at least, implies such a conclusion, see Johnson 2003, 2004; Harvey 2003).

REFERENCES

All URLs are live at the time of printing.

Ahuja, V., Bidani, B., Ferreira, F. and Walton M. (1997) *Everyone's Miracle? Revisiting Poverty and Inequality in East Asia,* Washington DC: The World Bank.

Akamatsu, K. (1962) 'A historical pattern of economic growth in developing countries', *The Developing Economies*, 1(1): 3–25.

Alden, C. (2007) *China in Africa*, London: Zed Books.

Alexandroni, S. (2007) 'NATO's rival in the East', *New Statesman*, 20 August.

Amsden, A. H. (1979) 'Taiwan's economic history: a case of "etatisme" and a challenge to dependency theory', *Modern China*, 5(3): 341–79.

—— (1985) 'The state and Taiwan's economic development' in P. Evans, D. Rueschemeyer and T. Skocpol (eds) *Bringing the State Back In,* New York: Cambridge University Press.

—— (1989) *Asia's Next Giant: South Korea and Late Industrialization*, New York: Oxford University Press.

—— (1990) 'Third World industrialization: "global fordism" or a new model?', *New Left Review*, I/182: 5–31.

—— (2001) *The Rise of "the Rest": Challenges to the West from Late-Industrializing Economies*, New York: Oxford University Press.

Amsden, A. H., Kochanowicz, J. and Taylor, L. (1994) *The Market Meets its Match: Restructuring the Economies of Eastern Europe*, Cambridge, MA: Harvard University Press.

Anderlini, J. (2008) 'China's angry youth vent their feelings', *Financial Times*, 2 May.

Appelbaum, R. P. and Henderson, J. (1992) (eds) *States and Development in the Asian Pacific Rim*, Newbury Park: Sage Publications.

—— (1995) 'The hinge of history: turbulence and transformation in the world economy', *Competition and Change*, 1(1): 1–12.

Appelbaum, R.P., Gereffi, G., Parker, R. and Ong R. (2006) From cheap labour to high technology leadership: will China's investment in nanotechnology pay off? Paper to the *Annual Conference of the Society for the Advancement of Socio-Economics*, Trier, Germany, 30 June – 2 July.

Appelbaum, R.P. and Parker, R.A. (2007) China's bid to become a global nano-tech leader:

advancing nanotechnology through state-led programs and international collaboration. Unpublished paper, Center for Nanotechnology and Society, Santa Barbara: University of California, (September).

Arnold, W. (2005) 'International business: Accusations in Malaysia amid trade policy dispute over cars', *New York Times*, 2 August , Available from: http://query.nytimes.com/gst/fullpage.html?res = 9F03E5D91E3FF931A3575BC0A9639C8B63 (accessed 3 February 2010)

Arrighi, G. (1996) The rise of East Asia: world systemic and regional aspects', *International Journal of Sociology and Social Policy*, 16(7/8): 6–44.

—— (2007) *Adam Smith in Beijing: Lineages of the 21st Century*, London: Verso.

Arrighi, G., Hamashita, T. and Seldon, M. (2003) (eds) *The Resurgence of East Asia: 500, 150 and 50 Years Perspectives*, Abingdon: Routledge.

Asia Monitor Resources Center (1988) *Min-Ju No-Jo: South Korea's New Trade Unions*, Hong Kong: Asia Monitor Resources Center.

Ba, A.D. (2003) 'China and ASEAN: renavigating relations for a 21st century Asia', *Asian Survey*, 43(4): 622–47.

Bair, J. (2005) 'Global capitalism and commodity chains: looking back, going forward', *Competition and Change*, 9(2): 153–80.

—— (2008) (ed.) *Frontiers of Commodity Chain Research*, Stanford: Stanford University Press.

Balassa, B. (1981) *Newly Industrialising Countries in the World Economy*, New York: Pergamon Press.

—— (1991) *Economic Policies in the Pacific Area Developing Countries*, London: Macmillan.

Baran, P. (1957) *The Political Economy of Growth*, New York: Monthly Review Press.

Bauer, P. T. and Yamey, B. S. (1957) *The Economics of Underdeveloped Countries*, London and Cambridge: James Nisbet and Cambridge University Press.

Bello, W. (1998) 'The Asian financial crisis: causes, dynamics and prospects', Paper for the Workshop on Assessing the Asian Crisis, Institute of Development Policy and Management, University of Manchester, April 7.

Berger, P. (1986) *The Capitalist Revolution: Fifty Propositions about Prosperity, Equality and Liberty,* New York: Basic Books.

Bergsten, C. F. (2008) 'China and the collapse of Doha', *Foreign Affairs*, 27 August.

Bernard, M. and Ravenhill, J. (1995) 'Beyond product cycles and flying geese: regionalization, hierarchy and the industrialization of East Asia', *World Politics,* 47(2): 171–209.

Best, M. (1997) 'Electronics expansion in Malaysia: the challenge of a stalled industrial expansion, *IKMAS Working Papers*, 11, Universiti Kebangsaan Malaysia.

Best, M. and Rasiah, R. (2003) 'Malaysian electronics at the crossroads', *Small and Medium Enterprise Working Paper*, 12, Geneva: United Nations Industrial Development Organization.

Boekestein, B. and Henderson, J. (2005) Thirsty dragon, hungry eagle: oil security in Sino-US relations. *IPEG Papers in Global Political Economy*, 21. British International Studies Association. Available from: http://www.bisa.ac.uk/groups/18/ipegpapers.htm

Boyer, R. (2000) 'Is a finance-led growth regime a viable alternative to Fordism? A preliminary analysis', *Economy and Society*, 29(1): 111–45.

Braudel, F. (1984) *Civilisation and Capitalism 15th – 18th Century, Vol. III: The Perspective of the World*, London: Fontana.

Brenner, R. (2003) *The Boom and the Bubble: The US in the Global Economy,* London: Verso.

—— (2005) *The Economics of Global Turbulence*, London: Verso.

Buzan, B. (2008) 'A leader without followers? The United States in world politics after Bush', *International Politics*, 45(5), 554–70.

Castells, M. (1992) 'Four Asian tigers with a dragon head: a comparative analysis of the state, economy and society in the Asian Pacific Rim', in R. P. Appelbaum and J. Henderson (eds) *States and Development in the Asian Pacific Rim*, Newbury Park: Sage Publications.

—— (2000a) *The Information Age: Economy, Society and Culture, vol. I: The Rise of the Network Society*, 2nd edn, Oxford: Blackwell.

—— (2000b) *The Information Age: Economy, Society and Culture, vol III: End of Millennium*, 2nd edn, Oxford: Blackwell.

—— (2003) *The Information Age: Economy, Society and Culture, vol II: The Power of Identity*, 2nd edn, Oxford: Blackwell.

Castells, M., Goh, L. and Kwok, R. Y. (1990) *The Shek Kip Mei Syndrome: Economic Development and Public Housing in Hong Kong and Singapore*, London: Pion.

Chang, H-J. (1994) *The Political Economy of Industrial Policy*, London: Macmillan.

—— (1998) 'Korea: the misunderstood crisis', *World Development*, 26(8): 1555–61.

—— (2000) 'The hazard of moral hazard: untangling the East Asian crisis', *World Development*, 28(4): 775–88.

—— (2002) *Kicking Away the Ladder: Development Strategy in Historical Perspective*, London: Anthem Books.

—— (2003) *Globalisation, Economic Development and the Role of the State*, London: Zed Books.

—— (2007a) *Bad Samaritans: Rich Nations, Poor Policies and the Threat to the Developing World*, London: Random House Business Books.

—— (2007b) 'State-owned enterprise reform', *National Development Strategies: Policy Notes*, New York: United Nations Department of Economic and Social Affairs (UNDESA). Available from: http://esa.un.org/techcoop/documents/PN_SOEReformNote.pdf (accessed 15 March 2010)

Chang, H-J. and Grabel, I. (2004) *Reclaiming Development: An Alternative Economic Policy Manual*, London: Zed Books.

Chang, H-J., Park, H-J. and Yoo, C. G. (1998) 'Interpreting the Korean crisis: financial liberalisation, industrial policy and corporate governance', *Cambridge Journal of Economics*, 22(6): 735–46.

Chang, M. H. (2001) *Return of the Dragon: China's Wounded Nationalism*, Boulder: Westview Press.

Chee, Y. H. (2003) 'Malaysia's Proton struggles on', *Asia Times*, 26 August. Available from: http://www.atimes.com/atimes/Southeast_Asia/EH26Ae01.html (accessed 3 February 2010)

Chen, E. K. Y. (1979) *Hyper-growth in Asian Economies: A Comparative Study of Hong Kong, Japan, Korea, Singapore and Taiwan*, London: Macmillan.

Chen, J. (2007) 'Poverty and income inequality in China: urban-rural income disparity and migration in an era of economic reform', unpublished PhD. thesis, Manchester Business School, University of Manchester.

Chen, T-J (1998) (ed.) *Taiwanese Firms in Southeast Asia: Networking Across Borders*, Cheltenham: Edward Elgar.

Cheung, S. N. S. (1986) *Will China Go 'Capitalist'?*, London: Institute of Economic Affairs.

Choung, J.Y. (1998) 'Co-evolution of national systems of innovation and sectoral systems of innovation: a case study of Korea and Taiwan', unpublished DPhil. thesis, Science Policy Research Unit, University of Sussex.

CIA (2010) *The World Fact Book*. Central Intelligence Agency, US Government. Available from: https://www.cia.gov/library/publications/the-world-factbook/geos/ks.html (accessed 8 March 2010).

Clark, R. G. (1995) 'More evidence on income distribution and growth', *Journal of Development Economics,* 47(2): 403–27.

Clarke, R., Driffield, N. and Noor, H. M. (2002) 'Technological activities of MNEs in developing countries: evidence from the electronics and electrical industry in Malaysia', *Working Paper*, Cardiff Business School.

Coates, D. (2000) *Models of Capitalism*, Cambridge: Polity Press.

Coe, N., Hess, M., Yeung, H.W.C., Dicken, P. and Henderson, J. (2004), 'Globalizing regional development: a global production networks perspective', *Transactions of the Institute of British Geographers*, 29(4): 468–84.

Cumings, B. (1987) 'The origins and development of the Northeast Asian political economy: industrial sectors, product cycles and political consequences', in F. C. Deyo (ed.) *The Political Economy of the New Asian Industrialism,* Ithaca: Cornell University Press.

—— (1997) *Korea's Place in the Sun*: *A Modern History,* New York: W.W. Norton.

—— (1998) 'The Korean crisis and the end of "late" development', *New Left Review,* I, 231: 43–72.

Dahrendorf, R. (1968) *Essays in the Theory of Society*, London: Routledge and Kegan Paul.

Davis, M. (2006) *Planet of Slums*, London: Verso.

Deacon, B. (1997) *Global Social Policy: International Organisations and the Future of Welfare*, London: Sage Publications.

Department of Statistics (ND) *Proportions of Semi and Unskilled Migrant Workers in Malaysian Manufacturing, 1981–2000*, Government of Malaysia, Malaysia Manufacturing Census.

Depner, H. and Bathelt, H. (2003) 'Cluster growth and institutional barriers: the development of the automobile industry cluster in Shanghai, P.R. China', *Spaces*, 09. Available from: http://www.spaces-online.uni-hd.de/include/SPACES%202003–9%20Depner-Bathelt.pdf (accessed 3 February 2010).

Deyo, F. C. (1987) (ed.) *The Political Economy of the New Asian Industrialism*, Ithaca: Cornell University Press.

—— (1989) *Beneath the Miracle: Labor Subordination in the New Asian Industrialism*, Berkeley and Los Angeles: University of California Press.

Dikötter, F. (1992) *The Discourse of Race in Modern China*, Hong Kong: Hong Kong University Press.

Dollar, D. and Kraay, A. (2001) 'Growth is good for the poor', *Policy Research Working Paper,* 2587, The World Bank.

Dore, R. (1986) *Flexible Rigidities: Industrial Policy and Structural Adjustment in the Japanese Economy, 1970–1980*, Stanford: Stanford University Press.

—— (2000) *Stock Market Capitalism – Welfare Capitalism: Germany and Japan versus the Anglo-Saxons,* Oxford: Oxford University Press.

Driffield, N. and Noor, H.M. (1999) 'Foreign direct investment and local input linkages in Malaysia', *Transnational Corporations*, 8(3): 1–24.

East Asia Analytical Unit (1995) *Overseas Chinese Business Networks in Asia*, Canberra: Department of Foreign Affairs and Trade, Commonwealth of Australia.

Elliott, L. and Atkinson, D. (2008) *The Gods that Failed: How Blind Faith in Markets has Cost Us Our Future*, London: Bodley Head.

Engels, F. (1892) *The Condition of the Working Class in England in 1844*, London: Allen & Unwin.

Ernst, D. (2003) 'How sustainable are benefits from global production networks? Malaysia's upgrading prospects in the electronics industry', *Working Paper*, 57, East-West Center, Hawaii.

Evans, P.B. (1995) *Embedded Autonomy: States and Industrial Transformation*, Princeton: Princeton University Press.

—— (2008) 'In search of the 21st century developmental state', *Working Paper*, 4, Brighton: University of Sussex, Centre for Global Political Economy.

Evans, P. B. and Rauch, J. (1999) 'Bureaucracy and growth: a cross-national analysis of the effects of "Weberian" state structures on economic growth', *American Sociological Review*, 64(4): 748–65.

Felker, G. (2003) 'Southeast Asian industrialisation and the changing global production system', *Third World Quarterly*, 24(2): 255–82.

Frank, A.G. (1969) *Capitalism and Underdevelopment in Latin America: Historical Studies of Chile and Brazil*, Harmondsworth: Penguin Books.

—— (1982) 'Asia's exclusive models', *Far Eastern Economic Review*, 25 June: 22–23.

—— (1998) *ReOrient: Global Economy in the Asian Age,* Berkeley and Los Angeles: University of California Press.

Friedman, M. and Friedman, R. (1982) *Free to Choose*, Harmondsworth: Penguin Books.

Fullbrook, E. (2004) (ed.) *A Guide to What's Wrong with Economics*, London: Anthem Press.

Gereffi, G. and Kaplinsky, R. (2001) (eds) *The Value of Value Chains*, Special Issue of *IDS Bulletin*, 32(3).

Gereffi, G. and Korzeniewicz, M. (1994) (eds) *Commodity Chains and Global Capitalism*, New York: Praeger.

Gereffi, G., Humphrey, J. and Sturgeon, T. (2005) 'The governance of global value chains', *Review of International Political Economy*, 12(1): 78–104.

Glancey, J. (2003) 'Our last occupation: gas, chemicals, bombs: Britain has used them all before in Iraq', *The Guardian*, 19 April.

Globalsecurity (NDa) Guatemala coup, Globalsecurity. Available from: http://www.globalsecurity.org/military/world/war/guatemalacoup.htm, (accessed 23 October 2007).

Globalsecurity (NDb) Allende's leftist regime, Globalsecurity. Available from: http://www.globalsecurity.org/military/world/war/allende.htm, (accessed 23 October 2007).

Glyn, A. (2006) *Capitalism Unleashed: Finance, Globalization and Welfare*, Oxford: Oxford University Press.

Gold, T. (1986) *State and Society in the Taiwan Miracle,* Armonk: M. E. Sharpe.

Goldstone, J. A. (1995) 'The coming Chinese collapse', *Foreign Policy*, 96: 35–52.

Gomez, E.T. (1998) *Chinese Business in Malaysia*, London: Curzon Press.

Gomez, E.T. and Hsiao, H.H.M. (2003) (eds) *Chinese Business in Southeast Asia: Contesting Cultural Explanations, Researching Entrepreneurship*, London: Routledge.

Gomez, E.T. and Jomo, K.S. (1997) *Malaysia's Political Economy: Politics, Patronage and Profits*, Cambridge: Cambridge University Press.

Gottschalk, R. and Prates, D. (2005) Macroeconomic challenges of East Asia's growing demand for primary commodities in Latin America. Unpublished Paper, Institute of Development Studies, University of Sussex. Available from: http://www.ids.ac.uk/ids/global/pdfs/RGMacro%20Challenge.pdf, (accessed 23 August 2007).

Gough, I. (2001) 'Globalization and regional welfare regimes', *Global Social Policy*, 1(2): 163–89.

Gries, P. H. (2005) *China's New Nationalism: Pride, Politics and Diplomacy*, Berkeley and Los Angeles: University of California Press.

Gu, J., Humphrey, J. and Messner, D. (2008) 'Global governance and developing countries: the implications of the rise of China', *World Development*, 36(2): 274–92.

Haggard, S. (1990) *Pathways from the Periphery: The Politics of Growth in the Newly Industrializing Countries*, Ithaca: Cornel University Press.

—— (2000) *The Political Economy of the Asian Financial Crisis*, Washington DC: International Institute of Economic Affairs.

Haggard, S., Li, L. and Ong, A. (1998) 'The hard disk drive industry in the northern region of Malaysia', *The Information Storage Industry Center Working Paper*, 98–04, University of California, San Diego.

Hall, P. H. and Soskice, D. (2001) (eds) *Varieties of Capitalism*: *The Institutional Foundations of Comparative Advantage*, New York: Oxford University Press.

Halliday, F. (1979) *Iran: Dictatorship and Development*, London: Penguin Books.

Halliday, J. (1974) 'Hong Kong: Britain's Chinese colony', *New Left Review*, I, 87–88: 91–112.

Harris, N. (1987) *The End of the Third World: Newly Industrialising Countries and the Decline of an Ideology*, Harmondsworth: Penguin Books.

Harvey, D. (1978) 'The urban process under capitalism: a framework for analysis', *International Journal of Urban and Regional Research*, 2(1): 101–31.

—— (1982) *The Limits to Capital,* Oxford: Blackwell.

—— (2003) *The New Imperialism,* Oxford: Oxford University Press.

—— (2005) *A Brief History of Neoliberalism,* Oxford: Oxford University Press.

Hass, R. N. (2008) 'The age of nonpolarity', *Foreign Affairs*, 87(3): 44–56.

Hayter, R. and Edgington, D.W. (2004) 'Flying geese in Asia: the impacts of Japanese MNCs as a source of industrial learning', *Tijdschrift voor Economische en Sociale Geografie*, 95(1): 3–26.

Hayter, T. and Watson, C. (1985) *Aid: Rhetoric and Reality,* London: Pluto Press.

Held, D., McGrew, A., Goldblatt, D. and Perraton, J. (1999) *Global Transformations: Politics, Economics and Culture*, Cambridge: Polity Press.

Henderson, J. (1989) *The Globalisation of High Technology Production: Society, Space and Semiconductors in the Restructuring of the Modern World*, London: Routledge.

—— (1991) 'Urbanisation in the Hong Kong-South China region: an introduction to the dynamics and dilemmas', *International Journal of Urban Research*, 15(2): 169–79.

—— (1993) 'Industrial policy for Britain: lessons from the East', *Renewal*, 1(2): 32–42.

—— (1994) 'Electronics industries and the developing world: uneven contributions and uncertain prospects' in L. Sklair (ed.) *Capitalism and Development*, London: Routledge.

—— (1998) (ed.) *Industrial Transformation in Eastern Europe in the Light of the East Asian Experience*, London: Macmillan.

—— (2010) 'Neoliberal globalization' in N. Young (ed.) *The Oxford International Encyclopedia of Peace Vol III,* New York: Oxford University Press.

Henderson, J. and D. Hulme (2002) *Globalisation, national economic governance and poverty elimination: insights from East Asia and Eastern Europe.* Final Report to the Department for International Development, British Government (Available from: www.gapresearch.org/governance/DFIDFinalreport3.pdf)

Henderson, J., Dicken, P., Hess, M, Coe, N. and Yeung, H.W-C. (2002a) 'Global production networks and the analysis of economic development', *Review of International Political Economy*, 9(3): 436–64.

Henderson, J., Hulme, D., Phillips, R. and Ainur, N.M.N. (2002b) 'Economic governance and poverty reduction in Malaysia', *Working Paper*, 440, Manchester Business School.

Henderson, J., Hulme, D., Phillips, R., and Kim, E.M. (2002c) 'Economic governance and poverty reduction in South Korea', *Working Paper*, 439, Manchester Business School.

Henderson, J., Hulme, D., Jalilian, H. and Phillips, R. (2007) 'Bureaucratic effects: "Weberian" state agencies and poverty reduction', *Sociology*, 41(3): 515–32.

Hewison, K. (1997) 'Thailand: capitalist development and the state' in G. Rodan, K. Hewison and R. Robison (eds) *The Political Economy of Southeast Asia: An Introduction*, Melbourne: Oxford University Press.

Higgott, R. (1998) 'The Pacific and beyond: APEC, ASEM and regional economic management' in G. Thompson (ed.) *Economic Dynamism in the Asia-Pacific*, London: Routledge.

Hill, H. (1996) *Southeast Asia's Emerging Giant: Indonesian Economic Policy and Development since 1966*, Cambridge: Cambridge University Press.

Hilton, R. H. (1976) (ed.) *The Transition from Feudalism to Capitalism*, London: New Left Books.

Hirst, P.Q. and Thompson, G. (1999) *Globalization in Question: The International Economy and the Possibilities of Governance* (2nd Edition), Cambridge: Polity Press.

Ho, S. Y. (1990) *Taiwan – after a Long Silence*, Hong Kong: Asia Monitor Resources Centre.

Hobday, M. (1995) *Innovation in East Asia*, Aldershot: Edward Elgar.

Hobsbawm, E. (1994) *Age of Extremes: The Short Twentieth Century, 1914–1991*, London: Michael Joseph.

Hodder, R. (1996) *Merchant Princes of the East: Cultural Delusions, Economic Success and the Overseas Chinese in Southeast Asia*, Chichester: Wiley.

Hodgson, G. (2001) *How Economics Forgot History: The Problem of Historical Specificity in Social Science*, London: Routledge.

Holton, R. J. (1985) *The Transition from Feudalism to Capitalism*, Basingstoke: Macmillan.

Houtzager, P. and Moore, M. (2003) (eds) *Changing Paths: International Development and the New Politics of Inclusion*, Ann Arbor: University of Michigan Press.

Hsiao, H. H. M. (1995) 'The state and business relations in Taiwan', *Journal of Far Eastern Business*, 1(3): 76–97.

Hsing, Y.T. (1998) *Making Capitalism in China: The Taiwan Connection*, New York: Oxford University Press.

Huang, Y. (1995) 'Why China will not collapse', *Foreign Policy*, 96: 54–68.

Hung, H-F. (2008) 'Rise of China and the global overaccumulation crisis', *Review of International Political Economy*, 15(2): 149–79.

—— (2009) (ed.) *China and the Transformation of Global Capitalism*, Baltimore: Johns Hopkins University Press.

Hutchinson, T.W. (1994) *The Uses and Abuses of Economics: Contentious Essays on History and Method*, London: Routledge.

Hutton, W. (2002) *The World We're In*, London: Little, Brown.

—— (2007) *The Writing on the Wall: China and the West in the 21st Century*, London: Little, Brown.

Hutton, W. and Desai, M (2007) 'Does the future really belong to China?', *Prospect* 130: 26–30.

Ikenberry, G. J. (2005) 'Power and liberal order: America's postwar world order in Transition', *International Relations of the Asia-Pacific*, 5(2):133–52.

ILO (1998) *The Social Impact of the Asian Financial Crisis (Technical Report for the High Level*

Tripartite Meeting on Social Responses to the Financial Crisis in East and South-East Asian Countries, Bangkok, April 22–24), Bangkok, International Labour Office Regional Office for Asia and the Pacific.

Ishida, A. and Hassan, S. (2000) 'Why do migrant workers intend to extend their stay in host countries? The case of Bangladeshi workers in Malaysia's manufacturing sector', *International Migration,* 38(5): 99–115.

Ismail, M. N. (1995) *Transnational Corporations and Economic Development in Malaysia,* Kuala Lumpur: University of Malaya Press.

—— (2001) 'Foreign direct investments and development: the Malaysian electronics sector', *CMI Working Paper,* 2001–4, Chr. Michelsen Institute: Bergen.

Jacques, M. (2009) *When China Rules the World: The Rise of the Middle Kingdom and the End of the Western World,* London: Allen Lane.

Jenkins, R. and Edwards, C. (2006) 'The Asian Drivers and Sub-Saharan Africa', *IDS Bulletin,* 37(1): 23–32.

Jenkins, R., Dussel Peters, E. and Mesquita Moreira, M. (2008) 'The impact of China on Latin America and the Caribbean', *World Development,* 36(2): 235–53.

Jesudason, J. (1989) *Ethnicity and the Economy: the State, Chinese Business and Multinationals in Malaysia,* Singapore: Oxford University Press.

JICA (2001) *Study on Strengthening Supporting Industries through Technology Transfer in Malaysia,* Tokyo: Japan International Cooperation Agency /Penang Development Corporation.

Jin, N. K. (1996) 'Singapore as a financial center: new developments, challenges and prospects' in T. Ito and A.O Krueger (eds) *Financial Deregulation and Integration in East Asia,* Chicago: University of Chicago Press.

Jin, S. (1998) 'The causes of the financial crisis in Korea', unpublished paper, School of Economic Studies, University of Manchester.

Johnson, C. (1977) 'MITI and Japanese international economic policy', in R. S. Scalapino (ed.) *The Foreign Policy of Modern Japan,* Berkeley and Los Angeles: University of California Press.

—— (1982) *MITI and the Japanese Miracle: The Growth of Industrial Policy,* 1925–75, Stanford: Stanford University Press.

—— (1988) 'The Japanese political economy: a crisis in theory', *Ethics and International Affairs,* 2: 79–97.

—— (2003) *Blowback: The Costs and Consequences of American Empire,* New York: Henry Holt.

—— (2004) *The Sorrows of Empire: Militarism, Secrecy and the End of the Republic,* New York: Metropolitan Books.

Jomo, K. S. (1990) *Growth and Structural Change in the Malaysian Economy,* London: Macmillan.

—— (1998) (ed.) *Tigers in Trouble: Financial Governance, Liberalisation and Crises in East Asia,* London: Zed Books.

—— (2001) 'From current crisis to recession' in Jomo, K.S. (ed.) *Malaysian Eclipse: Economic Crisis and Recovery,* London: Zed Books.

—— (2007) (ed.) *Malaysian Industrial Policy,* Singapore: Singapore University Press.

Jomo, K.S., Chen Y.C., Folk, B.C., ul-Haque, I., Pasuk P., Simatupang B. and Tateishi, M. (1997) *Southeast Asia's Misunderstood Miracle: Industrial Policy and Economic Development in Thailand, Malaysia and Indonesia,* Boulder: Westview Press.

Jomo, K.S., Felker, G. and Rasiah, R. (1999) (eds) *Industrial Technology Development in Malaysia,* London: Routledge.

Jullien, F. (1999) 'A philosophical use of China: an interview with Francois Jullien', *Thesis Eleven*, 57: 113–30.

Kanbur, R. (2000) 'Income distribution and development' in A. Atkinson and F. Bourguignon (eds) *Handbook of Income Distribution*, Oxford: Elsevier.

Kaplan, R. (2009) 'Center stage for the twenty-first century: power plays in the Indian Ocean', *Foreign Affairs*, 88(2): 16–32.

Kaplinsky, R. (2005) *Globalization, Poverty and Inequality: Between a Rock and a Hard Place*, Cambridge: Polity Press.

Kaplinsky, R. and Morris, M. (2008) 'Do the Asian Drivers undermine export oriented industrialisation in SSA?', *World Development*: 36(2): 254–73.

Kay, N. M. (1984) *The Emergent Firm: Knowledge, Ignorance and Surprise in Economic Organisation*, London: Macmillan.

Keidel, A. (2007) 'The limits of a smaller, poorer China', *Financial Times*, 14 November.

Kennedy, P. (1989) *The Rise and Fall of the Great Powers: Economic Change and Military Conflict from 1500 to 2000*, London: Fontana Press.

Kim, E. M. (1997) *Big Business, Strong State: Collusion and Conflict in South Korean Development, 1960–1990*, Albany: State University of New York Press.

Kim, W. J. (1997) *Economic Growth, Low Income and Housing in South Korea*, London: Macmillan.

Kim, E. M. and Mah, J. S. (2006), 'Patterns of South Korea's foreign direct investment flows into China', *Asian Survey*, 46(6): 881-97.

Ko, A. and Redding, S.G. (1998) 'Chinese capitalism in Hong Kong: a business system adapted to threat', Paper for the Workshop on East Asian Development Models in Crisis?, Manchester Business School, June 9.

Kojima, K. (2000) 'The "flying geese" model of Asian economic development: origin, theoretical extensions and regional policy implications', *Journal of Asian Economics*, 11(4): 375–401.

Komesaroff, M. (2008) 'China eyes Congo's treasures', *Far Eastern Economic Review*, April.

Koo, H. and Kim, E. M. (1992) 'The developmental state and capital accumulation in South Korea', in R. P. Appelbaum and J. Henderson (eds) *States and Development in the Asian Pacific Rim*, Newbury Park: Sage Publications.

Krugman, P. (1994) 'The myth of Asia's miracle', *Foreign Affairs*, 73(6): 62–78.

Lal, D. (1983) *The Poverty of 'Development Economics'*, London: Institute of Economic Affairs.

Lall, S. (1995), 'Malaysia: industrial success and the role of the Government', *Journal of International Development*, 7(5): 759–73.

Lall, S. and Albaladejo, M. (2004) 'China's competitive performance: A threat to East Asian manufactured exports?', *World Development*, 32: 1441–66.

Lane, D. and Myant, M. R. (2006) (eds) *Varieties of Capitalism in Post-Communist Countries*, London: Palgrave Macmillan.

Lakhera, M. L. (2008), *Japanese FDI Flows in Asia: Perspectives and Challenges*, London: Palgrave Macmillan.

Lanteigne, M. (2005) *China and International Institutions: Alternate Paths to Global Power*, London: Routledge.

—— (2008) 'China's maritime security and the "Malacca dilemma"', *Asian Security*, 4(2): 143–61.

Lau, B.K.F. (2007) 'A tale of two regions: how China affected the textiles and clothing exports of other Asian economies', Paper to the *Conference on Southern Engines of Growth*,

Helsinki: United Nations University World Institute for Development Economics Research, 7–8 September.

Lazonick, W. (1991) *Business Organization and the Myth of the Market Economy*, New York: Cambridge University Press.

Lee, S.Y. (1990) *Money and Finance in the Economic Development of Taiwan*, London: Macmillan.

Liew, L.H. (2006) 'China's engagement with neo-liberalism: path dependency, geography and Party self-reinvention' in K. Hewison and R. Robison (eds) *East Asia and the Trials of Neo-Liberalism*, London: Routledge.

Lim, L. and Pang, E. F. (1991) *Foreign Direct Investment and Industrialization in Malaysia, Singapore, Taiwan and Thailand*, Paris: OECD Development Centre.

Lim, L. Y. C. (1983) 'Singapore's success: the myth of the free market economy', *Asian Survey*, 23(6): 752–64.

Lin, J.Y. (2003) 'Development strategy, viability and economic convergence', *Economic Development and Cultural Change*, 51(2): 277–308.

—— (2005) 'Viability, economic transition and reflections on neo-classical economics', *Kyklos*, 58(2): 239–64.

Lin, K. S., Lee H.Y. and Huang, B.Y. (1996) 'The role of macroeconomic policy in export-led growth: the experience of Taiwan and South Korea' in T. Ito and A.O. Krueger (eds) *Financial Deregulation and Integration in East Asia*. Chicago: University of Chicago Press.

Little, I., Scitovsky, T. and Scott, M. (1970) *Industry and Trade in Some Developing Countries*, Oxford: Oxford University Press.

Lo, D. and Radice, H. (1998) 'Institutional chance and economic development in East-Central Europe and China: contrasts in the light of the "East Asian model"' in J. Henderson (ed.) *Industrial Transformation in Eastern Europe in the Light of the East Asia Experience,* London: Macmillan.

Lubeck, P. (1992) 'Malaysian industrialization, ethnic divisions and the NIC model: the limits to replication' in R.P. Appelbaum and J. Henderson (eds) *States and Development in the Asian Pacific Rim*, Newbury Park: Sage Publications.

Lüthje, B. (2002) 'Electronics contract manufacturing: global production and the international division of labor in the age of the internet', *Industry and Innovation*, 9(3): 227–47.

Mahbubani, K. (2008) *The New Asian Hemisphere: The Irresistable Shift of Global Power to the East,* New York: Public Affairs.

McCormack, G. (1991) 'The price of affluence: the political economy of Japanese leisure', *New Left Review*, I, 188: 121–34.

McGregor, R. (2006) 'Up for the job? How India and China risk being stifled by a skills squeeze', *Financial Times*, 20 July.

McVeigh, K. (2007) 'The sweatshop high street – more brands under fire', *The Guardian*, 3 September.

Miller, S.C. (1984) *Benevolent Assimilation: The American Conquest of The Philippines, 1899–1903*, New Haven: Yale University Press.

Milne, S. (2008) 'Georgia is the graveyard of America's unipolar world', *The Guardian,* 28 August.

Mirza, H. (1986) *Multinationals and the Growth of the Singapore Economy*, New York: St Martin's Press.

Moore, B. (1966) *Social Origins of Dictatorship and Democracy: Landlord and Peasant in the Making of the Modern World*, Boston: Beacon Press.

Morishima, M. (1982) *Why has Japan 'Succeeded'?,* Cambridge: Cambridge University Press.

Moulder, F. (1977) *Japan, China and the Modern World Economy*, New York: Cambridge University Press.

Murphy, R. T. (2006) 'East Asia's Dollars', *New Left Review*, II/40: 39–64.

Muscat, R. J. (1994) *The Fifth Tiger: A Study of Thai Development Policy*, Armonk: M. E. Sharpe.

Nee, V. and Opper, S. (2007) 'On politicized capitalism' in V. Nee and R. Swedberg (eds) *On Capitalism*, Stanford: Stanford University Press.

Nee, V. and Su, S. (1998) 'Institutional foundations of robust economic performance: public sector industrial growth in China' in J. Henderson, (ed.) *Industrial Transformation in Eastern Europe in the light of the East Asia Experience*, London: Macmillan.

NIC (2004) *Mapping the Global Future*, Washington DC: National Intelligence Council.

Nolan, P. (1995) *China's Rise, Russia's Fall: Politics, Economics and Planning in the Transition from Stalinism*, London: Macmillan.

—— (2001) *China and the Global Economy: National Champions, Industrial Policy and the Big Business Revolution*, London: Palgrave Macmillan.

—— (2004a) *China at the Crossroads*, Cambridge: Polity Press.

—— (2004b) *Transforming China: Globalisation, Transition and Development*, London: Anthem Press.

Noor, H. M., Clarke, R. and Driffield, N. (2002) 'Multinational enterprises and technological effort by local firms: a case study of the Malaysian electronics and electrical Industry', *Journal of Development Studies*, 38(6):129–41.

OECD (2009) *OECD Factbook 2009: Economic, Environmental and Social Statistics*, Paris: Organization for Economic Cooperation and Development. Available from: http://lysander.sourceoecd.org/vl = 11371257/cl = 21/nw = 1/rpsv/factbook2009/06/03/02/index.htm (accessed 25 February 2010).

Offe, C. (1975) 'The theory of the capitalist state and the problem of policy formation' in L. N. Lindberg, R. Alford, C. Crouch and C. Offe (eds) *Stress and Contradiction in Modern Capitalism*, Lexington: Lexington Books.

Ong, A. (2000) 'Penang's manufacturing competitiveness', Economic Briefing to the Penang State Government, July.

Onishi, N. (2007) 'Japan sets referendum on Pacifist Constitution', *New York Times*, 14 May.

Park, N-H. (2001) 'Poverty rate and poverty line in Korea', Conference paper, Philippine Institute for Development Studies (April).

Parsonage, J. (1997) 'Trans-state developments in Southeast Asia: subregional growth zones' in G. Rodan, K. Hewison and R. Robison (eds) *The Political economy of Southeast Asia*, Melbourne: Oxford University Press.

Pasuk, P. and Baker, C. (1997) *Thailand: Economy and Politics*, Kuala Lumpur: Oxford University Press.

Pei, M. (2006) *China's Trapped Transition: The Limits of Developmental Autocracy*, Cambridge, Mass: Harvard University Press.

Perera, Q. (2006) 'Sri Lanka should strive to gain additional garment export markets', *Asian Tribune* 11 May. Available from: www.asiantribune.com, (accessed 23 August 2007).

Persson, T. and Tabellini, G. (1994) 'Is inequality harmful to growth?', *American Economic Review*, 84(3): 600–621.

Phillips, R. and Henderson, J. (2009) 'Global production networks and industrial upgrading: negative lessons from Malaysian electronics', *Journal für Entwicklungspolitik (Austrian Journal of Development Studies)*, XXV(2): 38–61.

Phillips, R., Henderson, J., Andor, L. and Hume, D. (2006) 'Usurping social policy: neoliberalism and economic governance in Hungary', *Journal of Social Policy*, 35(4): 585–606.

Pieterse, J. N. (2008) 'Globalization the next round: sociological perspectives', *Futures*, 40: 707–20.

Pirie, I. (2007) *The Korean Developmental State: From Dirigisme to Neoliberalism,* London: Routledge.

Polanyi, K. (1957) *The Great Transformation: The Political and Economic Origins of Our Time* (2nd Edition), Boston: Beacon Press.

Pontusson, J. (2005) *Inequality and Prosperity: Social Europe versus Liberal America*, Ithaca: Cornell University Press.

Porter, M. E. (1990) *The Competitive Advantage of Nations*, London: Macmillan.

PSPD/UNDP (2000) *Poverty Status and Monitoring of Korea in the Aftermath of the Financial Crisis,* Seoul: People's Solidarity for Participatory Democracy and the United Nations Development Programme.

Pun, N. (2005) *Made in China: Women Factory Workers in a Global Workplace*, Durham, NC: Duke University Press.

Qian, Y. and Weingast, B. R. (1997) 'Institutions, state activism and economic development: a comparison of state-owned and township-village enterprises in China' in M. Aoki, H.K. Kim and M. Okuno-Fujiwara (eds) *The Role of Government in East Asian Economic Development*, Oxford: Clarendon Press.

Rapa, A. (2007) *The Socio-economic Impacts of Logging in Papua New Guinea*, MSc Dissertation, School of Environment and Development, University of Manchester.

Rasiah, R. (1995) *Foreign Capital and Industrialization in Malaysia,* London: Macmillan.

—— (1999a) 'Regional dynamics and production networks: the development of electronics clusters in Malaysia', Paper to the conference on *Global Networks, Innovation And Regional Development: The Informational Region As Development Strategy*, University of California, Santa Cruz (November 11-13).

—— (1999b) 'Government-business co-ordination and the development of Eng Hardware' in Jomo, K.S., G. Felker and R. Rasiah, (eds) *Industrial Technology Development in Malaysia: Industry and Firm Studies*, London: Routledge.

—— (2001) 'Pre-crisis economic weaknesses and vulnerabilities' in Jomo, K.S. (ed.) *Malaysian Eclipse: Economic Crisis and Recovery*, London: Zed Books.

—— (2002a) 'Systemic coordination and human capital development: knowledge flows in Malaysia's MNC-driven electronics cluster', *INTECH Discussion Paper*, 2002–7, Maastricht: United Nations University.

—— (2002b) 'Manufactured exports, employment, skills and wages in Malaysia', *Employment Paper*, 2002/35, Geneva: International Labour Office.

Rauch, J. and Evans, P. (2000) 'Bureaucratic structure and bureaucratic performance in less developed countries', *Journal of Public Economics,* 75(1): 49–71.

Ravenhill, J. (2006) 'Is China and economic threat to Southeast Asia?', *Asian Survey*, 46(5): 653–74.

Redding, S. G. (1990) *The Spirit of Chinese Capitalism,* Berlin: de Gruyter.

Reddy, S. (2007) 'Death in China: market reforms and health', *New Left Review*, 45: 49–65.

Ritchie, B.K. (2005) 'Coalition politics, economic reform and technological upgrading in Malaysia', *World Development*, 33(5): 745–61.

Robison, R. (1993) 'Indonesia: tensions in state and regime' in K. Hewison, R. Robison and G. Rodan (eds) *Southeast Asia in the 1990s: Authoritarianism, Democracy and Capitalism*, Sydney: Allen and Unwin.

Robison, R. (1997) 'Politics and markets in Indonesia's post-oil boom' in G. Rodan, K. Hewison and R. Robison (eds) *The Political Economy of Southeast Asia: An Introduction*, Melbourne: Oxford University Press.

Rodan, G. (1989) *The Political Economy of Singapore's Industrialisation: National State and International Capital*, London: Macmillan.

Roslan, A. (2001), 'Income inequality, poverty and development policy in Malaysia', Paper presented to the *Conference on Poverty and Sustainable Development*, Universite Montesquieu-Bordeaux IV (November).

Runciman, W. G. (1995) 'The "triumph" of capitalism as a topic in the theory of social selection', *New Left Review*, I/210: 33–47.

Sachs, J. D. and Woo, W. T. (1994) 'Structural factors in the economic reforms of China, Eastern Europe and the former Soviet Union', *Economic Policy*, 18: 101–31.

Salih, K. (1988) 'The new economic policy after 1990', *Discussion Papers*, 21, Malaysian Institute for Economic Research.

Salih, K. and Young, M.L. (1987) 'Social forces, the state and the international division of labour: the case of Malaysia' in J. Henderson and M. Castells (eds) *Global Restructuring and Territorial Development*, London: Sage Publications.

Salih, K. and Yusof, Z.A. (1989) 'Overview of the New Economic Policy and framework for the post-1990 economic policy', *Malaysian Management Review*, 24(2): 13–61.

Sassen, S. (1991) *The Global City: New York, London, Tokyo*, Princeton: Princeton University Press.

Sayer, A. (1984) *Method in Social Science*, London: Methuen.

Schiffer, J. (1991) 'State policy and economic growth: a note on the Hong Kong model', *International Journal of Urban and Regional Research*, 15(2): 180–96.

Scott, A. J. (2002) 'Regional push: towards a geography of development and growth in low and middle-income countries', *Third World Quarterly*, 23(1): 137–61.

Seagrave, S. (1985) *The Soong Dynasty*, New York: Vintage Books.

Seagrave, S. (1996) *Lords of the Rim: The Invisible Empire of the Overseas Chinese*, London: Corgi Books.

Shafaeddin, S. (2004) 'Is China's accession to WTO threatening exports of developing countries?', *China Economic Review,* 15(2): 109–44.

Shirk, S. L. (2007) *China: Fragile Superpower*, New York: Oxford University Press.

Singh, A. and Weisse, B.A. (1998) 'Emerging stock markets, portfolio capital flows and long-term economic growth: micro and macroeconomic perspectives', *World Development*, 26(4): 607–22.

Slaughter, M. (2002) 'Skill upgrading in developing countries: Has inward foreign direct investment played a role?', *Development Centre Technical Paper Series*, 192, Paris: OECD Development Centre.

So, A.Y. and Chiu, S.W.K (1995) (eds) *East Asia and the World Economy*, Newbury Park: Sage Publications.

Staples, A. J. (2008) *Responses to Regionalism in East Asia: Japanese Production Networks in the Automotive Sector*, London: Palgrave Macmillan.

Stigler, G. J. (1984) 'Economics – the imperial science?', *Scandinavian Journal of Economics*, 68(3): 301–13.

Stiglitz, J. (2002) *Globalization and Its Discontents*, London: Allen Lane.

—— (2010), *Freefall: Free Markets and the Sinking of the Global Economy*, London: Allen Lane.

Strange, S. (1998) *Mad Money: A Sequel to 'Casino Capitalism'*. Manchester: Manchester University Press.

Sturgeon, T. and Lester, R. (2002) 'Upgrading East Asian industries: new challenges for local suppliers', *Industrial Performance Center Working Paper,* 03–001, Massachusetts Institute of Technology.

Taylor, I. (2006) *China and Africa: Engagement and Compromise,* London: Routledge.

Taylor, M. (1995) 'Dominance through technology: Is Japan creating a Yen block in Southeast Asia?', *Foreign Affairs,* 74(6): 14–20.

The Economist (2006) 'Badawi's grand plan', *The Economist,* 7 April: 66.

Thompson, G. (1998) (ed.) *Economic Dynamism in the Asia-Pacific,* London: Routledge.

Thornton, J. (1995) 'The Japanese Bureaucracy and economic development: are there lessons for Russia and the reforming socialist economies?' in H-K. Kim, M. Muramatsu, T.J. Pempel and K. Yamamura (eds) *The Japanese Civil Service and Economic Development,* Oxford: Clarendon Press.

UNCTAD (2001) *World Investment Report 2001: Promoting Linkages,* Geneva: United Nations Conference on Trade and Development.

UNCTAD (2002) *World Investment Report 2002: Transnational Corporations and Export Competitiveness* Geneva: United Nations Conference on Trade and Development.

UNDP (1994) *Technology Transfer to Malaysia: The Electronics and Electrical Goods Sector and the Supporting Industries in Penang,* Kuala Lumpur: United Nations Development Programme.

Vartiainen, J. (1995) 'The state and structural change; what can be learned from the successful late industralizers?' in H-J Chang and R. Rowthorn (eds) *The Role of the State in Economic Change,* Oxford: Clarendon Press.

Viner, J. (1953) *International Trade and Economic Development,* Oxford: Clarendon Press.

Wade, R. (1990) *Governing the Market: Economic Theory and the Role of Government in East Asian Industrialization,* Princeton: Princeton University Press.

Wade, R. (1996) 'Japan, the World Bank and the art of paradigm maintenance: the East Asian miracle in political perspective', *New Left Review,* I, 217: 3–36.

Wade, R. (1998) 'The Asian debt-and-development crisis of 1997-?: causes and consequences', *World Development,* 26(8): 1535–53.

Wade, R. and Veneroso, F. (1998a) 'The Asian crisis: the high debt model versus the Wall Street-Treasury-IMF Complex', *New Left Review,* I/228: 3–23.

Wade, R. and F. Veneroso (1998b) 'The gathering world slump and the battle over capital controls', *New Left Review,* 231: 13–42.

Wang, C-I. (2009) 'The changing nature of China's economic governance: local variations, institutions and state-private sector relations', unpublished PhD. thesis, Manchester Business School, University of Manchester.

Wangle, A. (2001) 'Manufacturing growth with social deficits: Environmental and labor issues in the high tech industry of Penang, Malaysia', *IPL Technical Report,* 294–01, Danmarks Tekniske Universitet.

Watts, J. (2010) 'Drought turns southern China into arid plain', *The Guardian,* 7 April. Available from: http://www.guardian.co.uk/environment/2010/apr/07/drought-southern-china (accessed 8 April 2010).

White, G. (1988) (ed.) *Developmental States in East Asia,* London: Macmillan.

White, H. (2002) 'Combining quantitative and qualitative approaches in poverty analysis', *World Development,* 30(3): 511–22.

Whitley, R. D. (1992) *Business Systems in East Asia: Firms, Markets and Societies,* London: Sage Publications.

Whitley, R. (1999) *Divergent Capitalisms: The Social Structuring and Change of Business Systems,* Oxford: Oxford University Press.

WIDER (1990) *Foreign Portfolio Investment in Emerging Equity Markets*, Study Group Series No 5, Helsinki: World Institute of Development Economics Research.

Wilkinson, R. and Pickett, K. (2009) *The Spirit Level: Why More Equal Societies Almost Always Do Better*, London: Allen Lane.

Winters, L.A. and Yusuf, S. (2007) (eds) *Dancing with Giants: China, India and the Global Economy*, Washington DC. and Singapore: The World Bank and the Institute of Policy Studies.

Wong, S. L. (1988) *Emigrant Entrepreneurs: Shanghainese Industrialists in Hong Kong*, Hong Kong: Oxford University Press.

Woo, J. E. (1991) *Race to the Swift: State and Finance in Korean Industrialisation*, New York: Columbia University Press.

Woo, M. J. E. (2007) (ed.) *After the Miracle: Neoliberalism and Institutional Reform in East Asia*, Basingstoke: Palgrave Macmillan.

Woo, W.T. and Hirayama, K. (1996) 'Monetary autonomy in the presence of capital flows: and never the twain shall meet, except in East Asia' in T. Ito and A.O Krueger (eds) *Financial Deregulation and Integration in East Asia*, Chicago: University of Chicago Press.

Woo-Cumings, M. (1999) (ed.) *The Development State*, Ithaca: Cornell University Press.

World Bank (1981) *Accelerated Development in Sub-Saharan Africa*, Washington DC: The World Bank.

World Bank (1983) *World Development Report 1983*, Washington DC: The World Bank.

World Bank (1993) *The East Asian Miracle*, New York: Oxford University Press and The World Bank.

Yamashita, S. (1991) 'Economic development of the ASEAN Countries and the role of Japanese direct investments' in S. Yamashita (ed.) *Transfer of Japanese Technology and Management to the ASEAN Countries* Tokyo: Tokyo University Press.

Yang, Y-R. and Hsia, C-J. (2011) (in press) Local embeddedness of trans-border production networks: the case of IT clusters in the Greater Dongguan area of China', *Global Networks*, 11 .

Yang, Y.H and Shea, J.D. (1996) 'Money and prices in Taiwan in the 1980s' in T. Ito and A.O. Krueger (eds) *Financial Deregulation and Integration in East Asia*, Chicago: University of Chicago Press.

Yanus, K. (2000) 'Malaysia praised for forging good TNC-SME ties', *New Straits Times*, Kuala Lumpur, 4 September.

Yeung, H.W.C. (1999) 'Under siege? Economic globalisation and Chinese business in Southeast Asia', *Economy and Society*, 28(1): 1–31.

Yoshihara, K. (1988) *The Rise of Ersatz Capitalism in Southeast Asia*, Kuala Lumpur: Oxford University Press.

Yusuf, S. (2003) *Innovative East Asia: The Future of Growth*, Washington DC: The World Bank.

Yusuf, S. (2008) 'How China is reshaping the industrial geography of Southeast Asia', Washington DC: Development Research Group, The World Bank. Available from: www.foreignaffairs.org

Yusuf, S. and Nabeshima, K. (2009) *Tigers Under Threat: The Search for a New Growth Strategy by Malaysia and its Southeast Asian Neighbors*, Washington DC: The World Bank.

Zajek, O. (2008) 'China's naval ambitions', *Le Monde Diplomatique* (English Edition), September.

Zhao, H. (2007) 'Contesting Confucius', *New Left Review*, II, 44: 134–42.

INDEX